THE POINT OF THE NEEDLE

The Point of the Needle

Why Sewing Matters

BARBARA BURMAN

REAKTION BOOKS

'By better understanding the tangible things in our lives,
we better understand our fellow humans.'

GLENN ADAMSON

Published by

REAKTION BOOKS LTD
Unit 32, Waterside
44–48 Wharf Road
London N1 7UX, UK
www.reaktionbooks.co.uk

First published 2023
Copyright © Barbara Burman 2023

Printed and bound in Great Britain by TJ Books Ltd, Padstow, Cornwall

A catalogue record for this book is available from the British Library

ISBN 978 1 78914 719 3

Contents

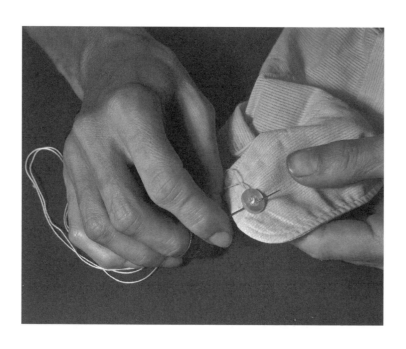

Introduction

If you're dressed when you read this, you'll know why sewing matters. Even simple jeans, shirts and trainers entwine us with row upon row of thousands of stitches holding everything together as we move though our day. And we use all kinds of other goods from the vast commercial output of sewing workers around the globe. But there are also millions of other people who sew for themselves purely for the love of it. In the UK 18 million amateurs participate in crafts, with sewing among their favourites. In North America, home quilters alone number between 9 and 11 million people and generate a market worth $4.2 billion. For all these people, sewing's place in their creativity and well-being is what matters.

The manufacturing of textiles and clothing constitutes one of the world's largest industries with the fourth heaviest environmental impact. It is estimated that between 60 and 75 million people are employed internationally sewing our clothes, mostly females, forming one of the world's biggest but least protected labour forces. Many work in poorer nations, but it is increasingly obvious that these labourers suffer employment malpractices in rich nations too. In this context alone, as part of a vast international complex involving commerce, technology, politics and the environment, sewing commands our attention. Its sheer size shapes our everyday consumer practices. At the same time, it forms the context for those who like to sew things for themselves and maintain their sense of personal agency. Rich nations continue to buy and then throw away factory-made fast fashion at frightening speed and home sewing and crafting are enjoying a lively renaissance. Whichever way you look at these parallel trends, sewing represents human endeavour on a giant yet also an intimate scale.

We all depend on what is sewn. How and where it takes place and indeed who does it and what it signifies at a collective or individual level are mostly absent from public discourse. It has been said that 'ordinary people make history through the smallest acts of everyday life. But people make history not only in the work they do and the choices they make, but in the things they choose to remember.'[1] I want to celebrate those who sew and to reinstate their largely untold narrative into what we choose to remember of today and the recent past. The aim here is to understand stitching – making clothes and other things – as a phenomenon with its own history and cultural memory. Indeed, people who choose to sew, especially alongside friends or family, often say they are making memories. It is an invitation to see sewing in a fresh light, to stimulate thought and prompt discussion about this multi-faceted practice.

Despite its prehistory, which is almost as long as the history of humankind itself, and its everyday presence in our lives, sewing's written history is sparse. Recognition of its importance is emerging in the media and in academia, as we will see in the following chapters, but for the most part working with a needle either by choice or necessity has been an overlooked story. Why is this so? Part of the problem is that it is usually thought of as a predominantly female undertaking; an increasing number of men are taking it up as a hobby, but it remains tethered to preconceptions of women's work as being less worthy than their male counterparts'. Whether sewing happens in a factory or in the home, the work is undervalued, or unseen. Virginia Woolf wrote about erasure in women's 'infinitely obscure lives' in *A Room of One's Own* of 1928. 'For all the dinners are cooked; the plates and cups washed; the children sent to school and gone out into the world. Nothing remains of it all. All has vanished. No biography or history has a word to say about it.' As if to emphasize the silence, Woolf does not mention sewing. But although the domestic work she describes has indeed vanished without trace, countless sewn artefacts survive from the late nineteenth and early twentieth centuries. In fact, Woolf had friends and family who sewed, and she herself frequented dressmakers and enjoyed fashion, so her omission underlines how easily such things are overlooked.

To makes matters worse for its profile, domestic sewing is tinged with amateurism, a word that damns with faint praise. Sewing as a home-based craft is encumbered with an equivocal reputation. It is assumed to produce serviceable but dowdy things condemned as 'homemade', to be an anachronistic hobby confined to those dull or old-fashioned folk who ought to get out more. The long bias against women's work and domestic work is further enshrined in the commonplace misapprehension that hands and head are independent of each other and working with your hands is less interesting and less valuable than working with your head. This position is too often reinforced within formal education since many schools privilege the academic over the vocational, and sideline practical skills. In so doing they disregard contemporary thinking that the hand may well be 'as much at the core of human life as the brain itself'.[2] To redress the balance, it's my intention in this book to insert sewing into an expanded and more inclusive perspective, to draw attention to it as an activity of consequence with its own language and story and with increasing contemporary relevance. It was no surprise that those who sew, when consulted when I was writing this book, often said to me, 'About time too.'

More ready-made clothes than ever before are consumed but kept for less time; cheaper items are discarded after a mere seven or eight wears (that's wears, not years). Given this easy availability of fast and super-fast fashion and the broader setting of a commodity culture in which personal consumption can seem boundless, why make things for yourself? Sewing for self and family has always been an important practice, deeply embedded in everyday life, but these days it is also a countercultural one. So its renaissance over the past decade or two looks all the more intriguing in the context of our contemporary throwaway culture and raises further questions about what lies behind it. The anthropologist Tim Ingold asks what it is like to live in a world where everything is ready-made for us: 'At the very same moment when the whole world is at our fingertips, it also seems completely out of our hands.'[3] Sewing people often say that this is precisely what motivates them: a desire to regain some personal control and take something back into their own hands.

The large numbers of people who make things for themselves demonstrate that throwaway fashion culture may not be as impregnable as manufacturers and retailers would like it to be. The lockdowns caused by the recent COVID-19 pandemic gave sewing at home a huge boost, as testified by the jump in sales of sewing machines, but its popularity was on the rise before then: there was a surge of interest in it during the financial crises of 2008, for example. It happened alongside growing awareness of the stresses caused by long hours of work and the difficulty of maintaining a work–life balance. Current steep rises in the cost of living add yet another concern. With more understanding of the ill-effects of 24/7 lifestyles on mental and physical health, there came a new willingness to talk more openly about such matters, and studies are now showing the benefits of craft and its real and measurable contribution to human health, shedding more light on why people enjoy sewing. Google 'sewing and well-being' and the immense international recognition of this interconnection becomes immediately obvious. People who sew at home, of course, have always felt it.

Sewing offers a sense of community, real or virtual, and brings otherwise disparate people together through common interests and aspirations. The significant rise of anxiety and loneliness felt by all generations in today's societies makes this shared aspect of the practice topical and ever more valuable. It is increasingly the case that the climate crisis is fuelling public anxiety and it is common now to hear sewing described as a means to respond actively, for example when buying natural fabrics or upcycling old items in the search for more sustainable living, a trend reinforced by evidence of substantial, often shocking social injustices within the textile and clothing industries. It seems that our world is becoming a more difficult and unsettling place. It is not surprising that sewing has become part of new conversations about these broader issues and the challenges we face. The practice of sewing gives us a framework for thinking about human resilience and well-being in the here and now, as well as approaches to more sustainable living and our connections with the past. In this day and age, the work of hands and eyes and the flourishing of human ingenuity and creativity become ever more important.

The book's attention centres on sewing that is plain or structural. Not surprisingly this focus involves practices that can feel diverse to those who do them, including quilting, dressmaking, tailoring, soft furnishing and work by 'thing makers' and hobby crafters busy on all manner of different things. Yet these affiliations overlap, and a love of stitching, making and experimentation often draws people into more than one area of interest. Embroidery is a form of needlework not featured here. Its practitioners often do plainer work as well, but it is a specialism that is loved and admired by many, and already gets ample limelight elsewhere. We need to dwell on 'plain' for a moment. My *Shorter Oxford English Dictionary* devotes seventeen column inches to 'plain'. It embraces unaffected, unadorned, unpretentious, candid, simple, frank, open, all words used to describe behaviour, actions, speech and things. In these definitions, there are as many that involve what it is *not* as define what it *is*. It goes on to define plain sewing as 'needlework that does not involve embroidery or ornamental work'. But as we know, whatever is being ventured when sewing, even a simple running stitch can be configured into an ornamental surface pattern. Quilting with plain stitching can result in something strikingly imaginative. Beyond functional concerns, many needleworkers these days who identify as textile or fibre artists use stitches on the wilder shores of plain, plying their needles in ways that transcend plainness. To cut a long thread short, the focus here is on unadorned sewing that constructs things we wear on our bodies, use in homes and other settings or are intended as uniquely expressive artefacts. But, like seam allowance on a paper pattern, our boundaries have some leeway, because this book is first and foremost about people in all their diversity; it is not a how-to book.

On these pages stitching and stitches are valued precisely because they embody human life and invention and cloth itself is inseparable from them. Explicitly and implicitly, cloth affects the perspective of this book because textiles are one of the most dizzily multi-faceted markers of humankind's ingenuity. They are 'beautiful, inventive, expressive, and more. They reveal the human compulsion to engage with texture, colour and story-telling. They record our ever-changing feelings of play, joy, wonder and profound thoughtfulness. They preserve skills, encourage creativity and represent continuity.'[4] So, a stitch may be plain but its story is enriched by cloth. Or, as one historian puts it, the 'history of needlework and textiles is deliciously complex'.[5]

For sewing, the mute button has been on for a long time. No official body or organization has been interested enough to gather information consistently to provide an overview of amateur sewing. Sporadic market research concentrates on commercial trends, not lived experiences. There is some quali-tative research used in the following chapters that gives access to what sewers think and do but it is limited. So it takes many different sources to tell the story of what might otherwise be forgotten. Hoping to unmute sewing, to some small degree at least, I undertook two projects designed to hear more voices, and they have been a valuable compass and inspiration for this book. Unreferenced quotations in the following chapters are taken from my interviews with participants in both projects in the course of my research; some names have been changed.

The first was an oral history project based in Hampshire, England, in 1995 with twenty retired women of whom several were in their eighties and nineties. With the not-so-snappy title *Home Dressmaking Reassessed*, it was designed to capture more about the then obscure history of home dressmaking and resulted in over sixty hours of taped conversations leading eventually in 1999 to my edited volume *The Culture of Sewing: Gender, Consumption and Home Dressmaking*. These wonderful and articulate participants welcomed me into their homes but nevertheless needed some persuasion to believe that their stories, their sewing, could possibly be of interest to anyone else. Once persuaded, they talked freely at length and often movingly about how sewing fitted into their long and eventful lives, why they did it, what they did, how they learnt, about coping in wartime, saving money for themselves or their families, about making clothes to higher standards than the ready-made garments they could afford, about dressmaking because they were not a standard body size, the pleasures of choosing their own styles and fabrics and the satisfactions of applying and advancing their skills. It was touching to hear how their sewing opened vivid memories for them and became a vehicle for their wider autobiographies and striking how sharp their recall was of fabrics, seams or their first sewing machine. Putting their own, their mothers' and even their grandmothers' sewing into words slipped both speaker and listener back in time with extraordinary ease and clarity.

Twenty-five years later, confined by the COVID-19 pandemic, I turned to written testimonies to reach more participants in a second project named *Our Sewing Stories*. Most of its stories came from within the UK but others were from mainland Europe, North America and Australia. It has been a joy to read the stories they penned. Of all ages and diverse backgrounds, rural and urban, contributors wrote openly to set out their own sewing autobiographies for the first time. Sewing is a field of knowledge, a process and practice but also a part of selfhood and identity, as these testimonies reveal. The motives, memories, achievements, challenges, disappointments, rewards and aspirations involved in their sewing underline how what they *do* is part of who they *are*. The stories are another point of departure for these chapters, helping to ground the book in everyday realities.

It was clear that many aspects of sewing at home had not changed over that quarter century, that sewing is thriving, that sewing machines still elicit strong emotions, that people continue to experience great satisfaction from sewing, that the love affair with fabrics remains alive. None of the participants used the term 'mental health' in 1995, but their terms 'enjoyment', 'absorption' and 'pleasure' match the more recent 'well-being', 'flow' and 'being in the zone'. The most marked new theme to emerge in the intervening time is best called the new politics of stuff – when sewing for yourself is part of the desire to reduce ready-made consumption, to be a thoughtful and well-informed consumer mindful of the potential exploitation of people and the planet. Nobody saw that coming.

Neither of these projects was quantitative or large in scale. Both emphasized the subjectivity of sewing experiences and the autobiographical context. The youngest story belonged to a five-year-old girl; the oldest to a woman just shy of her hundredth birthday. The first project was regarded by some of my male university colleagues as barely, if at all, acceptable as serious research, though others appreciated the use of oral history methods to retrieve everyday experiences that would otherwise be lost. Over a hundred voices and stories collected by the projects will be preserved in the public domain as a small corrective to gaps in sewing's history. Alongside other sources and approaches, the two projects were steered by my wish to meet history up close.

What follows in the book shows continuity and change in sewing over time. It gives voice to sewing people in the here and now and also a sense of their heritage and intergenerational connections. My intention is to balance historical insights with an emphasis on what people do and feel as they sew today, what they make and why, and to explore their processes of making and what it means to them. In these pages, historical material is mostly drawn from the eighteenth century onwards, to convey key legacies but for brevity's sake amounting to a mere snippet of sewing's long history. Sewing for a living has a presence here as part of the economic and political dimensions of sewing but the tilt of this book is towards other more intimate aspects of the practice that have not been much acknowledged or understood. There are different cultural and social emphases around the world that impact the degree to which sewing is considered a practice of choice or a habitual necessity. Although the main focus of this book is the Anglo-North American experience, it is important to keep such differences in mind.

The book starts with thinking about the most complex of all tools used to sew – the hands that hold the needle. By focusing on the partnership between hands and brain that enables stitching, a marvel we so easily take for granted, the aim is to describe the absolute fundamentals of how we sew and how it relates to well-being. The book moves on to how sewing is learnt and the cultural tropes, obstacles and gains that shape the experience for children and adults. Getting further into more tangible aspects of sewing, cloth itself and then sewing tools and their storage emerge as more affective and contested than they appear at first sight, involving sentiment and memory. The second half of the book takes a look at the things people actually make when they sew and the varied motives behind their craft, when it becomes clear that sewing is alive and well and plugged into far more aspects of life than meet the eye. Not only does it offer makers stuff to wear and use with immediate rewards and pleasure, but it builds confidence. It serves all manner of purposes, causes and charitable acts. It is a means of affirming kinship and friendship and enables engagement in real-world issues, when the needle often becomes an instrument for change and defiance. The book ends with the needle in action in the new yet also very old culture of mending and recycling. These specific forms of making by remaking reveal themselves to be creative statements of care and optimism.

After a career of research and teaching in UK art schools and universities, I continue those activities but at my own pace, which gives me time to reflect. I grew up in another golden age of home sewing. A copy of Dora Seton and Winifred Parker's *Essentials of Modern Dressmaking* lies on my desk. In my father's bold hand, it bears an inscription to my mother 'with love', dated on her birthday in 1953. Underneath are the youthful signatures of my older brothers and, bringing up the rear, my own determinedly neat autograph, by a five-year-old obviously not ready to risk joining up the letters of her name. Somehow, in our tiny pre-Internet village miles from a bookshop, my father had secured the book in time, then marshalled us with fountain pens for a signing session. The gift was a measure of his admiration for handiwork in general and particularly my mother's determination to acquire teaching qualifications in dressmaking and soft tailoring. As a country parson on a small stipend, raising four children, he well knew the economic value of her capabilities. Countless times as a child I stood on a kitchen chair while my mother measured, tucked and pinned to form a garment around me. The memory of a dirndl skirt in red cotton printed with large black-and-white zebras galloping round the lower half still makes me smile. I slept on sides-to-middle sheets and wore shorts made by my mother from old curtain material. Anything new was an unusual treat. As a witness to years of dressmaking, upholstering and tailoring, I learnt a lasting respect for her skills, but my mother aimed high and lost me on the way. Finely made garments and quality fabrics still catch my eye, but good sense tells me that while my upbringing alerts me to the craft involved, it doesn't mean I can make anything fit to be seen. But something of her lingers in what she left behind – boxes of sundries, buttons ancient and modern, tape measures and set squares, triangles of tailor's chalk in soft pastel colours nestled in a little box of bran, cloth and more cloth – and helped to shape me and my career. Perhaps making a book *about* sewing will be as close as I get to the real thing, although maybe it's a prompt to thread my needle again.

Published memoirs, numerous conversations and oral history work about sewing over the years tell me that many people share these kinds of early experiences of sewing mothers, aunts and grandmothers, not forgetting those fathers who sew. But what about younger people who sew? The world changes, but it seems to be well understood that sewing, and crafts in general, make a positive contribution to the well-being of younger generations as they try to slow the pace of their lives and find pleasure in handiwork. For these future consumers and citizens there is a widespread sense that 'enough is enough'. In keeping with Extinction Rebellion, the #MeToo movement and Black Lives Matter, awareness of environmental and social injustices is increasing. For many people craft as a form of self-reliance will play a part in how they re-imagine more assertively the future of their own lives and their communities.

It will be clear by now that this book isn't going to tell you how to sew. Today there are numerous books, magazines, local classes, blogs, Instagrams and websites offering excellent support and advice for beginners and experienced alike. Their welcome is broad and their enthusiasm infectious. Today's amateur sewing community, real and virtual, makes a new sewing movement totally unlike what many people remember from their school lessons, so if you haven't picked up a needle since then, maybe now is the moment. The needle truly is a tool for our times.

1

Hands, Hearts and Needles

The human hand, with its fabricating capabilities, is unique, although using and making things out of found materials occurs across the animal world. Some birds weave their intricate nests exquisitely well. One parasitoid wasp appears to do something akin to felting and the Australian green ant works in family groups to stick leaves together to form a durable nest. Perhaps the most proficient true stitch-maker is the Asian common tailor bird. Wondrously this little songbird, working alone, uses its sharp beak to pierce holes in leaves and systematically pull through plant fibres, insect silk or even stolen household thread to stitch them together to form a sheltered cradle, in which it then builds its nest. But as impressive as these behaviours are, it is the creature with the opposable thumb who leads the way with stitches.

Stitching is a way of joining pieces of textile and other materials such as leather, felt, paper or bark. It may not be essential for human life, like breathing or eating, but it is hard to conceive of a human society without the things that sewing produces and the evidence of humans stitching stuff together pre-dates the emergence of writing. We call ourselves *Homo sapiens* and *Homo faber*, man the maker, encapsulates our particular capabilities. We can make stitches because, while we share plenty of characteristics with the other seven great apes, we are the only one with a fully opposable thumb that can touch our index and other fingers.

There is a wizardry in the working partnership between our hands and brains. Except when we are babies and toddlers learning the rudiments of moving and acting in the world (seemingly a full-time job for them), or suffering from injury or illness, we are rarely conscious of ourselves in this way. The marvels of the brain's plasticity and those 128 billion neurons at work inside our skulls are the domain of neuroscientists and their exciting new insights, yet if we further consider what we ourselves experience daily as we work and think with our hands, the wizardry becomes more familiar. When we reach out to steady that child or pick an apple off a tree or thread up a sewing machine, our hands are conveying something more than mere touch. In fact, there is really no such thing as 'mere' touch, because touch informs how we know, explore, frame, express and remember our world and our place in it. It is said that 'through the sense of touch, the hand brings a dimension to the understanding of the external world that is unobtainable through vision, reason or imagination.'[1]

And today, more than ever, making something with our hands is acknowledged as a key element in a well-balanced human life. The full reach of this encapsulates 'the inherent satisfaction of making; the sense of being alive within the process; and the engagement with ideas, learning and knowledge which come not before or after but within the practice of making'. No wonder that making can be compelling and should never be thought of as 'an inferior or second-class kind of activity'.[2] When we situate sewing in this conversation about the tangible and non-tangible benefits of making, we can see its significance and complexity more clearly and give it the greater respect it merits. Lots of sewing people describe their stitching as a form of equilibrium for them, a restorative practice that compensates for certain forms of monotonous work that their day jobs may demand, including computer screen time. Helen is an author, teacher, fashion curator and keen sewer. She says she needs to 'balance' her head and screen work with handwork. 'If I don't keep either of these in balance, I get antsy. They complement each other and maintain my inner harmony.' For Jimmy, a younger sewer, their concerns about the ill-effects of fast fashion means that sewing and mending their own clothes brings another kind of balance and engagement. The 'repetitive, therapeutic, tactile process' of stitching is 'very soothing' but, at the same time, 'it is also a response to the world around me.' Many others appreciate that their stitching brings a sense of agency that provides its own coherence and ballast in their lives. In these terms alone, sewing demonstrates the 'inherent satisfaction of making', yet of all craft practices it is still the one most likely to be overlooked in debates about making and makers.

It is not easy to formulate plain sewing outside its own explicit knowledge and dominant vocabulary about itself. This consists chiefly of practical information, such as the documentation of named stitches and how to form and use them, or procedural sequences for cutting and assembling cloth into articles for use. Beyond this language of technique and method, sewing has also been recruited into moral and religious terms, as we will see. Today it is beginning to appear in conversations about feminism, mental health or sustainability, so some elements of the craft are heard in public discourse, but even among its most skilled practitioners there has been no easily identified public voice to proclaim its full value. As a senior craft in its own right, it seems curiously mute and set apart in its own world. It has long been demoted as 'women's work' despite its substantial history and essential place in our lived experience. Perhaps some practitioners enjoy their privacy in the margins, out of the public eye. Maker and writer Amy Twigger Holroyd views this quietness as something positive, as 'the strength of making'. Within this strength she sees all kinds of individual, social and cultural potential. 'Craft can fly under the radar of dominant forces and therefore potentially be more transgressive than more flamboyant acts of resistance.' She situates stitching in particular where 'non-confrontational acts' can be generated that offer 'accessible and appealing' benefits to individuals.[3] But from whatever angle sewing is seen, it has in common with all crafts the '*drive* to make and share things', brought to the fore in contemporary discussions about craft as both a social practice and one 'as old as the hills'.[4] It is in these more universal terms that sewing reveals its connections and engagement with what it means to be human. At the same time the specificities of that stitching hand can tell us about the magic that happens when we see with our hands and touch with our eyes, when we exercise our tacit as much as our explicit knowledge.

Perhaps we should add hearts to the working partnership between hands and brains. Science may not agree that hearts are a site of feeling, but nevertheless we know what people mean when they say that they put their hearts into making. For some the maxim of the faith group The Religious Society of Friends known as the Quakers – 'Hands to work and hearts to God' – fits this experience. The partnership of hands, brains and hearts not only makes sewing possible and functional, but recruits and realizes those dimensions of the maker's intelligence that are seldom acknowledged as part of manual work. Yet these are always a vital presence, facilitating the handling and management of processes, material and tools. Sewing also depends on our human capacity to focus, reflect, experiment, imagine, diagnose reiteratively, each of these abilities informing the manipulation of the cloth and needle as the task proceeds. What might look like routine needlework is in fact a journey that deploys the full marvel of our brains and bodies within social and cultural contexts. And recognizing that sewing, and touch, are entwined with the inner life of feelings and emotions is becoming ever clearer from science and from those who work in community and therapeutic settings. Working with our hands really matters to who we are and how we feel about ourselves.[5] 'We have now come to a point where we can more fully sense the convergence of the neurologic, linguistic, developmental, and anthropologic perspectives in our search for an understanding of the role of the hand in human life.'[6] Insights in these fields of knowledge move on apace, but for our purposes we return for the moment to our central point – the stitch and stitching.

Stitching by hand is a process that employs the simplest of tools that need no further mediation to achieve functional stitches. The fingers grip and push a threaded needle though the cloth and pull it out again at an appropriate distance from its point of entry and repeat that as often as required. The action and results of stitching by hand are all there in plain sight, no mystery, no tricks. Of course, the novice will make it look more laborious than the experienced needleworker who can achieve accuracy and neatness with apparent ease. But in its fundamental elements there are few crafts simpler. Picture the domestic hand sewer bent over their work, intent on their stitches. They use only small repetitive movements with their hands, wrists and arms. Their needle and thread and maybe a thimble are hard to spot unless you are watching closely. You are observing an age-old practice. The seated figure is not working on a heroic scale, not guiding and striking a chisel into wood or stone, not thumping clay or working the wheel, not treadling and managing the fast-moving parts of a loom with their hands and feet. In their attentive, more sedentary pose – it is curiously difficult to sew standing up – the stitching figure appears closer to a writer or an illustrator, working without overt muscularity in more or less silent concentration. To break the spell, they may be listening to their favourite radio station, or get up and down to attend to other tasks or shift to use their sewing machine or iron. Yet their application to their craft encapsulates something else, a cultural legacy packed with associations formed over generations. It invokes skill and resourcefulness, domesticity and care or the enjoyment of leisure, but it can also conjure up the grinding necessities of poverty. Today it can also signal a desirable immersion in slowness: the hand stitcher may have turned their back deliberately to consumerism and fast fashion, asserting their right to alternative ways of making and an alternative mode of being. The philosopher, poet and clinical neuroscientist Raymond Tallis underlines how our facility is about much more than the biomechanics of dexterity. As the hand becomes a tool so 'the body becomes an instrument' and we become 'true agents'. Tallis sees this leading to something profound: 'The development of the sense of oneself as an agent, acting directly or indirectly through the instrument of one's body, lies at the root of the emergence of human self-consciousness and the sense of self.'[7]

Fundamentally everything rests on the sewing figure using nothing but the simple needle with no intermediary, in one of the purest connections imaginable between hand and tool. Or so it seems. The needle could hardly take a form more spare, a function more elementary. It has no moving, adjustable, composite or modifiable parts, and perhaps this immediacy of contact between hand, cloth and needle lies at the root of the pleasure and absorption so many ascribe to sewing, something akin to hand knitting. The immediacy of this touch is not found in all crafts; there is little in sewing that requires the maker to work their hands and bodies at a distance from the materials with which they are engaged, unlike in glassblowing. Requiring only a simple thimble for protection, stitching is not like welding metal. There is little if any need to outsource the work to finishing processes, as when even the most experienced studio potter fires up their kiln, and the results are never 100 per cent guaranteed. In sewing, the hand is always the close guide, even when using a sewing machine.

The sewing machine is not a machine that requires mere watching or occasional tending as it accomplishes its work. It is more like a moving car: it needs hand, eye and foot coordination to steer and control the speed and direction of its stitching. Like cars, in due course sewing machines may be fully automated, but not yet. They remain, like the handheld needle, a form of tool that is still deeply integrated with the human body, unlike many other powered tools which now perform their tasks at one remove from us, perhaps just needing the press of a fingertip on a button. UK quilt artist Sara Impey machine-stitched a quilt with lines of text about her thoughts on stitching. It begins: 'In the negative space between the stitches your thoughts can run free – the sewing machine comes to feel like an extension of the body – hand and foot and eye work in harmony to control the movement of the needle until the rhythm becomes almost as natural and involuntary as a heartbeat and the thread flows through the system like blood.'[8] These are the words of an expert machine stitcher who describes how 'the words travel straight from my brain to my needle'. But anyone using a sewing machine for the first time will be quickly disabused of the idea that it simply does their sewing for them. They may be perplexed at the number of decisions and actions needed to thread it up and set the required stitch properties and tension even before stitching begins. They may be startled to find how closely they must pay attention through their hands and feet to work even the simplest machine. The proximity of their fingers to the steel point of that rapidly pounding and unforgiving needle means that, for a novice, the best advice is to proceed with caution and accept that even the most up-to-date machine cannot tell you what to do. It will be a while before 'your thoughts can run free.' But eventually something happens: a bond forms such that many sewing enthusiasts speak of an enduring affection for their machine.

The human hand is complicated, the opposite of the manufactured needle it manipulates to sew. But regardless of the needle's simple little form, it represents 'toolness' and 'a huge conceptual advance'. Stitching took humankind 'beyond the universe of even the most versatile tool-using chimpanzee'.[9] It has been observed in numerous contexts – archaeology, anthropology, biology, evolutionary theory, philosophy – that the tool, and therefore toolmaking, are fundamental components of human culture, both a means and a sign of agency, collective thinking and transformation in and of the physical world. When our hand holds the needle, what do we see? According to Raymond Tallis again, we are observing, and participating in, something profoundly and uniquely human. 'The hand . . . is both less than a tool, being more of a precursor or precondition of distinctively human tool-use (and toolmaking), than a tool in its own right; and more than a tool, for there is no tool yet devised (or likely to be devised) by man that will come anywhere near the prodigious versatility of the human hand.'[10]

Few people are likely to be conscious of these ancient cultural roots and their mental cogs and biomechanical shifts as they work at sewing or anything else. In fact, to many people, holding and plying a needle and the creativity it enables is almost second nature, so familiar that it can be hard for them to articulate what it entails. Many think sewing an irrelevance – other people do the sewing, they don't – and others find it an achingly difficult challenge, but it can still be an exhilarating thought that in picking up any tool – needle, spade, pencil, hammer – we are exemplifying a crucial evolutionary success story. The experiment and creativity served by tools are 'the hidden miracle at the heart of the ordinary in every field of art'.[11]

Our intimate knowledge of our hands, and they of us, is mediated through our skin, the largest organ we have. It is a thin but expansive and flexible all-over self-renewing layered barrier, regulator and communicator, fitted like a glove over the muscles, cartilage, blood vessels, nerves and bones of the hands. There are normally a total of 27 bones below the wrist that form our fingers and thumbs, but the sewing hand is also dependent on the workings of the wrist and its arm. For sewing, the top pad of our famously opposable thumb pairs itself with the same part of the forefinger on one hand to grip the thread for the squinty job of guiding the thread through the eye of the needle that is held in the same fashion by the corresponding digits on the other hand, usually the lead hand of the duo. Tallis names this specialist grip 'the pad-to-pad two-jaw chuck'. The same two fingers of the dominant hand will then ply the threaded needle through the cloth but often frequently form 'a three-jaw chuck',[12] with the next finger used for extra control and often chosen to bear the thimble and apply extra assistance to the needle's passage through thicker fabrics. The hand's grip is adjusted continuously in different dimensions as required. The other hand is in assistive mode, readied to hold and arrange the cloth and offer some guidance for the needle's entry and exit points. We see the wonder of our hands when we stitch or observe others doing it. Their 'prodigious versatility' in using the needle is a distinctive and remarkable part of who and what we are. We are both human *beings* and human *doings*, and perhaps these are inseparable components of selfhood.

Fingertips touch the needle, the thread, the fabric and all the other components the stitcher is utilizing. Their touching supplies a constant flow of information. Touch deepens our understanding of our task as we 'see' with our fingers. 'All of this – intentionality, transcendence, and general classification with general expectations, *a general sense of possibility* – is present in touch. What is given to us in tactile experience goes beyond what we are currently experiencing: touch puts us in touch with more than we are currently touching.'[13] The perception embodied in our hands is clearly evident in numerous ways that are specific to sewing, although those who don't sew may be unaware of what is going on. Those who do sew are well aware that their sewing hand is indeed a cognitive hand. The maker's initial choice of cloth asks their touching hand to judge how it will feel against the user's skin, how it will behave when it lies next to another layer of cloth and how it will drape on a moving figure. The inquisitive sewing hand informs the maker about the inherent properties and quality of the cloth, its heft and elasticity and its likely tolerance or otherwise of certain steps they need it to take to achieve their desired result. This is 'probably the greatest challenge facing any good craftsman: to see in the mind's eye where the difficulties lie', notes sociologist and musician Richard Sennett.[14] The choice made and with their work in progress, the maker's touch reckons the tension and strength of the stitches they are piercing through it to gauge their future durability. Theirs is a purposeful and sure hand because it is also a questioning and deliberative hand. The sewing hand illustrates Sennett's notion of 'a dialogue between concrete practices and thinking; this dialogue evolves into sustaining habits, and these habits establish a rhythm between problem solving and problem finding'.[15] The seated figure intent on their work appears composed and placid but at the same time, their calm is dependent on these ceaseless biomechanical and neural interconnections. It is easy to take for granted that our sense of touch is busy allowing us to make countless judgements at immense speed in any situation: 'We all become adepts at this, just as we do at judging mood from the look of a face.'[16]

Sewing is affective and takes us into the domain of emotions and feelings, where the heart enters the picture. We speak of tension in stitches, an apt term. Some children and adults find sewing with hand or machine entirely unsatisfactory: it just fails to connect with them. For others it is worse, even discombobulating, like a sweaty nightmare when all their normal capabilities and coordination seem to fail them. Who knows why this aversion strikes some people so strongly? Sewing instruction usually assumes right-handedness, so that can be tough for the significant minority of people whose left hand is the more dextrous, and there are further clues in how sewing is taught at school, as we'll see in the next chapter. One school sewing teacher was irritated by Jane's left-handed work. The effect lasted: 'To this day I struggle to remember which side of a project I need to start my work from.' One clothing machinist who chooses to sew part-time to earn money because she finds it pleasurable told me her sister would rather scrub floors for a living than sew. Emotion can leave its visible imprint on plain utilitarian stitching, often in the stitches themselves. A simple running stitch can be as expressive as embroidery, plain sewing's showier counterpart. What it communicates is as obvious in historical artefacts as it is in something made today. It may be hasty, stabbed, uneven, strained, sloppy, botched, meandering or erratic, or disciplined, deliberate, considered, regular and fluent, as when the appropriately named running stitch travels with the controlled grace of an athlete. Stitches are not inconsequential: they are an enduring trace of the maker and their mind.

'We think with the objects we love; we love the objects we think with,' writes psychologist Sherry Turkle about our relationship to things.[17] To an attentive stitcher, their staples – a thimble or length of cloth – are not just any old stuff; they are much more than that. There is a mental, emotional engagement with them, as with a sewing machine. This is heightened during handwork, when practical progress and the final outcomes of the craft are defined by the properties of the working objects we love and think with. For example, tailors and dressmakers all know the essential role played by the fit of their favourite shears in their hand as they cut into expensive fabric. Bodily connectivity of this kind is plainly visible to the observer as the perfect cut emerges behind the moving hand, yet the trusty hand and shears generate an extra dynamic for the maker; no doubt relief the cut's result is good, but also a special pleasure in the process as much as the result. What exactly is this and how can it be put into words?

Participants in *Our Sewing Stories* were quick to express how much this engagement and process mean to them. Hazel, a young student, feels 'the process of sewing is like singing and breathing, you can relax and feel super happy when you are doing them. In this case it's not the end thing you are enjoying, but something you are enjoying doing.' This experience of making means that while the perfect cut or perfect stitch may be satisfying, the *process* of the cutting or stitching is at the heart of this relaxed and 'super happy' thing. Hazel tells us to look at the means, not the end, if we want to understand what's going on: the doing can matter as much as the finishing.

Perfection isn't always the ultimate measure. Capabilities differ and there is such a thing as good enough. Speed over perfection is called for when rushing to finish a small child's costume the night before the school play. But for many people their sewing brings a private tranquillity because of its outcomes. Andrea feels her sewing is 'a peaceful activity (until a corner simply won't turn!) and a solitary indulgence. It demands focus, patience and discipline but, unlike many of our daily pursuits, shows results very quickly.' For others, sewing and making offer the further emotional satisfactions and release of sociability. Many stitchers will acknowledge that they need other people's presence to help shape or inspire their projects. A keen stitcher in her thirties who founded a textile group ten years ago with 42 members said that during their separation in COVID-19 lockdown their 'creativity seems to be stifled – we need each other to bounce ideas around'. Going to sewing workshops and courses together or arranging get-togethers offers mutual stimulus and encouragement and brings increased confidence as well as companionship. When Laura was a PhD student in a UK university, she organized a sewing project with fellow students for when the going was tough. They came together to make square appliqué images to form a quilt that represented their research topics. It was an alternative kind of public engagement to communicate their studies that also allowed them to have fun and relax together. Laura felt they enhanced their 'own well-being through mindful creativity'.[18] There is a growing understanding today of the importance of groups and group work, often seen as a counterbalance to the negative side of a culture that casts individualism as a priority: 'Finding your tribe is a powerful validation of your own interests and passions. It affirms and reinforces your commitment to what you're doing and can relieve the sense of isolation that people sometimes feel without such a connection.'[19]

'Flow' is the term often used nowadays as a shorthand way to describe the absorbing and immersive experience felt by many as they undertake activities such as handicraft and the outside world disappears. Alex finds that sewing slows her down and 'quietens' her brain. Teaching young offenders to sew in prison, Susanna observed how the boys 'liked sewing, it calmed them. There were lots of things that agitated them, but this didn't, it was very pleasant.' Cathy, a dressmaker, has an almost involuntary response to cloth itself: it is 'like a medicine' and 'enough to lift your mood.' In the context of domestic sewing, those who talk about the 'flow' or being 'in the zone' during their time stitching say it is often a cherished episode eagerly carved out of their day, even an antidote to everyday life. Stitching is often likened by them in its allure and rewards to certain other activities, particularly gardening or cooking. It remains a discrete activity that beckons them, especially when they are under stress. It is sometimes not possible to claim or negotiate the necessary space; it is certainly not seen as a right, however beneficial. Professor Sarah Gilbert was at the centre of the race in the UK to develop a viable vaccine against COVID-19. At a time of 'a rising sense of pressure within the team', 'worn out', she saw her daughter at home preparing for Christmas by getting the sewing machine out for 'a day of sewing'. 'I would have loved to have spent the day at home with fabric, ribbons and wool,' but the urgency of her professional obligations denied her that chance.[20] As an indication of how deeply entwined sewing can become with the self and the unconscious, some people have told me they dream about sewing. One individual had a dream about eating 'little pieces' of fabric. Lauren thinks about the process of sewing when she has difficulty falling asleep; others daydream about it, another way of claiming space for it.

The numerous and interlinked benefits of sewing so readily described by its practitioners today have been well understood for generations. In the past people may not have used the terms 'well-being' or 'mental health' but they knew all about the ways that working with a needle could be comforting and recuperative. The American author of an 1844 sewing manual, in addition to giving 'clear and practical instructions', wrote at length about the wider benefits of plain and fancy needlework: 'No one can look upon THE NEEDLE, without emotion; it is a constant companion throughout the pilgrimage of life. We find it the first instrument of use placed in the hand of budding childhood, and it is found to retain its usefulness and charm, even when trembling in the grasp of fast declining age.'[21] As in many other such instructional books, sewing was represented here as an intergenerational craft. The author further extols needlework as a unifying language that spoke of the domestic economy, benevolence, charity and Christian values that were seen as the proper sphere of womanhood. These connections between sewing and women's idealized sphere are found in other cultures too. In this sort of needlework advocacy, the needle's 'usefulness and charm' not only had moral dimensions but brought deep and lifelong personal satisfaction. Needless to say, not everybody saw it that way. In describing how she kept her family afloat on a limited income, the Victorian author and editor Mrs Warren spoke for many faced with interminable making and mending. 'A work-basket is a fruitful source of misery; its contents have a habit of accumulating, and causing a depressing influence upon the temper and spirits.' She advised relentless discipline to keep on top of everything. '*What is to be done should be quickly done.*'[22] But despite these kinds of pressure, there is plentiful evidence, in women's own words, of the solace of needlework.

There were several elements in how women in the past articulated an understanding of their stitching as pleasurable and supportive, not least in the sense of knowing that their work fulfilled a central role in their family's domestic economy. Beyond these advantages came their enjoyment of the conviviality and exchange of technical guidance or specific patterns when sewing in company and in the social and emotional bonding this represented. Some of Jane Austen's 'merriest talk' was when she was doing plain sewing in company.[23] This vignette of Austen sewing and chatting echoes the letters between women which were an important part of their social tissue and so often contained shared sewing experiences or appreciation of gifts received of needlework, fabric or needlework tools. In 1760 Sarah Hurst, a hard-working assistant in her father's business, thought her sewing or 'work' was on a par with more bookish pursuits: 'I shou'd indeed be quite unhappy if it were not for my three favourite amusements, work, writing & reading.'[24] She did not intend 'amusements' to indicate frivolity or distraction, but was underlining those pursuits that engaged her creativity outside her business duties. Another widely acknowledged value of needle-work derived directly from the soothing nature of the needle's repetitive action, the rewards of progressing the project in hand, whether as a solitary or group occupation, and the space it gave for quiet reflection, particularly in times of sadness or anxiety.[25] Charlotte Brontë and other Victorian novelists knew a thing or two when they described their heroines bending over their 'work' to still their aching hearts.

As women's opportunities for new kinds of paid employment outside the home expanded the already numerous demands on their time, needlework continued to be commended as bene-ficial, even in the face of more ready-made goods in the shops. At a utilitarian level, it remained a way for women to make and repair their own garments to eke out meagre wages and keep up the requisite appearances for the increasing 'white collar' jobs open to them, for example as clerks or elementary teachers, but needlework's capacity to calm and soothe became for some even more important. Flora Klickmann (1867–1958), a journalist in London and prolific author busy editing two popular national magazines, published a book in 1914 called *The Cult of the Needle*. She struck a personal note among the pages of practical advice when she commended needlework as a stressbuster for women earning their living in commerce. 'I really don't know what I should do if I hadn't needlework to fall back upon, as a recreation, when I get over-done with the wear and tear and strain of work in our great city.' She felt 'sorry' for those who hadn't discovered the 'charm and solace' in needlework of any kind 'after a day spent in wrestling with the stern commercial side of life'.[26]

A 'contemplative space, comfort, community and connection' is how the London-based textile artist Etka Kaul describes the substantial rewards she feels when she stitches, and many other voices echo her in their praise of sewing.[27] This range of positive and valuable effects is impressive and needs to be underlined in any context when the significance of sewing is in danger of being overlooked. It is confirmation that sewing should be counted among those practices which can contribute to human flourishing at many levels. More specifically, a large and expanding body of research to date confirms the many and various benefits of the arts and crafts to mental health and wellbeing. Whether listening to music or making it yourself, visiting an art exhibition or painting a picture, the benefits are evident. 'What better way to keep your mind in fine fettle [than sewing]?' asks the UK's Quilters' Guild; among other benefits, it improves fine motor skills, increases mental agility, releases dopamine and reduces anxiety.[28] These are also reported by those who work with people who have a range of mild to more severe mental illnesses. The benefits are not limited to individuals; there are also many reports of improved community cohesion. These are well enough known for the UK's National Health Service to use what is known as social prescribing, in which crafts and 'green' activities such as gardening can be used to help complex non-clinical problems. In this setting, arts and crafts are prescribed at a local level, distinct from art therapy. One recipient spoke of this service giving her life-changing access to art making: 'Art has given me a life, an identity, a voice and a future.'[29] Numerous charities and projects also work to make creative interventions aimed at helping vulnerable people, reducing loneliness and enhancing confidence, communication and self-esteem.

But these benefits are easier to describe than achieve. Of course, this has probably been true forever, although many women in the past were often so steeped in the sewing lessons of their youth that it may have seemed more like second nature to them, but in our world today new challenges get in the way. If, as Matthew Crawford, the American philosopher and mechanic, reminds us, we are wired to turn our attention towards the new – 'an important evolutionary adaptation in the world of predators' – then where does that leave us with the old?[30] The ancient work of sewing calls for sustained attention, the opposite of the other seemingly ceaseless calls on our time and concern. It requires us to set ourselves apart, moving in the channel of focus we choose. This isn't easy when the competing voices and hassles of the world are always seeking to appropriate our attention for their own commercial or political ends. In particular, women may experience further demands made by gendered assumptions about their role in supporting family life, at a time when sewing is no longer so central to domestic economy, as Marybeth Stalp found in her interviews with American quilters who felt their time spent on their craft was 'stolen' from family.[31] Crawford argues that to carve out and maintain 'a space for rational agency for oneself, against the flux of environmental stimuli' is a lifelong task to find our own personal 'narrative'.[32] If this is indeed the effect our complex modern world has on us, those who sew seem to have found a space for doing and being on their own terms and at their own speed despite 'the flux'. An accountant in the finance sector told me she loves sewing so much that she dreams of opening a fabric and haberdashery shop. 'I take so much joy in sewing. Since I have a demanding job, I find sewing as a way of escape.' It is clear what she means by this and why she values what happens when she sews, but it is also worth recognizing that what she describes is not always straightforward. Craft is not mere escapism or flunking the demands of the so-called 'real' world; in fact the proactive mental and physical processes and efforts of attention required are considerable. After all, what is called an escape is also a journey, a direction of travel that requires its own energy.

In the case of sewing, the maker is discovering and retrieving focus, they are contriving and claiming a way of their own, and through their own efforts they reap the benefits over time. As Nicola puts it, 'I feel that my childhood introduction to sewing has led me on a journey throughout my life.' Regardless of the levels of skill involved, this is an accomplishment, not bunking off. Not everybody can find the route into their own narrative. Those who think they can't but then find the key acknowledge it was worth the effort. Many people who sew would recognize arriving at the place that Crawford has described as their 'attentional landscape'.[33] One lively U.S.-based online membership organization that champions domestic sewing through practical classes, discussions, problem-solving and patterns – the

Seamwork Purpose – is forthright about its values and makes strong claims for what sewing can mean.

> It is a way to infuse creativity deeply into our everyday lives and feel connected to who we are and our impact on the world. We each have a limited amount of time in our lives. We simply can't make more of it. But we can choose what to do with it. We can make a choice to place our attention on the acts of creativity that fill us up and bring beauty into our lives. We can choose to pay attention to ourselves, and inspire others to do the same. We can connect around our passion, encouraging each other to become more thoughtful, aware, and self-sustaining.

They are not alone in claiming empowerment for sewing. This language shapes the 'new' sewing round the world to a considerable extent, with particular emphasis on community, shared support and the chance to change not just one's appearance but one's sense of self.[34]

Sewing provides an element of control. World and personal events can make us feel we have lost control over important parts of our lives, but choosing cloth, laying it out, measuring, cutting, constructing: these actions give us control over our medium as we elaborate and achieve the desired form and put it to use. Sewing also gives us control over our use of time: it can bring relief from fast culture by slowing things down, providing a purposefulness that restores us to ourselves. You may be sewing in a group around a work-table, making a commemorative or community or campaigning piece together, yet even as you feel involved in a supportive group, buoyed up by their talk and cake, sewing is at the same time a solitary act using your hands, your time. In these situations, sewing connects people together in a shared aim, a team effort, while also establishing an individual's sense of worth. Of course, choirs in halls, bellringers in belfries and relay sprinters on tracks all share this deeply satisfying duality of personal contribution to a collective achievement, and their endeavours are hard to miss. By comparison, stitching, especially by hand, is slow, quiet and easily overlooked despite its equivalent characteristics.

Sewing's personal and collective dimensions are moulded by two further considerations that tie it as closely to the realities of our physical world as they do to our imaginative possibilities and link it to the broader fellowship of making in general. First of these is that sewing requires cloth. In their focus on the specifics of materiality, the sewing-maker is like any craftsperson regardless of their medium. They are engaged in a dialogue with their cloth. Furniture maker and author Peter Korn's celebration of the multi-dimensionality of wood shows what stitching has in common with other heftier crafts. 'Among species of wood there are significant variations in color, grain, porosity, density, pliability, stability, strength, rot resistance, and other working qualities.' As any sewing-maker will tell you, precisely the same range of characteristics are present in each 'species' of cloth, from natural to synthetic, from heavy wools to gossamer silks. Success with both wood and cloth, despite their fundamental differences, calls for the same degree of commitment and understanding from the maker. Craft is rewarding, says Korn, because of its 'singular and pervasive materiality' and its 'tangible matter'.[35] We will see in Chapter Three how for many sewing practitioners this is one of its chief and enduring attractions.

The second of sewing's worldly realities lies in the way its materials and tools are formed by technical and cultural factors that makers have inherited over time. These are a template which fixes how we see and work with materiality. For example, tailors' and dressmakers' paper patterns are made along well-established lines and the cloth we buy is normally woven in specific widths for dress, suiting or furnishing on looms built for the purpose, so weaving and measuring cloth are prescribed in given units. Units of measure often derive from ancient formulae, many based on the scale of the human body, and have been used by political authorities to standardize and regulate trade and tax. Some were variable between national or local jurisdictions until early modern times. Like our biomechanical and cognitive skills, the ways in which our materials and tools are formed so shape our ways of thinking and making that they become second nature to us. Their particularities bind us to their own physical realities; they are the parameters of our sewing experience.

Calling these realities of cloth and tools to mind is part of thinking seriously about why sewing matters now as much as it has ever mattered, because we need to look at ourselves as makers in a real world. Following on from Crawford's idea of our 'attentional landscape' and the challenge of accessing and protecting it, he warns that autonomy is a deceptive goal. 'It suggests that freedom is something we are entitled to, and it consists in liberation from constraints imposed by one's circumstances.' Rather than running for the exit, or believing that happiness stems from the consumer or lifestyle choices concocted and presented to us by others, he makes a powerful argument for getting more actively engaged with the world as it really is: 'we find ourselves *situated* in a world that is not of our making, and this "situatedness" is fundamental to what a human being is.' This asks us to recognize that claiming agency for ourselves can have a powerful effect on how we can see and own the world. 'Encountering the world *as* real' can give 'pleasure' and 'wonder and gratitude'. In light of this, the ways in which others seek to represent the world or mediate it for us 'lose some of their grip on us'.[36] The act of sewing as a making process and the real things it creates together provide our own dynamic engagement with the world and an alternative lens through which to manage and enjoy it.

In some families sewing seems to be in the blood and the craft appears built-in and self-perpetuating. The practical craft of sewing can be learnt within families from elders and siblings, if not at school, as we will see in the next chapter. The para-phernalia of sewing when it is ever present and valued – the sewing machine, the store of cloth, the tools – forms a sort of household culture and resource for the next generation, some-thing many people acknowledge. A sewing enthusiast now in her seventies told me that if she was presented today with her mother's sewing machine she could 'thread it without hesita-tion, just from having watched her so much'. But the underlying satisfactions and enjoyments, the 'flow' of specific needlework projects, are internalized within the maker. The child can see a mother's hands at work and perhaps sense her concentration, but expressive as the hands are, they are silent about what the practice means to the maker. In families where sewing appears to be passed down from one generation to another, how does that happen: between learning the practice and the love of the practice, does one come before the other, or are they insepar-able? It is as if that love of sewing can be learnt in the same way that stitches can, although sometimes it skips a family member or two. Is there a making gene somewhere in the mix? In Hazel's case, she is already part of a sewing family whose stories tell us about family bonding between women reaching back to the 1920s and possibly before. Her mother, aunt and grandmother particularly recall several pairs of house curtains made by her great-grandmother when living in southern Africa and brought back to the UK. The curtains illustrated in appliqué the changing seasons and associated local activities. These curtains made long ago are a shared intergenerational memory, a treasured material reminder of past accomplishments. Does that kind of material family archive become a stimulus for future making?

As we will see later, it is often felt that we are connected by stitches and stitching across time to other stitches and stitchers. The past presents itself as shared, a sensed continuity as well as a visible legacy. Of course, stitching happens in the here and now and belonging deeply in the moment is also central to the fulfilment experienced by the practitioner. In another dimension, purposeful sewing looks forward hopefully in anticipation of the project's next stage, or its completion and the future place and value of the finished article in the life of the maker or recipient. So, making things with needle and thread can bring a satisfying convergence of past, present and future. Of course, when the versatile and knowing hand starts to sew, it connects more than time: it performs a kind of alchemy that joins together the maker's various tacit and explicit knowledge to realize their aspirations and bring their project to fruition. It draws on that intangible inner urge to make, to counterbalance and recalibrate the giddy world with something tangible, coherent and pleasing. The sewing hand is doing far more than meets the eye.

2

Learning to Sew

Two French sisters aged six and seven, under their mother's guidance, took up needles and thread for the very first time in their lives. In Paris, they were in unsettling circumstances confined at home by the COVID-19 pandemic. But they took to stitching like ducklings to water. Concentrating over two hour-long sittings, each completed their project to make a little cotton pouch and put them to use straightaway to stow their small private treasures. The older one described their experience of sewing as 'soothing', and said, 'it makes your head go better.' Her younger sister enjoyed backstitching most and 'talking to my head' as she worked. They both want to do it again and will recommend it to their friends. Their enjoyment of their project illustrates how age-appropriate handiwork can be mesmerizing and rewarding. Learning under a kindly eye, at their own speed, in company and with the prospect of realizing something prized and of immediate use: all these elements combined to give the girls an ideal introduction to sewing. If only this were available to every child.

Yet despite children's natural inbuilt desire to learn in general, and the specific value of utilitarian needle skills across a lifetime, attitudes to how, or even if, these should be taught have ebbed and flowed. For much of its history, the teaching of sewing to girls both informally at home and formally in schools around the world has been shaped by the belief that it was part of home-making and domesticity, which were the natural sphere of women rich and poor; indeed, these were seen as their core roles and duties. By association needlework became a moral issue. These values prevailed until recent times, though they are increasingly contested, and still affect, to some extent, how sewing is perceived today, particularly as a gendered practice. The teaching and learning of sewing are further complicated by another weighty legacy – that false division often made between intellectual and manual work. Despite the value placed on some craft production, the former work is usually esteemed more than the latter, a distinction enshrined in both social and economic life despite evidence it is a thoroughly misleading view of how humans actually function. Looking at it in homes and more formal settings past and present, it is clear that teaching and learning to sew are far from neutral processes.

Girls raised in the more affluent homes of the eighteenth and nineteenth centuries were accustomed to a large repertoire of home-fabricated informal garments and accessories then in everyday use by women, men, children, infants and domestic servants, including many that are now forgotten, such as indoor day and night caps, or those flannel petticoats so beloved of the Victorians. Formal or heavier outer garments were less likely to be attempted at home. Shirts for men and boys could occupy a significant share of home output, as could a greater variety of household linen than we are familiar with today. The labour of generating and maintaining such things continued in many households long after ready-made equivalents were available.

In households with servants, nursery maids were charged with making or repairing the young children's clothes. Other domestic servants could also be involved depending on the number employed. In wealthier homes a lady's maid cared exclusively for her mistress's wardrobe and augmented her dressmaker's output with small items and alterations. Up until the Second World War, there were dressmakers willing to live in for a few days while they made or repaired body and household linen. In addition to this endless back-of-house industry, girls in such households witnessed their mothers and other female relatives and visitors frequently stitching front-of-house with all the necessary paraphernalia present, such as sewing tables or baskets, and often saw them socializing as they did so, as these adults had in their own childhoods. So learning to make simple items at a very young age was to take part in a familiar domestic scene.

Despite the legacy of pious samplers, and tracts on needlework as a way to instil neatness and self-discipline, in practice many sources suggest teaching at home was often enjoyed as a child-centred activity. Commonly starting with small gifts for grandmothers or sets of simple clothes for their dolls, little girls learnt constructional sewing in plain materials and scaled-down age-appropriate ways, as evidenced by countless examples that survive in museum collections. A set of dolls' underclothing might include a chemise, shift, petticoat, night dress and perhaps a cap, even a pocket with a tiny pincushion or handkerchief made to fit inside. Museums also hold many examples of specimen miniature garment parts, which were sometimes carefully preserved on card to serve as a reference for particular stitches and methods. These show how various levels of complexity were taught in miniature, such as measuring and cutting out fabric, constructing sleeves, gussets, collars and cuffs, hemming, gathering, trimming, cording, and making frills, drawstrings and buttonholes. Running and back stitch were taught for seams, plus specific stitches for hemming, piecing and buttonholes. In the early nineteenth century, one young girl who loved utilitarian sewing at home also enjoyed what went with it: 'the amusement of either gossiping, or learning poetry by heart, from a book, lying open under my work'.[1]

Instruction within the family was common enough, though not often in print, making the 1833 *The Rudiments of Needlework* a rarity. It is dedicated by the anonymous author to her three 'dear little nieces'. It baldly lists thirteen rules to be observed and thirteen errors to be avoided, but when the girls discovered the tiny cotton specimens of real needlework glued inside their aunt's slim book, they must have wondered if they were stitched by elves. By contrast, in the USA in 1913 the popular, chunky *The Mary Frances Sewing Book; or, Adventures among the Thimble People* gave children fulsome sewing instructions entwined with stories of animated tools and lively illustrations on every page. The 'dear little nieces' would have loved it. It included tissue-paper patterns for making many items for a doll's wardrobe. Author Jane Eayre Fryer, though steeped in the values of traditional home-making, refrained from moralizing. Her book's fusion of instruction and entertainment demonstrates how pedagogy developed to embrace imaginative play as a means of learning practical skills.

Learning to sew at home was very different for girls in poor or less leisured households with fewer resources and no paid help. Here their mother's needlework was often a matter of improvised urgent repairs and making over one existing garment into another. The priority was often keeping the shirt on the back of the principal wage-earner, if there was one. For many children, even having a doll, let alone the time to make clothes for it, would have been an unknown luxury. In the context of small and precarious budgets that could force choices between paying the rent or buying food or clothes, making clothes for yourself and your family had real value. When feasible it provided some stability in combination with strategies that included acquiring clothing from other sources such as second-hand markets, occasional gifts from neighbours, family and charities, as 'perks' for domestic servants from their employers or theft in an era when clothing represented a significant proportion of stolen goods. But, again, female relatives and neighbours played their part in transferring sewing knowhow and perhaps encouragement. Children whose mothers and elder sisters were employed in sewing as waged homework were surrounded day and night by the activity and knew it was a relentless burden but one on which the family's most basic needs depended. They could grow up seeing mother working through '40 pairs of trousers in the corner – sixpence halfpenny a pair' as a witness recalled from her own childhood in Edwardian London. They were frequently recruited to lug the completed work back to the middleman and return with the next batches to keep the home stitching going without interruption. They often joined in the making, with negative impact on their schooling. 'At home children of eight and seven help their mothers to hem shirts, to stitch cloth caps and neckties, to sew tapes on crinoline skirts,' notes an 1864 report on the employment of children.[2] Learning to sew in cramped quarters, often with used or shoddy materials, repetitive tasks and cheap tools, may have been a necessity but hardly conducive to advancing greater skills or enjoyment. These conditions lingered in Britain despite efforts to prevent child labour and long after compulsory schooling was introduced in the late nineteenth century.

In more recent times, when children learn to sew at home it is in the context of a smaller range of garments and household items in daily use than in the past and in the sure knowledge that ready-made goods dominate clothing consumption in general. They know making things at home is now a deliberate choice, sometimes in contrast to the homes of their friends. As we will see in later chapters, adults who sew at home have many different motives and ambitions for doing so, and within this ambience of sewing, children learn indirectly by watching and listening as well as directly by doing. Women who sew keenly today frequently describe learning almost by osmosis at an early age. Alyson's mother 'sewed just about all the time, making things for me and my 3 brothers and the house, and I thought that was normal and what mothers did'. Sophie's mother 'didn't so much teach me as just absorbed me into her sewing'. In many homes, mothers, grandmothers, aunts, older sisters and friends have taught children to sew before school age and then continued by supplementing school lessons. Inadvertently it sometimes has caused problems when a child starts school sewing lessons with better levels of attainment than her classmates or even her teacher. Scottish drag queen Lawrence Chaney, the 2021 winner of RuPaul's Drag Race UK, benefited from their mother's sewing at home. Her tuition meant that, as a student, they could make their own 'fabulous dress' for their first drag outfit.[3]

Learning to sew at an early age is often recalled today as part of the world of play, an extension of the relationship to toys and imaginative worlds. New Yorker Stella remembers her mother making her Barbie clothes, 'and I would make some simple things, clothes for dolls and teddy bears, blankets and pillows for my doll house, bedding for a fairy house that my friend and I put in the woods'. Recollections of this kind echo the eighteenth- and nineteenth-century lessons in making sets of garments for dolls, a long continuum of needlework enabling and bonding with a child's own view of their world. Books and magazines also continue to play a formative part in the domestic ecology of stitching, as they have done for generations. Elaine recalls 'the sewing books that my wider family had were really inspirational. We used to holiday with an aunt who had, as well as *Jane Eyre* which I adored, a cloth-bound copy of *The Big Book of Needlecraft*. I loved the illustrations in that book.'

When sewing skills are taught directly or indirectly by example in a home where the work and paraphernalia of stitching is evident, by more internalized processes these also transmit the habits, the motivations and the rewards of the practice and a child absorbs it all. Ludvinia was taught to sew in school in her native St Lucia, but when she managed to make a pair of pyjamas there with only one leg it was her dressmaker aunt who intervened to ensure her niece eventually worked out the conundrum at home for herself. Ludvinia picked up skills quickly and went on to sew for a living. Other aspects of home life have an impact too. Those who sew with enthusiasm often say the support of a non-sewing but craft-loving partner, or a childhood spent in a household where people just liked making things, have directly influenced them. A skilled professional needleworker traces her work to paternal inspiration: 'I thoroughly enjoy making things and love [a] challenge. I get this I believe from my dad, a jobbing carpenter in the building trade who could turn his hand to all things practical.' So although we think of women as mainly responsible for the transfer of needle skills to children at home as well as in the classroom, it is also fathers who, without even threading a needle, make an impact by their example and attitude in other areas. Elizabeth, a doctor and lifelong sewer, thinks her particular 'obsessional' approach to following the instructions when making clothes is inherited from her engineer father's respect for precision. That background served her well in a more challenging setting. 'I learned a different sort of sewing when I was a medical student. I was initiated into the world of sutures: catgut, silk and nylon; and the various stitches needed to join tissues together: continuous, interrupted, subcuticular, mattress, purse string and so on.'

What is the future for learning to sew at home? There are families where the absence of sewing or craft of any kind means the seed may never be sown there. However, what happens in sewing or non-sewing households is shaped to an important extent by what happens in schools and, as we will see, way beyond school in the world of digital learning and other communities of support for those who stitch. In those families where sewing is second nature, it can flow across generations. Charlie is a thirty-year-old Londoner who grew up with the sound of his mother's sewing machine in the background. In his first post-school sewing project, he made himself a wearable shirt almost entirely *by hand*. Along the way, this 'mammoth task' was aided by his mother giving him 'invaluable' help via video call. She then wisely gave him a sewing machine of his own to support his aim to continue making clothes. Claire, another avid maker now in her mid-seventies, was also taught by her mother, Mary, who in turn learnt from her aunts in the 1920s. Claire taught her own children to sew, two of whom have taught sewing to people outside the family. 'My first memory is sewing,' says Susanna, whose sewing background now feeds into her work as an archaeologist studying ancient textiles. Claire's sewing granddaughter believes 'sewing is a habit you get into.' This family also treasures various sewing heirlooms, reinforcing a sense of themselves as 'a sewing family'.

The first instructional sewing books in Britain became available in the early nineteenth century before compulsory schooling was established. The readers of such books were those in charge of teaching poor children in schools, orphanages or other charitable institutions or budget-conscious women who wanted to teach daughters and servants. They were clearly not intended for the poor to buy for themselves, but these books may have helped improve the teaching they received. The jury is out on exactly how widespread sewing and cutting-out skills were in the period from the eighteenth to the early twentieth century, especially among the poor, whose lives show up less in the historical record and whose garments seldom survive in museum collections. But in general, it is safe to say that most women had rudimentary knowledge of sewing and many had more skill, and it is likely that the rise of cotton as the dominant lighter-weight, washable fabric during the industrializing period was a help to many who made utilitarian items at home. Until the arrival of cheap paper dressmaking patterns in the later nineteenth century, there is also evidence that cutting out fabric to make up into garments or furnishings was regarded as at least as big a challenge as making up. Cutting out accurately to avoid wastage was promoted as an obvious economy, both for those supplying the cloth and the learners themselves, and applied even to simple undergarments such as shifts. One book described measuring for cutting cloth as a kind of domestic mathematics, yet another educational benefit, and at heart moral.

Elementary schooling was compulsory in 1880 for children between five and ten and needlework instruction became more formalized and based on the belief that working-class girls should learn only plain needlework, a value inherited from earlier schemes of education.[4] Utilitarian needlework, including mending, was thought far more appropriate than decorative work for the children of the poor because it was seen as a suitable skill for their likely work in domestic service, or a means to supplement the income of their future family or support themselves independently if necessary. Elementary school teachers, predominantly women, were not well paid themselves so knew from personal experience that plain needlework was essential to make ends meet and maintain an acceptable appearance.

In classrooms where creativity or playful learning were not priorities, nineteenth-century teachers followed the rule book and taught needlework by rote, starting with drill.[5] Daily lessons were common. It was thought that a tough learning regime was required because in times past the binding structures of social class meant there seemed no choice but that working-class girls must learn to sew usefully. A kindly Victorian vicar, the Reverend Glennie, when serving as a school inspector, was however perturbed by what he observed during a sewing lesson in 1858. Children's needlework was taken away from them at the end of the day. It could be issued the next day to another child or even taken apart so the fabric could be re-used for further work, a method he says was likely to 'break the hearts and chill the sympathies' of children. He took a child-centred approach, calling for a personalized lap-bag for each child for all the time she was in school, so that her work could be easily stored and redistributed to her. He saw the benefits of learning needlework in a system that secured an 'interest in her own performance, on the part of each individual girl. What she begins, she is to complete. The particular article of dress, when finished, will, in its integrity, be the result of her own industry, perseverance, and successful contrivance.'[6] Nevertheless, teaching that aimed at conformity in needlework across a whole class of children was widespread in English classrooms of the period. It was almost inevitable when payment to schools was based on results in the compulsory curriculum and some of its disheartening effects reached well into the last century. When I sat down to listen to an elderly participant in my 1995 oral history of home dressmaking, her story about trying to make a buttonhole depicted teaching practices indeed likely to 'break the hearts' of children. At school in Southampton in 1918, ten-year-old Constance, a carpenter's daughter, was in trouble. 'I made mistakes all along the line,' so the needlework teacher 'had me stand outside of the class, in the classroom, but separate from the rest of the girls and I had to go on working at my buttonhole, because my buttonhole wasn't finished,' and 'this buttonhole that I was working on became so dirty and wet, mostly wet with my tears I think and ... I was left standing, working ... standing up, which wasn't the easiest of things to do and working at my buttonhole. I wasn't allowed to move on to the next lesson. I had to just stand there and get on with it.' The grim experience recalled by Constance had taken place almost eighty years before, but it was clear as she spoke that it still hurt.

In larger population centres the number of vocational learning opportunities outside schools increased and diversified during the nineteenth century. Developments in London exemplify how funding became available for vocational courses in the nineteenth and early twentieth centuries. The London County Council set up evening classes in spacious workrooms leading to dressmaking qualifications, shown in photographs of the time complete with sewing machines and the elaborately finished garments proudly displayed. Needlework was taught in the newly emerging teacher training colleges. Surviving samples of student work from Whitelands College in London, for example, show how the best could achieve the very highest standards in fine and decorative stitching; by the start of the twentieth century the training there shifted from that ultra-fine work to plainer sewing exercises on more utilitarian items such as garments better suited to the likely lifestyles of the future teachers and their pupils.[7] After the First World War, war widows were among the first intake for a course in 'Dressmaking and Ladies' Tailoring' at London's Chelsea College, hoping the training would help them find work to eke out their government pensions. Trade schools were established in London in the early twentieth century to train workers for the city's extensive clothing trade, which ranged from the city's cheaper East End garment workshops to the upmarket dressmakers and tailors of the West End. Like other big cities, London also had its share of small private teaching establishments for adults, set up by women who sometimes also traded in haberdashery or paper patterns or published their own instruction books. They were themselves an example to their customers how competence in needlework and dressmaking could offer independent career opportunities for women. Tailoring schools for men proliferated too on a commercial basis, often specializing in particular systems of cutting.

What has happened in schools in more recent times? How did we arrive at a place where many children today cannot even thread a needle and certainly could not help a modern Constance with her buttonhole? A survey in 2017 in the UK revealed that almost a quarter of adult participants cannot sew on a button properly, half need to ask their mothers to help them and a third were never taught to sew at all, yet over half wish they *could* sew and are prepared to learn, including over half of the men who responded.[8] Behind the findings of this dipstick survey lies a history of educational debate. In the nineteenth century the state took increasing control of the teaching of needlework along with other subjects because of its perceived importance. We may no longer talk much of the proper sphere of womanhood or its religious significance, though some still do, but shifts in the school curriculum now, as in the past, continue to be shaped by broader cultural values and politics.

In the case of girls' education, the push for academic success derived from the belief that the earlier over-domesticated model for their more limited education was out of touch with modern life, notably the rise in women working outside the home. Like many other subjects, needlework in the UK became something of a battleground about curriculum content and pedagogical methods between progressives and traditionalists, education professionals and the state. What was called 'home economics' or 'domestic science', the home of needle crafts in school, was taught mostly to girls as a self-contained curriculum and its critics accused it of banality, of chaining girls to outmoded ideas of domesticity, of suppressing their ambitions, of pseudo-science being applied in an attempt to raise the status of the subject. Some wanted its components, all useful life skills in their own right, to be integrated more meaningfully into other subjects. In England and Wales, the 1944 Education Act was a major step in articulating a fresh philosophy of how state education should meet the needs of modern society, including secondary level – needlework in schools survived that Act.

What followed from the 1970s onwards was the arrival and then the departure of compulsory study at secondary level of design and technology, a newly conceived subject area and something of a catch-all. It absorbed previously separate craft subjects and in this mixed context needlework became increasingly marginalized. With new emphasis on design using different media taught in schools and the rise of computer studies, there is even less emphasis on hand and craft skills. One teacher in the UK recently told me that sewing machines were getting a bad press in her secondary state-run school not only because they took up space and resources but because they could harbour infections. Another said that reductions in funding means larger class sizes, which exacerbates the difficulties of teaching practical life skills – especially sewing, since it involves potentially dangerous equipment such as hot irons, scissors and sewing machines. The long-term effect of this drift is worrying. Roger Kneebone, a UK professor of surgical education, is concerned that students of surgery today have spent too much time in virtual worlds, making them noticeably less comfortable doing things with their hands than they used to be. 'Partly it stops [students] being aware in three dimensions of what's going on around them, because their focus is much narrower. But also it takes away that physical understanding you get by actually doing things . . . That has to be done in the real world with real stuff.'[9]

But teaching a hand skill 'in the real world with real stuff' is not easy, though it helps if the learner is handy in the first place. Even when an explicit instruction, demonstration, diagram or video has laid out the task required, it still needs another kind of learning for a practical skill to be fully absorbed. Compared to sharing explicit knowledge, the tacit knowledge required across the craft in using tools and fabrics as well as the structural sewing methods themselves is often beyond the capacity of ordinary language to describe in any meaningful sense, so space and time are needed for embodied knowledge of this kind to take root. For some learners this may be testing and require more frustrating repetition than expected to get a feel for what's happening as they work. For others it is easily mastered. Some abilities are transferable, and age is no barrier. At the age of 81, Bruce bought his first sewing machine. With many years of fine-cabinet-making behind him, wood is his area of expertise. But already being dextrous, with a well-honed capacity to think in three dimensions and respect for hand and power tools, he needed only brief instruction on his machine to start his new hobby. It is perhaps no coincidence that he had a sewing mother and several seamstresses tucked away back in his family tree. But for both teachers and students, perhaps precisely because of these different cognitive processes, success, in all its various forms, is particularly rewarding. One sewing teacher, Natalia, says she enjoys her students' achievements as much as her own sewing and gets 'enormous satisfaction from the pleasure that learning to sew gives most people'.

Despite the explicit and tacit knowledge involved, working with the hands has often been valued less than non-manual or intellectual work. It is a persistent distinction enshrined in social class, education, politics and life choices that continues to frame perceptions of the world of work. By contrast, there have been those who valued manual work for its fundamental importance and specific skills, and some have recognized its capacity to bring spiritual insight. Although more radical educational theories and teaching practices past and present have seen past the false hand–head division by approaching the intellectual and practical development of children as inseparable and mutually supportive, most have done the opposite. The educationalist Mike Rose saw this play out in education in the USA and it is apparent in other countries – the distinction 'between the academic and the vocational' – and describes it as 'one of the most long-standing and visible institutional manifestations of our culture's beliefs about hand and brain, mind and work'.[10] As an example, Jane is now a lifelong sewing fan, but this damaging binary idea coloured her schooldays in the UK: her own mother's struggle to get an education meant she thought it wrong 'to spend valuable school time making aprons to cook in' in hours of sewing lessons when all that could be taught at home. Numerous experts on education, learning and human intelligence argue that hand work is central to a properly integrated and mutually reinforced approach to learning. The advice from that quarter is 'any parent or teacher who hopes to awaken the curiosity of a child, and who seeks to join the child who is ready to learn, is simply to head for the hands.'[11]

And yet, talk to adept craftspeople and they will underline the link between creativity and the discipline behind it. Repetitive practice might not always bring perfection, and perfection isn't everyone's goal, but there's no perfection without it. Teachers of plain needlework have always made this clear one way or another.

The graft behind the craft can indeed lead to 'the joy of creation' as described here by a needlework expert in 1932:

[Needlework's] value from the cultural and practical aspects makes it essential that the approach to the subject should be on the right lines. All good Craft-work depends largely on the thorough grasp of the technique of the subject, and the person who masters the details will be more than repaid for the time and thought expended in the process, when the monotony, and perhaps the drudgery, of practice will have turned into the pleasure of accomplishment and the joy of creation.[12]

This is not an easy lesson to teach in today's crowded school curriculum and in a world where gratification is so often instant. Yet sewing lessons are like any other – the attitude of the teacher is formative in and outside lessons. Ingrid's parents came from St Kitts to England as part of the Windrush generation. Aged about seven she was 'one of a few black children at the school' and endured harassment and bullying. Not being able to face the playground again, she heard her teacher say, 'That is a big sigh for a little girl – come and sit with me.' The teacher was sewing at her desk, recalls Ingrid, 'she showed me what she was doing, I copied her and that's where my love for sewing began.' As an adult she has gone on to teach sewing to children and adults including refugees. Despite her mother's anxieties about sewing being taught in lessons that could be devoted instead to academic subjects, Jane remembers a school sewing class in which pupils learnt poetry by rote as they worked: 'I only have to think of the first line of John Masefield's poem "Cargoes" to be transported back to a school classroom and my 8 year old self. I loved the poem and the association with stitch, the combination of having my hands busy while my mind wandered and I daydreamed of exotic places far beyond my home in suburban London.'

For every person who enjoyed their school needlework lessons, there is another who didn't, but it is not uncommon to find that the latter went on with the craft in one way or another in later life. Many people who sew proficiently and happily today came through less than effective formal teaching in schools. A museum fashion curator recalls needlework as part of domestic science classes: 'I made a corduroy dress, but, by the time I'd finished, it didn't fit.'[13] Elsewhere Peggy was a pupil who felt 'imprisoned' by lessons at school yet sewed enthusiastically as an adult for years afterwards at home for herself and her family. She was one of the older participants in my 1995 oral history of dressmaking who were mostly in school before the Second World War and were more likely to report unhappy needlework experiences in the classroom than those who told me their stories of more recent schooling. Their complaints included making items they didn't choose and wouldn't use when finished and teachers unable to support pupils who came in with higher levels of attainment acquired at home. Their negative classroom experiences could be overcome in homes where sewing or other forms of making were encouraged.

There have often been mismatches between what is taught in schools and what can be seen in the shops outside the school gates, magnified between the world wars when fashion magazines and films cast their own irresistible spell. Elsie told me how in 1930s Portsmouth, England, she had to make 'ghastly dresses' in school but once she got her first job aged fifteen at a ladies' tailor she developed a lifelong passion for good fabrics and making her own fashionable, well-cut suits and dresses. After the war, Dior's 1947 New Look blew her away and as for many others at the time her home dressmaking became the way to achieve fashionable outfits for herself that were affordable and fitted exactly to her figure. Despite her unhappy school experience, Elsie became very proficient and passed her stylishness and sewing knowhow on to her daughter and granddaughter in a lasting legacy. While some gave up sewing post-school in the face of affordable youth-centred fashions in the 1960s and ever faster cycles of change that fuelled a throwaway culture, others were encouraged to make their own clothes by the excitement of the new, simpler fashions. But more recently a younger generation has reported more enjoyment of school sewing within a broader syllabus that exposes them to a wider variety of designing and making in general. Although this approach reduced the time devoted to developing practical skill in any one specific craft, it seems to have resulted for some in a readiness to continue sewing after leaving school. Such personal stories give a flavour of sewing in schools, including ways in which strong positive and negative reactions to lessons can be coupled with some unpredictable long-term effects. Some never sew again; for others sewing becomes a lasting and pleasurable habit.

Learning to sew may be threatened by neglect within much of the formal secondary education sector, certainly in the UK, but in other settings where sewing thrives today, amateur practitioners and enthusiasts are busy learning for all sorts of reasons. There is a new mood in the air. Lockdown during the COVID-19 pandemic increased the sale of sewing machines and got many returnees and novices sewing, with one sewing-machine manufacturer claiming that in the UK young men slightly outnumbered young women in this take-up.[14] The positive effects of sewing on well-being were demonstrated during the pandemic but those involved in the retail side confirm that trade was growing even before COVID-19. The founder of a stylish London fabric and haber-dashery retailer has seen a 'great' increase since she started in 2008, particularly for garment-making rather than furnishing supplies, and including more male customers.[15] Sewing is undoubtedly benefiting from more relaxed teaching styles in new settings that foster a can-do attitude using encouragement and banish older prescriptive teaching methods. The simpler informality of gar-ments promoted by the new breed of independent paper pattern businesses feels less daunting for learners dipping their toe in for the first time and patterns can now be printed from PDFs at home. One sewing advocate with thousands of followers online advises: 'Honestly, just start. I think the best trait you can have to be good at sewing is not being afraid of failing. Sewing is a lot about trial and error. Things don't need to be perfect and you'll get there with practice!'[16]

In an echo of how Big Food's processed food industry and its remorseless advertising have eroded home cooking, Big Fashion and its monster offspring Fast and Ultra-Fast Fashion have gen-erated a consumer environment seemingly inimical to sewing clothes for yourself at home. So what incentivizes people to learn to sew for themselves? And what are the rewards for their efforts? The learning experience is affected for better or worse by the degree of ambition. For adults choosing to learn to sew and for those who want to take their activity beyond basic levels of attainment, strong motivation is required given how many other things compete for their time.

There hasn't been a lot of number-crunching on why people sew at home, but there is enough to establish some key markers. Allowing for changing perceptions of these issues at different times and places, the role played by personal economics, or thrift, shows as a consistent motive but is never the overriding incentive for everybody who sewed at home. In the USA in the mid-1920s, one of the earliest studies to explore motives found that thrift mattered more for poorer rural women and was overtaken by wanting to make better-quality and better-fitting clothing as income and community size increased. It was estimated that by 1958 in the USA 20 per cent of all female clothing was made at home, something of a post-war boom that is echoed elsewhere, indicating that domestic sewing was happening on a significant scale. Naturally enough, motives could vary: for example, age, occupation and marital status have always differentiated attitudes to home sewing, with older makers valuing thrift and fit more than their younger counterparts, but, despite these variables, personal enjoyment has remained a strong stimulus. A 1990s study revealed enjoyment to be 'significantly more important' than sewing for economy or fit. This top incentive was expressed variously in terms of 'accomplishment', self-reliance, being 'creative', immersion and the chance 'to learn from others of the same mind'.[17]

More recent research in the USA confirmed that personal fulfilment remains a lead motive for participants aged 22 to 40, with overt reference to taking control of their experience as consumers: 'The desire to be active in the creation process of their clothing and to escape mass-manufactured goods may explain why women are choosing to sew their own clothes.' In such cases, Big Fashion makes home sewing more attractive, not less. Computer-based jobs can lead people to make something 'tangible' in their own time 'when the majority of their time was spent on intangible outcomes'. The findings described a sequence of phases in how these sewing women moved through their practice, from the initial investment of money and time to feeling they were in control of their practice and eventually reaching a sense of 'empowerment' as it all came together. Although sewing practices may vary considerably and the specifics of community and culture will have their own impacts, these phases broadly map onto the experience of adult learning from first steps to proficiency. One important finding in this particular study is that thrift no longer played any part at all for any of the ethnically diverse participants, indicating a significant break with previous generations.[18] My own project in 1995 with older women who chose to make clothes at home in the UK found that, although thrift played a central role for them when they were younger, in their later years it did not. This was also emphasized by numerous older participants in *Our Sewing Stories* in 2020–22, who reported that home sewing was not a way to save money. But for how long? Recent rises in the cost of living may mean that thrift becomes a more pronounced driver for home sewing again. Younger participants said that sewing with recycled fabrics at very little cost gave them great satisfaction for both thrift and environmental reasons. Growing public awareness of the unsustainability of the fashion and textile industries, compounded by increasing unease about the climate crisis, may act as a fresh impetus for learning to sew in the context of adopting other more self-reliant practices.

Numerous part-time non-award-bearing sewing classes for adults have sprung up in recent years in many towns and cities, sometimes associated with fabric and haberdashery shops. They often teach 'make and take' craft projects to be completed inside a day, hold short courses for absolute beginners – such as how to use a sewing machine and apply its various functions to make simple items – or offer further levels of dressmaking such as making a whole garment. For more aspiring sewers there are workshops focused on one specialism such as bridalwear or pattern drafting, sometimes as a step towards first qualifications and work in the industry. A common element across these commercially run classes is their promotion of their other less tangible advantages, such as meeting real people in the same 'tribe', sewing's role in reducing stress and the chance to unleash an individual's creativity. Their claim for this triple helping of benefits now forms a widely shared narrative about this kind of informal learning experience, which offers beginners or improvers undogmatic, personalized approaches through self-selected and self-paced projects. This approach to positive teaching is often accompanied by an online follow-up presence with tutors who can offer continuing support and group contact. There are now sewing retreats where those who can afford it enjoy an immersive stay in comfortable surroundings together with a tutor.

Loneliness and anxiety are on the rise in society, becoming a public health issue exacerbated by the known links between these psychological problems and physical illness. It is no coincidence that the desire to undertake hand and craft work through shared learning opportunities is growing at such a time. There are specific rewards in learning to sew in groups; sitting side by side without direct eye contact helps people to talk openly, and sewing together with other learners, especially by hand, can facilitate listening and sharing, thus not only making and valuing what is made but creating a particular ambience that is often described by participants as having mental health benefits. These informal learning environments in the UK may be a response to cuts in local authority funding for public evening classes, although some continue to offer free enrolment at sewing classes leading to initial qualifications, billed as preparation for employment or further levels of education. However, Claire, a teacher who runs her own short courses for small-group classes near London, told me she deliberately modelled her business on offering what more formal institutional courses cannot. She provides a homely and relaxed environment with a cuppa on the sofa and a choice of sewing small items such as bags or full-on dressmaking, other crafts such as knitting and crochet, day or half-day machine-based classes for time-poor learners who want to take a finished product home on the same day, weekend or longer workshops for more ambitious projects such as making a pair of jeans, and a Friday-night online sewing club. Numerous short online courses are also available, giving her students flexibility in how and when they learn. She feels her teaching is inseparable from the emotional support she gives. A well-used collection box for a mental health charity sits in a prominent spot near the sofa. Ultimately, she is 'building a community' where people feel enabled but also safe, something reiterated by the students I met on my visit. Claire is an energetic businesswoman who believes that without the glue of social media for both marketing and holding this community together, she simply wouldn't have a viable teaching business. Men are in a very small minority here: a man might come with a specific technical craft need or a dad might bring his young daughter for a shared treat, but, although welcome, they are less likely to seek the social intimacy on offer.[19]

Sewing's online profile is now immense. For many adults, learning to sew these days is well-nigh unimaginable without it. Countless websites and blogs make it abundantly clear how engaging, rewarding and social sewing can be. One home sewing enthusiast told me her iPad was her favourite sewing tool – a testament to how much instruction, advice and support is now available at the tap of a finger. 'All of the women' in a recent survey said 'the Internet was essential to their learning to sew.'[20] Anyone who has turned to websites for assistance will know they vary in quality and users need to shop around for the most appropriate ones for their project. There is a certain irony in using them for those who like to enjoy their leisure time working with their hands, in contrast to their day-long screen-based jobs, but the sense of being connected to others in an online community of shared activity offers a powerful antidote to the slog of learning on your own. It is said that about 46 per cent of the USA's 9–11 million quilters 'are now searching online for quilting products and education every day'.[21] It is remarkable how many online special-interest sewing communities have emerged. Groups that support absolute beginners or more confident makers, creating clothes for and by men, the disabled, people with non-standard body sizes, those who seek more gender fluidity in their wardrobe, or people who just want to stand out from the crowd, make clothes for their children, rev up their style or slow their lives down – many of these groups underline their commitment to ethnic and gender diversity and their provision of a safe, non-judgemental space. These 'families' of makers are testimony to the sheer range of home stitchers and their motives.

For newcomers, the first steps in dressmaking in particular can be a bit of a gamble. The first time you open out a paper pattern envelope and lay out the contents you are faced with the baffling business of understanding how the future three-dimensional garment starts life in its various flat deconstructed constituent parts. Line drawings of the intended garment, advice on fabric type, sizing and any buttons or zips required (notions, as dressmakers like to call these small extra necessities) are printed on the outside back of the envelope and a detailed instruction sheet fits inside with all the requisite tissue-paper pieces or templates. Despite the growth of patterns in PDF form, over many years this has remained the traditional way of presenting a pattern. Each piece of the garment is represented by a tissue-paper pattern piece printed with symbols for folds, grain, darts, size and adjustment lines and so on, a code of essential information about the precise place and form the piece will take at both the cutting and assembly stages. In all, this can feel like a weird new kind of thinking, but once learnt, it makes sense. How-to books grew up alongside the advent of paper patterns in the nineteenth century, complementing their emphasis on style and fashion with the documentation of fundamental procedures. Today there is a new generation of such books aimed at younger sewers and starters, but, however inspiring these are, beginners will always be in need of learning through practice. Learning to think and act sequentially with the accumulated pattern pieces, fabric and tools takes time and inevitably mistakes occur. Whether or not a mistake is turned into a positive stage in the journey or remains a roadblock depends on the mindsets of the learner and the teacher. The academic Jade Halbert described her experience of making a dress from a paper pattern for the first time. 'In making just one simple dress a plethora of new intellectual skills have been developed; I've learned a new language, and translated and contextualised an entirely new vocabulary. I've learned how to drive a new machine and concentrated hard on solving difficult problems.'[22] While the maker must learn the detail, they must also build a sense of the whole. Learning to read the 'language' of a pattern, to cut cloth and to 'speak' garment construction, requires this active interplay of mind and matter.

One young woman told me that she learnt to use a sewing machine when her mother and a schoolteacher gave her mostly oral and tactile prompts. For machine sewing the exact coordination of the necessary movements of hands and feet evade even the clearest of manufacturers' instructions, a reminder that there is no truly precise vocabulary to convey the totality of learning to sew by machine. A teacher's apparently effortless economy of movement and composure in machine or hand sewing derives from tacit forms of knowledge, the kind of craft-specific understandings that can only be learnt by repetition. Technical instruction only goes so far. It is knowing by doing, embodied knowing, that develops the skills and satisfactions of sewing. If we imagine the teacher's left hand holding a length of cotton fabric with the intention of gathering it, perhaps to bring it to fit a waistband, and the right hand moving the needle and thread to tack the gathers evenly in place, there will be a visible movement of the fingers as they ease the cloth into place. Yet the change of pressure exerted by that movement and the natural limits of reach and control, and the degree of feel and push required behind the needle in the other hand, is unknowable to the novice watching. It is only by repeating the doing that you can retain and own that understanding and become independent at the task. In other words, experiential learning is central to the endeavour. Roger Kneebone thinks that to master a craft we must learn from others and also at the same time shift our attention inwards. 'It doesn't come from books and you have to experience it for yourself, stocking an internal library of sensations, muscular actions and familiarity with your materials.'[23] The stages of the journey to confidence and on to mature expertise involve these immersive experiences, and as we saw at the start of the chapter, even very young learners can enjoy the rewards of the concentration required.

What exactly is being taught in and through sewing? It is not just about stitches and practical matters, which themselves depend on deploying cognition, senses, motor abilities, intellect, memory, imagination and creativity. Called into action, these can lead beyond the initial steps to more confident and venturesome learning that in many cases is lifelong and involves a sense of personal growth. For those with few alternative opportunities, learning to sew can be a revelation. In Bukirasazi in Burundi a project in partnership with UNICEF provided a young woman in poverty with a sewing machine and training in 2020. She can now support her family and, with four friends, is earning enough to expand her business interests. 'I've never dreamed that one day I would get this far,' says Joselyne.[24] Learning to be a maker is a rich and fuzzy process that means different things to different people in different situations and at different stages of their lives. Yet it is generally true, regardless of standards or experience, that making leads the maker to new places. As Peter Dormer puts it, 'when craft is practiced as a disciplined piece of knowledge, it is inevitably an activity of self-exploration in the sense that one learns about oneself through searching for excellence in work.'[25]

We look askance at what went on in the schoolrooms of the past when rigid instruction methods were imposed and

Constance wept over her buttonhole. School rooms today may aim to be happier places, but making buttonholes is no longer a priority. Does that matter? The modern child may have modern skills in computing or electronics or design, but if they are then lost in the face of the rest of the everyday material world around them, they are disempowered. If they lose the option to shape their own consumption practices, or their own living space, to cope in any practical way with hardship, or simply enjoy making stuff, then what is gained? It is worth asking if the reduction in teaching manual skills in schools both for their own worth and for their role in engendering creativity as a habit correlates with the rise in anxiety and depression seen in society today. A child is built for learning, making, doing and exploring the world around them. Sue Stuart-Smith, a psychiatrist and psychotherapist, writes about the benefits of gardening, but her argument could equally apply to sewing, and craft in general. 'As children, and let us not forget it, as adults too, we need to dream, we need to do and we need to have an impact on our environment. These things give rise to a sense of optimism about our capacity to shape our own lives.'[26]

We squander human capabilities at our peril. The dependency that ensues is surely a deprivation, stunting the pleasures and rewards of practical skill, starving cognitive capability and creativity. We are reduced if we lose familiarity with the use of basic tools. You don't have to be a survivalist or extreme doomster to recognize that for humankind to thrive we are sorely in need of inventive minds and resourcefulness. Sewing belongs in this mix. But if we look ahead, although sewing may encounter ups and downs in education, there are plenty of causes for optimism. When we hear about the five-year-old who can already thread a sewing machine 'in the correct sequence with perfect accuracy' and enjoys making clothes for her favourite toys, it's time to celebrate. Setbacks aside, her mother believes 'overwhelmingly the experience of teaching her is positive – I love that she will have the option to make things and be creative and enjoy something which is practical yet also gives you a sense of fulfilment.'

3

A Material World

Sewing matters and cloth matters; it is hard to think of one without the other. All cloth, even the most ordinary sort in everyday use, is a material document of human innovation and endeavour past and present. To see this at work in our world, we must look beyond the finished fabrics we sew or wear to their hinterland of raw materials and production. But the immensity and almost incalculable impact of this global complex are normally invisible to us as consumers, except when they hit the headlines. A river runs full of toxic dye, cotton workers suffer exploitation: these stories come to our attention but fade all too fast. At the same time, from childhood onwards we all know through our five senses, emotions and memory that we experience cloth – its colour, texture and character – with an intimacy and immediacy like little else. But this is disconnected from the realities of the giant conglomeration of labour and industry that produces the cloth we touch. Yet if we want to see the distinctive realm of textiles for what it actually is, we need to recognize all its constituent parts, good, bad or ugly. It doesn't stop us loving textiles, but would it make us more savvy consumers?

Cloth, fabric, textile: as in everyday speech, all three words are used here more or less interchangeably. The word 'cloth' is very ancient, woven through several European languages. In modern English it resembles various Old English, Dutch and German words but Oxford's lexicographers admit it is ultimately of unknown origin. For 'fabric', they record origins in the Latin *fabricare*, meaning to make or fashion. The word 'textile' contains 'text', from the Latin *texere*, to weave, a close partnership of the etymological with the metaphorical, since we may read, decipher and understand a textile, just as we do a text. Textiles are woven with yarns, and after all, a yarn is also a story.

There is no doubt that the link between cloth and human emotions is dynamic and a powerful part of its significance. We first meet the affective capacity of human physical intimacy with cloth when, in their early years, children may form a profound bond with a comfort blanket, and can become distraught if it goes missing. It has been said that cloth's propensity to retain smell is important in these transitional objects. But once that attachment phase is passed, youngsters may grow up indifferent to cloth's many wavelengths – even budding fashionistas with unshakeable opinions on their appearance and brands *du jour* are often cloth-blind. Many adults know in forensic detail what's in their muesli but not what they sleep on or wear next to their skin. Yet despite a general unawareness of its origins, cloth can still cast a spell, less intense than the comfort blanket but nonetheless life-enhancing. The cosiness of a winter vest, the welcoming aroma of fresh bed linen, a good old-fashioned hanky in time of need, a familiar well-worn jacket that remembers our body shape in its creases: surely few people are immune to these sensations, even if they know nothing about how or where or by whom these things were made.

Ask somebody who sews for pleasure why they do it and they will tell you that their love of cloth is one of the main drivers behind what they do. However, within this almost ubiquitous answer, people describe different sensory responses to cloth. Many people find the sight of the colours of the material can lift their mood. Cathy, a professional dressmaker, says that when her favourite silks – 'heavyweight duchess satin silk and silk dupion' – arrive from the supplier she loves the 'luxurious and luscious' smell of them. Pino, an artist, hears fabrics and avoids sewing with them if their surfaces sound harsh when rubbed. Others dislike sewing with cloth that is cold to the touch. For me, Harris tweed takes the prize. Naturally water-repellent, it protects against thorns, insulates against the cold and is fully biodegradable in the unlikely event of anyone wanting to part with it. But as well as these utilitarian virtues, it is earthy and seductive, sturdy yet beautiful, and animated from within by the colours of its local island landscape. Like stroking a pet, handling Harris tweed is soothing. Can a cloth made from natural fibres communicate something of its biological origins?[1] Cloth may not be animate, but nevertheless it holds its own story.

The act of stitching to form something from cloth unites the mind and life of the maker with the 'mind' and life of the cloth. There are vast differences in the tastes and preferences of makers, just as there are countless physical differences across the plethora of fabric types. Many makers like to work with what they experience as responsive cloth. Another very experienced professional maker, Beatrice, likes sewing with cloth made of natural fibres, 'poplin, lawn, linen, silk, wool, Viyella', because they are 'easier to sew, respond well to steam and more stable when cutting out'. A retired academic looking back on her long life of amateur sewing has always liked to sew with them 'because of how they handle' but also feels there's 'something special about the depth and vibrancy of their colours' and they are comfortable to wear because they 'breathe'. Responses to fabric also depend on the aptitude of the maker, the capability of their sewing machine and, importantly, the thing they want to sew and the finish they seek. Lucy recalls, 'My mother made me a turquoise mini dress with a silver lurex thread to go to a party when I was a teenager. I loved it!' But her tastes changed over time, and now she loves to sew and wear natural fabrics. As a child of the seventies who 'grew up in synthetics', Julia remembers 'experiencing static regularly' and although that unpleasant prickly sensation, literally hair-raising, is now largely a thing of the past, Julia still prefers to avoid sewing with them. Nonetheless lots of stitchers are happy sewing with synthetic fabrics such as polyester or those with added glamour, sparkle or novelty finishes, or with natural yarns blended with synthetics to provide the extra stretchiness or harder-wearing properties they want. Regarded by others as unyielding, synthetics attract sewers not least because they are so readily available and offer immense choice, frequently at a lower cost. The popularity of knitted fabrics in the 1970s and '80s and more recently four-way-stretch dress fabrics are examples of how textile manufacturing innovations can keep home dressmakers on their toes, adapting to new techniques to manage the more unpredictable behaviour of these fabrics, which can fray and squirm under the needle. Alice was one who succeeded with knitted fabrics and loved the dresses she sewed in 'swishy, flowy jerseys'. Despite the fact that viscose (a semi-synthetic cellulose material) 'is hell to cut and sew', says Natalia, who teaches sewing, she counts it among her favourites for its drape and durability.

Even materials which can hardly be called cloth – such as neoprene, a kind of synthetic rubber usually sandwiched between stretchy knitted synthetic fabrics, used for wetsuits for example – though challenging, can be sewn by keen domestic makers. Now widely available, when neoprene appeared in the 1930s it mostly had military and industrial uses before emerging into sportswear and other more popular applications. Keen home sewers enjoy the fact it doesn't fray and meet its demands for heavy-duty thread, or a ball-point machine needle or so-called walking foot to give better movement through a sewing machine. They sew cases for their electronic devices, jewellery and clothing, following neoprene's emergence onto the catwalk, where fashion designers exploit its non-woven properties to form garments into eye-catching sculptural shapes. Given the chance, it seems somebody somewhere will use almost any material to sew almost anything.

Just as the maker relates to the material, traditional or innovative, the sewing thread that stitches and holds this maker–material partnership together also has distinctive properties and potentials of its own that respond to the maker's task in different ways. For stitching lingerie or carpets, gloves or sportswear, there's specific thread made for the job. In industry it might be flame-resistant, or muscular enough to sew a truck seat or a cricket ball. For ordinary domestic purposes, natural cotton, linen and silk sewing threads are also each manufactured to offer specific degrees of strength, give, suppleness and smoothness for different uses. Fossil-fuel-derived polyester sewing thread, used extensively, also has give, an important trait for accommodating the movement of the body inside the garment. Some stitching aims to match the thread so closely to the cloth that it becomes more or less invisible, but sometimes contrasting visible stitches are the name of the game, as in blue jeans. The story of thread, so often overlooked, complements the complexities of cloth itself.

The anthropologists Annette B. Weiner and Jane Schneider note how cloth around the world expresses status, sex, power, ideology, religion, wealth and poverty; they sum up how deeply cloth is interwoven into human life. 'In addition to its seemingly endless variability and related semiotic potential, cloth is a repository for prized fibers and dyes, dedicated human labor, and the virtuoso artistry of competitive aesthetic development.'[2] Sewing of course is an essential element in this 'dedicated human labor'. It is the work and skill of hand or machine stitching that transforms the diversity of cloth into garments and other articles of use and value, and it is stitching that mends or repurposes cloth to extend its useful life.

To see 'virtuoso artistry' at work, one of the most stunning manipulations of fabric occurs in the famous Delphos dresses developed by Italian Mariano Fortuny (1871–1949) in the first decade of the twentieth century. Each one was delicately engineered to resemble the fluted drapery on ancient Greek statues. They changed contemporary expectations of how a familiar fabric, made unfamiliar, could interact with the wearer. The dresses were assembled from simple rectangular shapes but by a still-secret pleating treatment of the silk these unique garments formed, in the words of a museum curator familiar with them, 'into rills like the delicate underside of a field mushroom . . . to create a shimmering, clinging tube of impossible lightness and loveliness . . . while the pleats skim the swell of stomach and curve of hips in a heavenly palette'. They were aimed at an elite but artistic market and for clients who so wished they could be 'dusted with gold'.[3] It was

Henriette Negrin (1877–1965), Fortuny's collaborator and later his wife, who ran the workrooms; she was a superb needlewoman who perfectly understood the expert hand stitching required to make these unique dresses.[4] The Delphos dresses exemplify the endless versatility of fabric and the enduring high value it can command when combined with fine needle skills; even today surviving examples fetch thousands of pounds at auction.

There are many ways for us to experience the affectivity and allure of textiles. The ancestors of artist Henri Matisse (1869–1954) had been weavers for generations. He was thus familiar with textiles, and his early depictions of them became pivotal to his new ways of seeing. 'Flowered, dotted, striped or plain, billowing across the canvas or pinned flat to the picture plane, textiles became in his hands an increasingly disruptive force used to destabilise the laws of three-dimensional illusion . . . to abolish the distinction between background and foreground.'[5] Many people were perplexed at first by these radical paintings, but they were taken up enthusiastically by a Russian patron. Sergei Shchukin ran a successful international cotton business that dealt in colourful printed goods, so he was in tune with decorative textiles around the world. He understood their rich heritage and the visual languages that Matisse was exploring as a means to disrupt pictorial space. Matisse collected textiles old and worn or new all his life – textile pieces, carpets, screens, costumes, Kuba cloth from the Congo, Tahitian bark cloth. He bought from 'oriental carpet shops and clothes stores . . . bazaars, souks and market stalls' in North Africa as part of an eclectic habit that included furnishing 'all his homes and studios from junk shops'. His textiles have been called his archive and toolkit; to him they were his 'working library'.[6]

Home sewers often keep quantities of unused fabric at home but they rarely refer to this treasure trove of fabrics-in-waiting as a 'reserve', 'store' or 'stock', let alone a 'library'. Instead, they mostly use 'hoard' or 'stash' to describe this precious resource, hinting at an addiction or illicit concealed bounty. But like Matisse, today's hoarders can have a powerful creative response to the colours, feel and decorative elements of cloth. One sewing enthusiast calls herself a 'fabricaholic'. Hoarding may happen for practical reasons, but hoarders still feel a special kind of pull towards their collection. In Munich, Barbara keeps her fabrics out of sight, but still feels 'a secret inner call to go on working with them'. Many makers have a strong desire to possess the tactile and visual pleasures offered by the un-made-up cloth, even when no immediate project presents itself, a desire that can outweigh practical considerations of cost or space. While collective or individual memories can be embedded in cloth, it can also represent anticipation. Poppy reflects that 'with all crafts there seems to be something about buying materials as a statement of intent – perhaps an optimism about a project that might be realised but often isn't.' She reports that acquiring a fabric that you like 'can be a now or never decision'. Many makers squirrel away their collections of fabric over considerable periods of time until, bingo, the right project comes along. For another Barbara, a retired local government planner and environmentalist, her opportunistic purchase of 'turquoise silk in Bangkok in 1975' had to wait 35 years to be made into a simple shift dress. Hoarding can be an insurance against possible future need or deprivation, a way to create surplus for future generosity or a kind of self-sufficiency. It can be a comfort and even an autobiography in that the hoard may be measured and savoured through memories of the places, people and past times from which it came. Buying cloth on trips away from home is often cited as a particular pleasure. A hoard may be private, even slightly secret, but expands and decreases over time as the hoarder's own life changes. In practice it is a constantly valued work in progress; its owner keeps a mental inventory of potential uses committed to memory. It is cloth-in-waiting, not cloth forgotten. One day its time will come.

Quantities of cloth kept together, be it in bales in a factory or shop, even in baskets of cut-offs or remnants for sale, or in lengths in the home, can create a particular physical environment. They can change or make more private a room or space by the way they act to muffle exterior sound. The surfaces of cloth interact with light in innumerable ways. In the domestic environment, by the accumulation of her maker's stash, the home sewer creates a notional territory and lexicon of her own. Just looking at a stash or turning pieces over in the hand can be a pleasure. There is comfort in this. Gaye lost a close friend with whom she had shared happy sewing times. 'Before she died her husband had her bed put into her sewing room so that she could be surrounded with all her materials and sewing things and a number of nearly completed quilts that were finished later by her many friends.'

Amassing cloth can be more pressing for quilters because assembling a pieced work on any scale is likely to call for variety and carefully managed colour ranges which need to be on hand if the project is not to stall. Sociologist Marybeth C. Stalp has studied in depth the hoarding tendency among American quilters who, despite the obvious rationale for accumulating fabric, often hide their stash. Hiding it is linked to feeling considerable anxiety about taking resources, time and space for themselves in the family home, highlighting what Stalp calls 'their diminished ability, relative to their spouses and their children, to pursue leisure activities without a stigma'.[7] The quilters Stalp talked to freely refer to their quilting and fabrics as simultaneously addictive and therapeutic despite the anxiety their stash might generate for them. My own second-hand copy of Stalp's book on quilting was signed and inscribed in her own hand – 'Embrace the stash' – a motto to preserve. Can these collections of cloth be an adult version of a child's comfort blanket? But in lockdown in the UK during the COVID-19 pandemic, some participants in *Our Sewing Stories* reported a new trend when they distributed their hoards as a whole or in part to charity shops, schools or friends. They seized lockdown as a chance to de-clutter and see their materials put to good purpose. For some, the hoard had reached its natural expiry date because no appropriate projects presented themselves before their tastes changed. For Natalia, her hoarding has been a negative experience. 'Having all that fabric just stresses me out. I feel I have to make things all the time, and I don't want to do that.' There is no doubt that cloth can engender strong emotions.

If keeping cloth can be a serious pleasure, guilty or otherwise, acquiring it in the first place is for sewers another kind of enjoyable recreation. Amy, a Londoner, speaks for many – 'Buying fabric is one of the great pleasures of sewing.' The days are long gone when the pedlar came to your door, a highlight for those in remote places, with goods such as cloth and haberdashery for sale, even singing their wares, as did Shakespeare's Autolycus in *The Winter's Tale* – 'Lawn as white as driven snow; Cyprus black as e'er was crow'.[8] Shopping in fixed shops was already a glamorized experience for richer folk in many eighteenth-century cities and the later nineteenth-century arrival of plate-glass shop windows increased the attraction and made goods seem even more accessible. By this time, more humdrum mail-order businesses were selling fabrics for local dressmakers or amateurs alike, often in bundles or dress or suit lengths, as did market stalls with ends of lines and remnants. Sewers today describe the fun of bins of different-sized remnants that offer the chance to rummage out an unexpected treasure. Generations of families have benefited from alternative ways of getting fabric, such as from local textile works that employed them or their neighbours. Muriel Sharples recalled the '4 shilling [20 p] bundles' of 'sub-standard material' as one of the monthly entitlements when she started work in 1959 at the old but soon-to-close United Turkey Red dyeing and printing works north of Glasgow: 'My Grannie was a dab hand with her ancient Singer's sewing machine, and made me quite a few skirts and dresses' out of these bundles.[9] Inheritance of unused fabrics, sometimes in significant quantity, when a female relative or friend dies is also a familiar story. Some quilters display instructions concerning their stash at home in a half-serious Last Will and Testament. Charity shops, garage and car boot sales are all rich hunting grounds for fabrics in lengths or in garment or furnishing form to be reused.

Buying retail fabric online, where countless different fabrics are offered on our screens, is the latest manifestation in a long history of alternatives to traditional shops. Some find online fabric buying unreliable because they can't feel it or verify the true colour, resonating with Gaye's sense that most women who sew, especially items for their own use, have 'an intense tactile response' to the fabrics they choose to buy. Teenager

Hazel says that in 'a fabric store I rub my fingers down the fabric and decide if it is right or too rough for what I want to make.' Some suppliers provide small sample pieces to help customers make their choices, a partial recompense for the limitations of the online experience that many sewing people bemoan. A top complaint for stitchers is the closure of their local fabric shops, a loss that includes informative chats with the people who staffed them. Others enjoy the bigger choice conveniently available online, a means of shopping also well suited to choosing haberdashery. But Natalia, stressed out by too much fabric, has now resolved to withstand the temptations, limiting purchases to what's required for a specific project because 'the urge to buy anything just takes over when you go into a shop or web site.' The international trade in fabrics is immense, seen in the many prominent international fashion textile trade fairs such as Premiere Vision, which now have specialist spin-offs such as those dedicated to denim or sportswear. In recent years numerous other national and regional fairs have emerged, often under the banner of hobbyist craft. The calendar bulges with big events showcasing a vast selection of fabrics and haberdashery, supplemented by workshops, demonstrations and competitions, all now a regular highlight for many amateurs and professionals alike.

When the fabric is in your hand, it reveals the character of its surface and handling qualities. In partnership, yarn and weave merge to form what we see and touch but under the lens of a microscope it becomes disconcertingly unlike what our senses lead us to expect as a wondrous transformation happens. It is a bit unsettling to find that the familiar surface of the cloth disappears and instead reveals quite unexpected dimensions.

Even the simplest weave is not flat at all: under the lens it is decidedly, even precipitously, un-flat. The lens reveals warp and weft yarns swooping up and down in their interlinking woven construction. The yarns themselves turn out to be astonishingly varied: silk fibres seem glassy and translucent, wool ones are scaly. The person who sews with confidence has a sense of the innate working properties of the fabric they are handling, using that knowledge we only learn fully by doing. They understand how to manipulate and lead a particular cloth to its best performance for the desired result. They will swiftly detect which way up and which side out a piece of woven cloth is intended to go, what weight of thread or size of needle it requires. For example, they know how to work with the fluid slinky nature of silk satin by cutting and stitching it on the diagonal to its woven grain – on the bias – if they want it to hang and mould more closely to the body. This kind of correspondence between maker and material is seen in other crafts too, such as ceramics or woodwork, and is inseparable from knowing which tools best suit the task in hand.

Sometimes the very best tool is the hand alone. I recall my mother helping me to set a sleeve. She showed me how the curved top of the sleeve must be eased into the corresponding curve of the arm scye (she was averse to 'arm hole') and persuaded into its proper alignment, ready to be pinned or tacked in position without being allowed to slip or wander off-true, an error, if stitched in, that no amount of skilful pressing afterwards would ever disguise. Up to that point, I had only sewn in straight lines and understood cloth as inert or passive. Setting in that sleeve, I felt it become something active that could respond to stroking or urging into position. My fingers were learning that the direction and grain, the drape, the weave, the weight and nature of its fibres added up to different handling characteristics, that a cloth could communicate these readily to experienced hands and that it would end in tears if they were misunderstood or ignored. A piece of cloth has a physique and language all its own. It can be cooperative or bolshy. The needle in the hand or machine cannot change that. To succeed, there must be mutual cooperation. And that is learnt by doing.

Cloth may communicate one thing to the hand, but another in public. It is a widely accepted idea that clothing and fashion express social status and personal identity, yet it is often overlooked on an everyday basis that cloth itself has a symbolic primary and cultural power all of its own. Cloth can 'speak' through its intrinsic material properties and its endowed meanings, as seen the world over in small and large societies alike, ancient and modern. Sometimes this is due to complex weaving, or expensive or rare dyestuffs and yarns. Sometimes cloth's potential to 'speak' can change, such as when neoprene journeyed from industry and water to catwalk. On occasion, a fabric selected by fashion designers or journalists can upgrade its status almost overnight. For example, the designer Hardy Amies (1909–2003) visited a tweed mill in the 1930s and noticed, in 'a pile of scraps of old material lying abandoned in the corner . . . a soft tweed made in a mixture of dark plum sprinkled with specks of vivid cerise and then criss-crossed with a fairly large overcheck in emerald green'. He fell in love with it. 'I know it sounds awful, but the whole tweed glowed.' In no time, at his request a similar tweed pattern was woven afresh. Then it was cut out in London to his design by his trained cutters and carefully sewn by his expert workroom 'hands', who brought it back to life again as a woman's stylish suit. Their craftsmanship was a crucial part of its journey from neglect all the way onto the April 1937 cover of British *Vogue*.[10]

Cloth can speak in more literal ways. In many African countries it has long been common to use lengths of cotton for dressing or wrapping, vividly printed with slogans, political portraits and commemorative images, such as one printed to celebrate Zambia's participation in football's African Cup of Nations in 2012.[11] African printed cottons in general attract stitchers in London and elsewhere who make curtains, cushions, skirts and shirts to enjoy the bright and exuberant patterns. By contrast, cloth made into simple garments can signal a departure from mainstream life. Cloth and sewing have long been part of monastic life. St Francis of Assisi (?1181–1226) and his religious order originally emphasized their unworldly identity by wearing habits stitched from lowly undyed cloth typical of the peasantry. As the son of a successful silk merchant, Francis probably had a good eye for the diverse languages of cloth. For her ordination, American Zen Buddhist priest Josho Pat Phelan was required to sew small pieces of material together to make her habit's neck-piece called a 'rakusu', regarded as a solemn reiteration of making Buddha's own robe, itself believed to have been sewn together originally from discarded rags. In this spiritual context, she came to experience her simple sewing as a 'meditation practice which unifies body, breath and mind.'[12]

Stitched-together pieces of cloth – patchwork – when melded in random or orderly patterns to form an entirely new entity is a kind of democratic clothmaking. Patchwork is a relatively uncomplicated way to create larger items such as bedcovers or garments from smaller pieces of cloth, whether new or recycled. It is surprising to learn just how many cultures across time and geography east and west have utilized these transformative assemblages of pieced cloth. Celia Eddy, a British writer and quilt-maker, points to the broad range of meanings of patchwork clothing as signifiers of 'holy poverty' and humility, 'alternative' political values, 'thrift associated with poverty and scarcity' and the Harlequin costumes redolent of 'disorder, trouble, or frivolity'. Eddy illustrates the 'particularly rich traditions' that attach to clothing of patchwork past and present in Islam, Buddhism and Japanese Shinto; for instance, the changes and continuity of various symbolic meanings of patchwork garments seen today within the Sufism sect known as Baye Fall are now widespread in Senegal and also spread to the West by migration.[13]

Cloth production was a driver of innovation in the Industrial Revolution and the subsequent massive global trade, but it had great range and variety even before the mass industrialization of spinning and weaving. Barbara Johnson (1738–1825) was an Englishwoman who left a remarkable legacy, now in London's Victoria and Albert Museum, that illustrates the diversity of available fabrics in her lifetime. She had carefully fixed into an album 121 samples of the fabrics she had chosen to be sewn for her garments from 1746 to 1823, along with fashion plates.[14] Some of those she identifies in her quirky Georgian spelling have names that are still recognized today, such as 'Callicoe', 'Muslin', 'Cotten' or 'linnen'. But her 'Blue and white strip'd lutestring', her 'Manchester Brunswick', her 'scarlet stuff shot with white', or 'brown fustian' for her riding dress: these names evoke the richness of past textiles manufacturing and consumer choice but have passed from common use. Even the names of colours and patterns vary over time, such as 'Devonshire Brown' and 'Massereen Blue'. Her samples demonstrate the variety of colours, weaves and patterns that went into women's clothes and enlivened the social scene. In her lifetime, there was an even longer rollcall of everyday textiles, such as Holland, dimity or linsey-woolsey, that are now mostly gone from our vocabulary. Such changes happened in part because cloth was often named for its place of manufacture, which might cease as technology and transportation changed. Improvements and innovations, coupled with fashion, diversified textile production and marketing too fast for some. A commentator even in 1662, struck by the vast output of Norwich, England, which exported world-famous worsteds and silks, wrote, 'Expect not I should reckon up their several names, because daily increasing, and many of them are binominous, as which, when they begin to tire in sale, are quickened with a new name.'[15] The tide has turned again with those consumers and stitchers who prefer the natural cottons, linens and wools so familiar in the past and avoid newly developed artificial fabrics.

Cloth and skin, cloth and stitching: these fascinating cultural and psychodynamic interactions express a duality in how cloth both covers and reveals us. It is found in societies rich and poor everywhere, with textiles in clothing marking a threshold between our bodies and the outer world and, in the case of curtains, screens, blinds or wrapping cloths, forming a threshold between private and public space, even between the living and the dead. Cloth may have these enduring cultural roles yet at the same time it is also inherently changeable, with innovation in its DNA. The fabrics in use today are made of fibres and techniques developed by our ancestors, such as plain weave linen and cotton, combined with established synthetics both familiar or new and experimental. Today's world is also 'quickened' with new names as it was in the past, but for materials that could never previously have been imagined, which have come particularly thick and fast over the last hundred years. They give stitching ever broader scope as a practice that is rooted in the immensely prolific and technically complex histories of textile invention and manufacturing. There is now a litany of brand and generic names, including nylon, Terylene, Crimplene, acrylic, acetate, polyester, viscose, Tencel and other regenerated fibres such as bamboo. Velcro, made from nylon, has made itself indispensable. We might know what these fabrics do and what can be sewn with them but most of us don't know what they're made of, and now smart and e-textiles offer startlingly new avenues for wearable technology. Fibres and fabrics have long been a meeting of science, technology and art and today this is ever more in evidence.

Stitching has been transformed by these developments. People who sew for pleasure or for a living are now doing so in a world in which synthetics make up almost 70 per cent of the world's production of fibres, the majority of which are made in China. The days are long gone when sewing involved locally or regionally made cloth. Who could have anticipated 3D scratch denim that permits surface patterning of all kinds, or the successful laboratory formation of fibre from a fungus mycelium or from food waste? Some of us may even have textiles inside us generated by the fast-growing field of bio-textiles, such as heart replacement parts, sutures, artificial skin and tissue scaffolding of various kinds. Who knows what spin-offs these may have for more general use? There are countless initiatives in fibre development and more in the pipeline. 'As science delves deeper and deeper into the subject of fibre production, many of us will know materials more by what they do, than by what they are . . . When considered as a totality, it is as if we are creating a quite radical, fundamental, evolution of textiles and clothing; a genuine quantum leap without historical parallel.'[16]

Cotton is one fabric familiar to everybody as wearers or makers. From denim to gauze, cotton is available in an infinite number of weights, weaves, finishes, colours and patterns. It is soft, breathable and comfortable to wear, strong and supple. It washes and irons well, it isn't costly and eventually it can bio-degrade. It is stable when being sewn. Sharon, a sustainable designer and textile lecturer, finds it is 'forgiving to beginners' in her workshops. What more could a maker want from a fabric to sew with? Yet looking beyond this well-deserved reputation as a friend to machine and hand sewing alike, cotton was, and still is, a big beast with a formidable and often disturbing foot-print around the world past and present. Cotton shows us how fabric we use connects us directly as stitchers and consumers to the huge hinterland of textiles. It may not be the world's most costly natural fibre – vicuna usually has that distinction – nor is it perhaps as beautiful as silk or warm as wool, but its story exemplifies how fabric, any fabric, is embedded in global eco-nomics and deeply entwined in human lived experience. It has been calculated that globally today the livelihoods of 350 mil-lion people are tied to cotton at all its stages from growing to sewing.[17] In 2020–21 almost 35 million hectares of land around the globe were devoted to the cultivation of cotton, distributed across more than ninety countries, producing over 26.5 million metric tonnes of the crop. Statistics on this scale may be out of mind as we choose our length of cotton to make something at home or buy a shirt sewn by somebody somewhere else. They are even more staggering when the scale of wool, silk or linen production is added, let alone synthetics. Nevertheless, this is the material world as it really is, the one we inhabit and share and in which we stitch.

The production of textiles and the associated products for sewing, such as small 'notions' – buttons, zips, pins and needles and the like – has over the centuries shifted from one place to another, one country to another, but even when the work has gone elsewhere, former centres of production are left with many unmistakeable marks on their built environment and landscapes that continue to contribute to local, regional and national identities and remain part of a community's shared memories. Closely associated with sewing's history, two sites have a particular resonance. Singer's colossal sewing machine factory built in Scotland's Clydebank in 1882 became the world's largest, and was said at one stage to be making 80 per cent of the world's sewing machines. It shaped life and work in that community for a hundred years until its closure and eventual demolition, but the memory of it is strong among the families of its workers, the railway station still bears the name Singer, and a sewing machine even features in the design of the town's coat of arms. The giant international thread manufacturer Coates began life in Paisley and dominated the town for generations with its monumental sewing thread mills, regarded as architectural wonders in their day, until production and thousands of jobs moved elsewhere round the world, leaving only a handful of buildings standing. They serve new uses now, at the same time acting as often painful reminders of manufacturing's global shifts.

Some old textile mills continue to work as museums and offer visitors a full-on experience of the noise, the evocative sights and smells of mills as they once were, retrieving the past more dramatically than words or photographs ever can. There are many examples of these unique buildings in former textile centres that were once the mainstay of local and regional economies, now preserved for new functions; for instance, in the USA the Massachusetts Museum of Contemporary Art is located in what was once a textile printing works. On a local scale, the buildings themselves can embody powerful stories about their communities for those who worked in them. The many oral histories that now exist for textile places recall the good times of fellowship and fun in the mills, with canteens used for dances or laughter when a kipper was nailed under an unpopular supervisor's bench. The bad times make for difficult reading today. In Oldham's cotton mills, children were employed to squeeze under the moving machines to brush them clean, known as 'fettling'. 'When I got my fingers fast it was awful. I went through so much pain and I was only a little girl . . . I lost four fingers in all.' In a similar mill an adult operative died when his legs were caught by a moving strap which 'took him up and smashed him on the roof'.[18] The buildings in their various ways around the world are monuments to technical ingenuity, exceptional products, the rise of capitalism and industrialization and the geopolitics of empire and global trade, and memories of them reveal how textiles are deeply embedded, for better or for worse, in human lives.

Cotton, like all fabric, embodies continuity and change globally and locally over a long timescale. For example, in India in the 1920s, cotton cloth became weaponized from the bottom up by Mahatma Gandhi in pursuit of radical political change.

Referring to the vast quantities of cotton cloth exported by the industrial mills of Manchester, Gandhi thought that these had done immense damage to India's indigenous cloth crafts. For Gandhi, in his mission to drive out the British from India by non-violent means, *khadi*, home-woven cloth using home spun yarn, was important at a political but also a spiritual level. Zealously promoted, it was his express intention that this simple cotton cloth would help to galvanize Indian identity. It was envisioned as a national cloth capable of asserting moral standards and uniting all Indians regardless of caste or religion. It resulted in the early independence movement depicting a spinning wheel at the centre of their flag, a reference to their belief in Indian self-reliance and their aspiration that India should separate itself from Western industrial and economic dominance. Who knows if this is what Gandhi would have wanted, but the tables have turned. The Manchester mills are gone, and India is to date the second largest cotton producer in the world, after China.[19]

Of all the cloth, clothing and other goods made of cotton, it is in familiar blue jeans that we can see continuity and change most clearly. Over time the cultural journey of blue jeans has taken them across the work–leisure and gender divides and transformed them into an international language, exemplified at the fall of Kabul to Taliban rule in August 2021: a distraught young Afghan woman reported: 'My brother bought me a burqa, I burned my jeans today . . . I burned my hopes with them.'[20] Jeans have their origins in nineteenth-century American workwear and jeans aficionados love traditional 'heritage' selvedge denim, made on antique narrow shuttle looms. In recent years its production mostly shifted to Japan, meaning that less of this iconic American cloth is now made in America. Blue cotton denim itself has its roots in earlier times and the production of cotton and indigo for dye as separate raw materials take us back to antiquity.

Today cotton and indigo both remain freighted with complex references to colonialism, slavery and exploitation in European and African American history. In India under British rule all stages of indigo's production were often marked by abusive practices. From the small farmers who grew it to the labourers who processed it – pre-mechanization this was arduous, and working inside the vats was particularly unhealthy and unpleasant – although not technically slavery it was close to it and gave rise to such discontent that it contributed to wider political unrest. When colonial regimes started their production of indigo in the West Indies, along with cotton, tea, coffee and sugar, the African slave trade was what made it profitable, as became true of the indigo trade that was later based, like cotton, in the southern states of the USA. It is now clear that cotton historically was a major engine powering industrial innovation and wealth. It has been called the first global fibre, but its story is one of extremes of human and environmental cost, neither of which are yet over. The story is repeated yet again with terrible human suffering today in the cotton picking forced on Uyghur Muslims in China.[21] The region in which these inhumane and coercive practices, amounting to genocide, are found contributes 20 per cent of global cotton production. Forced labour is also used to pick cotton in one of the world's other major cotton-producing countries, Turkmenistan.[22] We may wish otherwise but to date complete global traceability in highly complex textile supply chains has been notoriously difficult to achieve. Raw cotton from different sources is often mixed together at the earliest stages of production, even before spinning and textile manufacturing, all of which may then occur in different countries, each with different labour and environmental laws and practices. Technical solutions to traceability at scale are still under development. More painful truths about the cost of 'the horrendous wrongs that have been done in the name of cotton' alone are revealed as each day passes.[23] Cotton and indigo also connect us in the here and now with urgent concerns about sustainability and the environment. Cloth is never just cloth; dye is never just dye.

If the great majority of cloth globally comes from synthetics, why does this plant hold such economic might, despite competition from synthetic fibres? Part of the answer is that the scale of its production brings its own impetus and imperatives. Vast investment in agri-chemicals and modified seed in cotton cultivation and other agricultural technologies, all in the drive to increase output, add to burdens of debt falling on dependent small- and large-scale farmers alike, with state subsidies for growers in some countries and coercive labour practices in others. Increasing the volume of production can drive down the prices to farmers, requiring yet more production to keep up with costs. The USA has sometimes spent more on its subsidies than the total GDP of Benin.[24] So, cotton production exemplifies how a tangle of unsustainable and conflicting interests can develop that may require global agreements to untangle, if the players have the will to do so.

Textile production of all kinds is now globalized; competition is acute, technology and markets change. From an environmental point of view, one country's consumption is likely to be based on another's environmental degradation and contribution to global warming and human exploitation. Nowadays fibre, natural or synthetic, may be produced in one country, then exported to another for processing, to yet another for clothing manufacturing, then re-exported to distant consumers, and this now happens on a scale unimaginable in the past. Trade from source to finishing is affected by interconnected and shifting factors such as labour and finance costs, government regulation and taxation, international trade standards and deals and now the emergency of climate change. There is no way around it: in thinking about cloth we can salute the creativity and ingenuity in its design and production but at the same time the destruction it causes in the world today is now an unavoidable fact. Cloth makes an immense impact on us and our planet because of the exploitation of people and man-made environmental transgressions involved.

Textile production in our Anthropocene era has in fact been a major contributor to the necessity for coining the term 'Anthropocene' in the first place. The textile supply chain is estimated to be responsible for 20 per cent of global water pollution through textile dyeing and finishing.[25] In the context of global fibre production now being largely synthetic, the European Environment Agency states that the 'carbon-intensive' production of polyester, the most common synthetic, requires 'more than 70 million barrels of oil each year'. The agency estimates that 3,500 chemical substances are used in making textiles. 'Of these, 750 have been classified as hazardous for human health and 440 as hazardous for the environment.' In addition, when we wash our plastic-based clothes, such as those made wholly or partly of polyester, nylon or acrylic, 'about half a million tonnes of plastic microfibres are released into the ocean annually.'[26] At the UK consumer level, a recent study of fast fashion sold online found that the average use of recycled plastic in plastic-based clothing by four large retailers amounted to only 3.2 per cent, despite sustainability claims. It was also found that consumers were ill informed about plastics used in their clothing.[27]

Their feelings for cloth are part of why people sew for pleasure but sometimes the immense human and environmental problems of cloth manufacturing can seem overwhelming to individual consumers, however much they love cloth and however committed to sustainability and social justice they may be. It can help to focus on examples of real changes that are already underway. The new hasn't driven out the old; perhaps the new has even made us value the old more. Just as there is a slow food movement, there are also radical moves to develop a kind of slow cloth economy. Fibershed is a California-based non-profit with affiliates across the USA, Canada and around the world that aims to create a new regenerative textile economy. This means that to protect people and the planet, within a circular flow of naturally grown and locally made yarn, cloth and clothing, we would wear things until they were worn out and then return them to the soil as regenerating compost. In other words, soil to soil in the same locality.[28] This particular concept of local making and using as a circularity goes beyond choosing to buy, for example, organic cotton or linen cloth because they still may be sourced from around the globe and may eventually become landfill. The Fibershed model requires consumer awareness of their bio-regional or local cloth and clothing and acceptance of natural dyes. Those old partners cotton and indigo, despite their bitter and tangled histories, can also demonstrate today some of the hopeful steps in the journey towards sustainability. Remarkable indigo production by Stony Creek Colors is an example of win-win sustainable production in the USA, capable of scaling up, where nitrogen-fixing indigo plants are grown without chemical interventions and can naturally replenish soil depleted by tobacco growing.[29] Mass-produced fabrics such as EcoVero by the company Lenzing show how semi-synthetics can become significantly more environmentally and user-friendly.

As we already find when we shop for cloth and clothes, the trend towards growing organic cotton is on the increase globally. Behind the scenes, there has been growth in the work of voluntary organic textile standards certified by bodies such as the Organic Content Standard (ocs) and the Global Organic Textile Standard (GOTS), though many argue for tougher frameworks of legislation to guarantee these standards.[30] These developments chime with the wish for sustainable practices and products that is uppermost in the minds of many consumers and manufacturers. In keeping with these developments, manufacturers now make organic cotton thread, various fully compostable products and recycled polyester thread, for example, so stitchers who want to engage with these issues can move more aspects of their craft towards better sustainability.

The fullest definition of sustainability and the one most likely to bring lasting benefit to humanity and the earth is one that embraces social justice as well as the environment. In these global challenges, the tectonic plates of textile production and consumption may just be moving slowly in the right direction. Many universities and companies around the world now have research centres working on sustainable fashion and textiles. True sustainability in textiles and clothing rests on sustainable production methods as well as sustainable materials, and, of course, consumer engagement. The more we know about the calamitous effects on people and on our planet caused by textile production, and the more we wish to change this, the more attractive the idea of compassionate consumption becomes. Their love of cloth and their sewing skills already give home sewers a head start on this route to the future. Choosing sustainable fabrics and making and mending isn't the whole answer to these ills, because they are global and systemic. But it certainly is one effective way to become a more knowing consumer, one who is willing to ask questions, make informed choices and enjoy the stitching journey.

4

In the Gently Closed Box

Nests and shells, boxes and houses: such spaces have a particular power to enchant us. It is their potential to shape our memories and encompass thoughts and dreams that fascinated French philosopher Gaston Bachelard (1884–1962), who named this quality 'the dimension of intimacy'. He saw 'the germ of [a] daydream contained in the gently closed box'.[1] This thinking leads us to what stitchers understand well – that an everyday vessel such as a sewing basket or even a thimble can have its own dimension of intimacy. Family memories gathered around an inherited sewing kit can magnify that intimacy. An artist and teacher who sews in personal and professional contexts describes an experience many will recognize. 'I have an old Russian biscuit tin from my grandmother's house which I keep threads in. The threads themselves are a mix of old and new, given to me or acquired at various points. They still hold a kind of magic for me.'

The tools and sundries we handle and cherish with easy intimacy are fundamental to sewing, yet while these utilitarian objects extend our practical capabilities, at the same time they all have their own specific histories of form and function. Sometimes these are rooted in a surprisingly distant past, even a prehistoric one, like the needle, or one that is more up-to-date, such as electric scissors. But the physical life of sewing tools is not just about technique or performance; they also belong to the wider ecosphere of humankind's evolution and the way tools can enhance or damage us and our world. Ruth Schwartz Cowan thickens the plot in her classic book *More Work for Mother*:

> Tools are not passive instruments, confined to doing our bidding, but have a life of their own. Tools set limits on our work; we can use them in many different ways, but not in an infinite number of ways. We try to obtain the tools that will do the jobs that we want done; but, once obtained, the tools organize our work for us in ways that we may not have anticipated. People use tools to do work, but tools also define and constrain the ways in which it is possible and likely that people will behave . . . This is precisely the lesson that the sorcerer was trying to teach his apprentice in the famous fable.[2]

Digital apps are one new species of tool that come to mind here. They are intended to support the home sewer to plan projects and organize their fabrics. They have many fans, but will they come to 'define and constrain' their users in unanticipated ways?

A good place to start thinking about the sewing equipment we use today in our homes and workrooms is how and where we store it, because this reveals something about underlying attitudes to sewing itself. Whether a container is an old Russian biscuit tin with its own family history, or an anonymous plastic crate, storage is a record of relationships to certain *stuff* in particular. It also speaks of how we value stuff in general, how we control it or sometimes how it becomes a millstone. This does not just affect us moderns living in a crowded world of proliferating consumer goods or Marie Kondo's disciples, but was something previous generations faced as well. A familiar housekeeping plea from 1743: 'See that every one keeps what is in their charge in there [*sic*] proper stated places, then nothing will be out of order, or to seek when wanted, nor any hurry.'[3] Modern attitudes to sewing inherit some enduring ideas from earlier generations, and storage is often central to these. For better-off girls and women, workboxes in the past were sometimes finely wrought and lockable, ingeniously packed with ornate and valuable tools and all the necessities of needlework. Such boxes, like today's handbag, were deeply female territories. While they embodied a morality of tidiness, they also hinted at intimacy, for they provided inner recesses where a private letter or memento could be locked away from prying eyes. These boxes exercise a certain fascination for collectors today, perhaps not only because they recall a time when good needlework was prized but in admiration for the cabinetmaker's skills that created these evocative spaces.

The title of *The Work-Box; or, Grand-Papa's Present*, an 1828 story for girls, alludes to the once-common practice of giving sewing boxes and sundries as tokens of love and affection. It was a familiar way for friends and family to sustain social ties and reinforce shared values within a community of everyday needlework practice. The box in the story is the pivot for extended moralizing on the importance of tidiness, addressed to the charming but disorderly Anna and intended to reform her careless ways. She is the kind of girl who 'would be searching for her scissors or bodkin, whilst she should have been carefully employed at her needle'. But will the new box be a remedy? The red Moroccan leather box stands on 'pretty' claw feet. It comes stocked with 'ivory winders filled with silks of different colours, and pincushions filled with pins, a thimble, some needles, an emcry cushion' and, exclaims delighted little Anna, 'everything I shall want'. But in no time, she has allowed her kitten to scatter the contents on the floor and damage them and so begins this educational tale. The tidiness, or otherwise, of the workbox stood for wider values in female education about order and duty and the author drums this home relentlessly to young readers.[4]

Fancy boxes were no match for all the needlework and desperate mending done in poorer households or in those better-off ones where quantities of household linen, clothing for men, women and children, including servants, required regular attention. In 1840 the no-nonsense matriarch of all sewing manuals, *The Workwoman's Guide*, devoted a chapter to tools and their organization, such was their importance. The advice was clear: 'A work-box, or basket, should be large enough to hold a moderate supply of work and all its requisites.'[5] The container should not be too big to carry around the house and should have the user's name on it (the author assumed a school or family household with servants), and should hold work in progress as well as tools.

Entirely different needs in less stable settings led to another popular way of storing needlework tools and notions – the small fabric or leather case or roll containing a basic sewing kit known for generations as a 'housewife' or 'husswif'. Still in use now in various forms, this is a reminder of the continuity of many sewing and making practices across time despite huge social changes. It got its name in pre-industrial times when housewifery was respected as a practice responsible for generating and organizing vital household resources. It was a praiseworthy role to be taken seriously. 'Husswifs' were made to be portable, easily stowed away in a pocket or bag to keep essentials ready to hand. They were used by men and women alike, rich or poor. Some were made in elaborately decorated silk, others from scraps; some were made as gifts to men or women and have stitched messages of affection from the maker, such as 'When this you see, remember me.' They also were a perfect place to secure little keepsakes or money. The material used in their construction can be significant; one made about 1800 is believed to be made of scraps from dresses belonging to Martha Washington (1731–1802), the first First Lady, putting the absent person and memories of her into tangible form.[6] Another fragile little husswif is an unlikely survivor of 'the worst disaster in the history of British polar exploration'. Sir John Franklin's last expedition of 1845–8 to further explore the Arctic Northwest Passage resulted in the loss of both his ships and all the men. A search expedition mounted in 1857–9 found an abandoned boat on a sledge at Erebus Bay, King William Island, containing two skeletons and the husswif, among other personal possessions. It still contained 'a thimble and a quantity of thread, a small package wrapped in cotton fabric held by a pin and a ball of wool'. It is made of blue velvet and ribbon woven with iconic English clover plants, oak leaves and acorns.[7] Its soft velvet and familiar motifs may have embodied emotional intimacy for the owner, perhaps Bachelard's 'germ of [a] daydream' connecting him to its maker and the comforts of home, even in the midst of the terrible conditions in which he and his companions eventually perished. Even the smallest things made for, and by, needlework can carry affective meaning across time, distance and gender.

Even when aids and tools no longer survive in physical form, they still retain a vast presence in literature and visual art, and frequently in the many plain sewing manuals that have been published in English for well over two hundred years. In these manuals, generations of domestic needleworkers get the same advice as wayward Anna in Georgian times. *The Workwoman's Guide* of 1840 was forthright as usual: 'much of the comfort of a good workwoman depends on the choice and arrangement of her tools.' Mary Brooks Picken said much the same over 120 years later. 'Successful sewing means having good equipment conveniently arranged. Expert workmanship requires the best tools you can afford, kept in AI condition.'[8] In 2020 a message to quilters also got straight to the point. 'The less time we have to spend searching for a specific fabric or notion, the more time we can spend actually creating.'[9]

The idea persists that tidiness is a virtue for those who sew. But what is tidy to one person can be exasperating or frustrating for another. A participant in my 1995 oral history project recalled her husband hating what he called the 'mess' of dressmaking when he returned from work. She described the disruption she felt when having to tidy it all away at the end of each day. There is a sense that what is being tidied out of sight is not just the project and its paraphernalia but an important part of the maker. The ideal encountered in many how-to books and websites is a sewing room of your own, or a corner of an infrequently used room with capacious cupboards and a sewing machine, a good working surface and a board ready for pressing, all to hand. This may be a distant dream for many makers, or inappropriate for what they want to do. But if our tools could speak, they'd probably ask for a place of their own at least, if they are not to be lost – a needle wants its case, a pin its cushion. Order and intimacy are not mutually exclusive when even a pincushion may contain memories.

The tools of all kinds we have in our hands are understood and used over much of the world and connect us to a community of makers, wherever we are. Tools embody remarkable continuity over time and place, yet they can also represent innovation. But surely in this day and age, all tools are the same and devoid of sentiment or character? Gone are the days of inlaid sewing boxes and turned wooden cotton-winders. Plastic hasn't got much patina, mass production doesn't lend itself to artistry. Yet if we take a closer look at the tools we work with today, we see they are more than the sum of the materials of which they are made. All tools, however complex, if they do what they are meant to do, and we use them well, have an attraction of their own. They are inert, but when we pick them up, they magnify our potential. We recognize this in them as they sit waiting. The promise embodied in the simplest of needlework hand tools is permanently available: they don't have to be assembled, or even plugged in; your scissors, pins and needles are ready for off. Their minimalism defines their character and beauty, but they can be affective too, and despite the abundance of choice on offer from tool manufacturers, makers often grow attached to particular favourites. 'I have a large pair of tailor's shears which I had for many years . . . sharpened numerous times. Once they were sent to Sheffield for sharpening, the postage cost could have bought me a new pair, but I couldn't bear to part with them,' a London-based professional designer-maker told me. Bringing some familiar tools into focus helps reveal how sewing has an intricate and evolved material culture of its own that connects makers to their tools, to other makers past and present and to the world beyond.

The pin has a long ancestry. Before woven or felted cloth came into being, early humankind used strong pins of bone, wood or thorn to fasten animal skins and fur coverings together. In early modern times, pins were closely associated with women not only for lacemaking or sewing but for a task now long gone – keeping their clothing and accessories neat through the day. Over 240 years ago, the author of the 1780s *The Adventures of a Pincushion* warned that 'in want of pins, and destitute of a *Pincushion*, she has quite undressed herself, and her cloathes are dropping off.'[10] For sewing today, a pin is a tool for temporary work, often used first to anchor pieces of cloth together and then removed after the needle has done its more permanent work. For those who don't stitch, the variety of modern sewing pins available can seem bewildering: steel, nickel-plated, brass, with round heads of glass or plastic, fine for light silks, stouter for coarser materials. Dressmaker pins vary in length and girth, 'lil' or sequin pins being the smallest. But for all its apparent simplicity, the pin represents strides in technology and industrial organization. The pin was in the limelight right at the start of Adam Smith's first chapter of his famous *An Inquiry into the Nature and Causes of the Wealth of Nations* in 1776. He drew attention to pin-making as exact proof of how production is speeded up by the division of labour.

> One man draws out the wire, another straights it, a third cuts it, a fourth points it, a fifth grinds it at the top for receiving the head; to make the head requires two or three distinct operations; to put it on, is a peculiar business,

to whiten the pins is another; it is even a trade by itself
to put them into the paper; and the important business
of making a pin is, in this manner, divided into about
eighteen distinct operations.[11]

Smith witnessed how just ten men working in this way could
produce 48,000 pins between them in a day, whereas he thought
if a single man made a pin from start to finish he'd be pushed
to get twenty made in the same time. However, even this was
not enough. A pin-making machine was patented in the USA
in 1841 by John Ireland Howe (1793–1876) to make pin heads
all of a piece with the shank. Further refinements included
mechanically fixing the finished pins into paper packaging, a
job once providing work for many girls and women, all of which
turned the USA into a global exporter of pins, so that the famous
English pin makers of Redditch were all but gone by the 1870s
and Birmingham's were much reduced. Modern pin making
advanced alongside the making of small arms, knives, nails,
clocks and locks and their manufacturers' improvements in the
principles and practices of precision production and the division
and increasing mechanization of work processes. In turn these
activities rested on the perfecting of machine tools, forging,
milling and gauging. The production of the chain-driven bicycle
is a familiar part of this manufacturing journey that eventually
led to mass production, the gospel of interchangeable parts and
the assembly lines of Henry Ford. When we hold a pin, we are
connecting to prehistoric people and to those ten Georgian
labourers watched by Adam Smith. We are also holding the
fruits of this period of dramatic world-shifting transformation
in how everyday things were made and in how we experience

work, for better or worse. That is, until we join those makers who now prefer to grip their fabric together ready to sew not with the humble pin but with little plastic clips and clamps made for the purpose – a popular choice because they don't leave holes behind, get lost in the carpet or prick your finger. So, what is the future for the classic little velvet pin pad? Attached by a strip of elastic to the left wrist, it has been the trademark of the professional dressmaker for generations, but away with romance: it can now be replaced by a magnetic pin holder on a plastic wrist strap.

In all the creative possibilities of plain stitching, it is the needle that is fundamental in both hand and machine work, with an austere beauty all of its own. Designer and craftsman David Pye aligns the needle with the pen as possibly the only hand tools in any field of work that can do their job fully without further aids or guides, in what he identifies as the 'workman-ship of risk'.[12] Like the pin, the needle family is ancient and extensive with many distinct forms and functions. Needles of quality require much expertise and precision in their manufac-ture. A pre-packed set of five large, stout needles found among my late mother's extensive collection of needles new and old contains one curved into a semi-circle for repairing upholstery, a rather less curved one with a bevelled shank for sewing pack-aging, and three different-sized straight ones for bookbinding, carpets and sails. Surgeons, vets, undertakers, glovemakers, tattooists, saddlers, milliners, cobblers, chefs and all manner of crafts require bespoke needles for their specialisms. The needle for hand sewing is a marvel of versatility. It requires two hands, one to grip, guide and propel it and one to control the material being stitched, but that is all. It can make functional movements in different planes and at different speeds; it can pierce cloth vertically or glide into it at a controlled angle in any direction across, towards or away from the user's body; it can follow a weaving action over and under several threads for much of its length; it can be used to pick apart single fine threads for white-work or fine darning. The needle will function in one way or another regardless of the dexterity of its user, though the results will soon reveal if it was in the hands of a novice. Differences in the size and shape of the eye, the dimensions of the shank and the shape and sharpness of the point will allow the needle to pull every known thread, hair-fine or coarse, through the puncture it has made in countless kinds of fabric, even vellum and leather. It is used to make diagonal, forward and backward stitches, the length of the stitch limited only by the length of the shank. Machine-made a metal needle might be, but still it can bear the mark of its user. For hand quilters it is often 'a source of pride if a favourite needle will last out the whole work, when it will have acquired a bend suited to the hand of the worker. Some quilters consider a needle is not in perfect condition until it is curved.'[13]

Needle traditions defined by local culture and environment show how sewing tools contribute to both change and continuity in everyday life. Inuit women bootmakers are still working within their various local traditions with animal skins such as seal, caribou or wolf to sew their distinctive products and formerly used needles made by their men from the bones of hunted animals and birds for this demanding work. These specialist needle practices continued well into living memory and remained within the zero-waste hunter-gatherer communities as a fallback if the traded supply of steel needles failed. Today these expert bootmakers select modern steel needles with brass eyes, and glover's needles with triangular points, to sew the boot parts together but often still with animal sinews prepared by age-old methods.[14] In early modern Japan needles were also valued for their essential work within a belief system that meant seamstresses annually offered their broken needles 'along with prayers for success in their work' to the 'deity of Awashima', a tradition that continues today in the festival called Hari-Kuyō. Specialist needles contribute to some of the old crafts still practised in modern Japan, such as needles with round rather than elongated eyes shaped to preserve the profile of fine thread, and there are certain needles preferred for the classic hand-sewn tatami mats and others with larger eyes made to work with the heavier threads used in sashiko, a type of stitched mending that is now a popular hobby in the West.

The U.S. inventor Elias Howe (1819–1867) is credited with having refined needles for sewing machines. When the eye migrated from the head into the point and the shank was ridged for fitting into the machine, reliable mechanized sewing finally had just what it needed to develop. The machine needle stays rigid; it is powerful, even in a domestic machine, stabbing into cloth at speed with such force that some say eight hours' work is all it should do before it is replaced. Machine needles, like hand needles, take many forms designed for specific fabrics and tasks such as needles with twin points on a single shaft for parallel lines of stitches or needles with two eyes allow more decorative top stitching. Big industrial machines need especially sturdy needles to sew at pace continuously.

The thimble is the needleworker's armour. It too has ancient origins, closely related to those of the needle.[15] Commonplace or precious, hard or flexible, this simple tool protects a finger when it pushes down on the needle. It allows increased pressure to be safely exerted when required and thimbles with side ridges can help to guide the needle's trajectory. In the past some were made with hard stone inset in the crown for extra protection and durability. Today they are versatile and accommodating tools for many different methods of sewing, made of metal, leather, rubber, rigid or flexible plastic. Some are designed to accommodate long fingernails; others have an open side to reduce perspiration or are shaped like a ring. On metal thimbles the rim can be a space to be engraved with sentimental messages or makers' marks. The case of Grace Stout, a housemaid who did sewing and mending, illustrates how even the little thimble can carry degrees of status. Convicted of theft of cash and goods in Massachusetts in 1682, Grace had 'previous', and it became clear that she was often in the habit of spending more than she earned, but it was the fact she possessed a high-status silver thimble that led to the conclusion that she had overstepped the mark.[16] The status of thimbles of precious metal, sometimes finely decorated, is reflected in the fact that they were often given in celebration. Lynn Knight writes about her grandma, Annie, the daughter of a shopkeeper in Chesterfield, England, who became a teacher. She was given a silver thimble about the time she came of age at 21 at the outbreak of the First World War, an accompaniment to a new sewing machine, indicating investment in her adult status and future.[17] My own father stretched his vicar's modest stipend to draw on the tradition of a thimble as a significant personal gift – in the 1960s he gave my mother a gold thimble in its own little satin-lined leather box. Keen stitchers, who often have a collection of thimbles, will have a favourite. Elaine's thimble is almost part of her: 'The one I use all the time is silver and has been trodden on at some time which makes it a perfect fit; I find I am actually unable to stitch unless I have the thimble on, even if I am not using it.'

A good pair of scissors has a clean elegance in its design and economy of movement. Our hands acquire an entirely transformed capacity from the appetite of scissors for cutting. Scissors are refined by the various lengths and shapes of blades and handles (bows), for different tasks and fabrics and they are made left- or right-handed to enable the appropriate 'lateral squeeze' and to allow the user to see what they are cutting. The long rollcall of different culinary and surgical scissors, and those for hairdressing and personal care, let alone other trades and crafts, is enough to remind us of the seemingly endless adaptability of this indispensable tool. Making his paper cut-outs, the artist Henri Matisse said his scissors were 'as sensitive a tool as a pencil, pen or charcoal – maybe even more sensitive'.[18] But who has not been told firmly never to cut paper with sewing scissors? Once, but only once, I took a pair to cut card, and learnt from my mother in no uncertain terms that this would quickly blunt the blades.

Fans of needlework will choose scissors according to budget as well as task. For buttonholes there are scissors with an adjustable length recess in one blade. Various lighter scissors made with both blades pointed are suited to delicate work. Embroiderers and lacemakers' fine scissors can be arched or angled, some with one blade ending in a little bump. Folding scissors are prized by those who sew or knit when they travel. Bent-handle scissors with small blades at an angle allow cutting inside difficult corners. To sever thread rather than fabric, there are little cutters with very short blades operated on a spring, or as a continuous bent piece of metal (like miniature hand-held sheep shears), in contrast to most scissors that depend on two separate blades joined at a pivot. Like any tools, scissors become a close partner in sewing not only when they are efficient and durable but when they are a memento. Alyson describes this attachment. 'I have my mother's very sharp pointed unpicking scissors which are in the shape of a bird, with the blades as its beak. I am sentimental about them as they remind me of her, and they are very good.'

The big players in the scissor world are the long-bladed scissors for cutting cloth used by tailors and dressmakers, and normally known as shears. They can be hefty, with off-set shanks to allow one blade to lie close on the cloth and the ability to cut cleanly along the full length of their blades. A good pair is costly but essential for anyone who wants to cut valuable cloth accurately without waste or damage. The resources embedded in cloth, its visual attractions, the difficulties in sourcing that elusive perfect piece, all these make cutting out one of the most nerve-wracking stages in making. However carefully considered, following the old adage 'measure twice, cut once', the risks involved as your shears begin to bite into the cloth bring a frisson quite unlike subsequent stages of assembly and finishing. The shears may make a pleasant crunching sound as they work but, although in many stages of sewing and assembling you can reverse a small mistake or even contrive to claw your way back from disaster, cutting cloth is a one-way street. Many cultures around the world wisely avoid this altogether when possible and show in their older forms of dress a preference for lengths of cloth just as the loom wove them, which are then sewn together with straight seams or left unsewn. Kimono, sari, sarong, the Malagasy lamba, poncho, shawl, turban: all depend on simple seams or skilful winding, draping or tying for comfortable wear instead of curved pieces.

In the West, fitted garments have been predominant since the advent of buttons, and so require shears to create the foundational curved pieces. Yet as shears begin their irreversible work of dismemberment, they also start their work of shaping the cloth, so bringing the excitement of anticipation. Scissors must sever and crop, but they are fundamental to the making that follows.

The human compulsion to measure runs through history. By now so many forms of knowledge are dependent on extremely accurate measurement that it is hard to imagine a modern world without it. For dressmaking and tailoring, the tools of measurement can be simple but the bodies they measure are not. The humble flexible tape measure, which first emerged in the nineteenth century, made it quicker and easier to measure all the ins and outs of the human form. Metric and imperial units often appear side by side on tape measures, echoing different traditions and preferences within the sewing community, and tape measures are not immune to change: there are non-stretch tape measures made of fibreglass and tape measures that adhere to cloth temporarily. At the other extreme, in the garment manufacturing industry body scanning can achieve a 3D image. For dressmakers and tailors there are numerous dimensions to consider, including body asymmetry, but to achieve a fitted garment that *looks* right, what a tape measure says often needs to be further refined by shrewd adjustments. One mid-twentieth-century domestic dressmaking manual advised using 'a full-length mirror, a brutal light, a kind but catty friend' and adopting a 'detached attitude of mind'.[19] In this scenario, height, weight, neck, shoulders, arms, bust, waist, hips, legs and ankles all get the once-over – a demanding attitude to womenswear in general that has prevailed for generations. It may now be rather less daunting for women who want to fit clothes to their own natural body and sense of self, not their body to fashion. The use of elastic and elasticated fabrics mean that there can be some leeway in body measurements. The battery of measuring and pattern-plotting devices includes a template for drawing curves accurately, known as a French curve, seam gauges, set squares, yard or metric sticks, measured cutting mats and more recently flexible rulers.

Even a multitude of measurements cannot give the keen dressmaker a sense of their true bodily self in the same way as a dressmaker's form, or adjustable dummy on a stand. It is the opposite of a standardized shop mannequin designed to project a body so idealized that the garments displayed on it are often pinned at the rear to take up the slack. The dressmaker interested in fit must by contrast start with bodily truth. The dummy, with shape-shifting mechanisms adjusted according to numerous direct measurements, copies the contours of the real living body, to become the faithful record and double of a person's torso, even if the dressmaker intends to flatter the real body afterwards by some wizardry in the construction of the eventual garment. Dummies don't complain when a sleeve-in-the-making is held in place by pins. Measuring a body, your own or someone else's, is an intimate process. During a visit some years ago to a London dressmaker who worked for senior British royals, I saw their dress forms were discreetly shrouded with loose cloth to protect them from dirt and damage but also to keep the royal dimensions from prying eyes. Not everybody has the resources or space for a dummy, but they can raise the maker's game and be transformative. When Amy used one for the first time, she found it made a 'big difference' and with it she produced her best ever work.

The most ephemeral tool in domestic needlework is a tissue-paper garment pattern. Called by a friend of mine 'a marvel of compression', the pieces come folded inside an envelope complete with every possible instruction for cutting and making up, as we saw in Chapter Two. In theory it can be used again and again, and with variations, if the results please the maker. What could possibly go wrong? A browse through paper pattern catalogues or websites with downloadable patterns is the stitcher's equivalent to a gardener looking at seed catalogues, full of promise but still needing to be weighed up in practical and budgetary terms. Development of the paper pattern industry in the nineteenth century gave domestic dressmaking a newly reliable platform for beginners and experienced makers alike, adding another step in the expansion of domestic sewing machine adoption. Without a paper pattern, the amateur maker was stuck with improvisation, something makers then and now are often very good at, or otherwise risking shapeless clothes or unpicking existing garments to replicate them. At first, widely available domestic paper patterns promised more and cheaper access to newly fashionable styles that could be changed every season if desired. They were accompanied by an explosion of popular how-to periodicals advising on sewing clothes and household items at home. Today, in an age of inexpensive ready-made fast fashion, the increased cost of paper patterns, even if they are used many times, coupled with the cost of new fabric, presents a different equation. However, keen home sewers know that a good paper pattern, if it meets their personal preferences, leads to quality in their workmanship and gives them pleasure, it is a prized aid.

The sewing machine is the biggest, most complicated and expensive stitching tool, a weighty investment in every sense.

The machine's now familiar form arose in the same period of manufacturing advances that produced its polar opposite, the modern pin. A relatively new invention – or, more accurately, series of incremental inventions – the sewing machine comes with a substantial story of its own, usually told in terms of technical and engineering progress, or celebrating its male inventors or entrepreneurs, such as the American Isaac Singer (1811–1875). But most accounts overlook what the machine could actually do and what impact it had on the lives of its users, so a full social history of the sewing machine has yet to be written. Victorians called it 'the Queen of Inventions'. At five hundred stitches a minute, the speed of the first reliable 1850s sewing machines mesmerized onlookers and excited manufacturers of clothing and accessories. The economies lay in the rapid stitching of long straight seams; anything else was inevitably slower. But manufacturers still applied the machine to all elements of garment construction. Probably the earliest surviving examples of machine sewing, in the UK at least, are women's cotton collars dating between 1857 and 1859.[20]

The dream of achieving mechanized stitching was an old one. The journey to arrive at the 1850s collars is thought to have begun with drawings made by a London tailor called Thomas Saint in 1790 (not discovered until 1874). The French tailor Barthélemy Thimonnier achieved some workable wooden framed machines in 1830, but his brief success ended in their destruction by other tailors fearful for their livelihoods. In 1846 the American Elias Howe patented his eye-pointed needle and shuttle and from this pioneering period until the end of the 1800s, inventions, patent applications and countless manufacturers' insolvencies and takeovers came thick and fast on an international scale. Even miniaturized machines that fitted into tin boxes for children and pocket-sized stitching gadgets that clamped to a tabletop came on the market. There was traffic in technical knowhow between metal sewing machine, bicycle and small arms manufacturing. Husqvarna of Sweden is a company whose long history exemplifies this. Two sewing machines stand out as landmarks for users – the Singer 1865 New Family and 1881 Improved Family. They established a template for enduring consumer expectations in terms of the capability of a domestic sewing machine, how it operated and what it should look like. Machinists today would have no trouble finding their way around any number of similar machines of all makes from this period which survive in working order. By 1890, when Singer was selling 150,000 machines a year in the UK alone, fundamental technology and design hurdles were largely overcome.

The domestic sewing machine is as complex as the hand needle is simple. At first powered by foot pedal or hand-turned drive wheel but by electric motor since the early twentieth century, it is engineered to do two different but interdependent tasks, which have been pretty much the same for about 170 years. If these two mechanisms fail to perform their tasks in perfect synchronicity, disaster rapidly piles up on a scale quite beyond anything in a hand sewer's worst nightmare. One crank and cam system sends the threaded needle down to take it through the cloth and loop it through another thread underneath, fed from a bobbin in a shuttle, to form the stitch and then up again to start the next stitch. For the first few decades of the machine's development, an oscillating hook mechanism beneath the sewing plate created a chain stitch from one single thread delivered by the needle. There was competition between the early makers of these chain stitch and lock stitch types. It is the lock stitch version we are more familiar with today at home, although chain stitching continues in other contexts such as making paper sacks. Unlike hand sewing, where the needle normally goes right through the cloth and returns a stitch's distance forward from its previous point of entry, a machine needle moves up and down without moving forward. So as not to keep stitching on the same spot, the machine's second task is then to shift the cloth forward after each stitch. This it does by means of a feed-dog on which the cloth lies and whose toothed surface rises forward and drops back, the feed-dog driven by another sequence of crank and cam shafts.

As one awestruck writer observed in 1890, all this works 'with a rapidity, a precision and a rhythmic symmetry of movement entirely beyond the reach of any merely human manipulation'. He thought all the constituent parts were remarkable, even the tables and cabinets made for housing them. He was struck, as modern observers often are, by just how versatile machines at this early date could be, with attachments 'for binding, braiding, cording, piping, ruffling, gathering, welting, quilting, hemming, and embroidering'.[21]

How did the Victorians arrive at the situation we know today when sewing machines, first developed for commercial use, now in some senses also symbolize domesticity itself and self-sufficiency? How did the manufacturers get their machines into the parlour, a female domain ideally far removed from noisy powered clothing workshops? Our unadorned machines, in their pallid plastic casing, are commonplace these days, with no need to justify their place in the home. But the first manu-facturers offered their products in well-made wooden covers or drop-down tables, making them as much a piece of furniture as a machine. Recognizing different newly emerging domestic settings, two Americans who had formed the company Willcox & Gibbs in the mid-nineteenth century enjoyed success with their affordable 'noiseless', light, easily portable machine. Advertised as 'so Handy, Adaptable and Silent', it was aimed at women office workers living independently in flats. Alongside the general expansion of the personal credit industry in the late 1800s came the Singer offer of payment by instalment or by part-exchange, and their well-drilled sales force, with agents or shops on every high street, meant widespread sales. These innovations in the Singer brand were the brainchild of Singer's far-sighted partner Edward Clark (1811–1882), who grasped that advancing domestic use and access to the machine was as important, if not more so, than state-of-the-art engineering or manufacturing processes.

The popular stove enamel known as 'Black Japan', hand-finished or transferred with gilt or sometimes coloured ornamentation or mother-of-pearl inlay, was an enduring feature of machines until the first plastic cases of the 1950s. Nicholas Oddy notes that the machine's unique aesthetic made its march over the domestic threshold easier than was sometimes supposed and indeed set influential precedents, as it became a leading model for decoration on bicycles, typewriters and other emerging office equipment of the day. Latterly sewing machine design has lost that lead and become instead a follower of fashion.[22] My own little black-and-gold 1907 Willcox & Gibbs 'Silent' model still chugs away quietly at its stitching when asked. Although its enamel and ornament are worn by years of handling by former owners, it continues to perform its work in a demonstration of the innovative machine design and sturdy engineering that characterized this period. David Pye makes the general point that with the durability of things comes the connection to the people of the past who made them and also that evocative quality of patina: 'age and wear diversify the surfaces of things in ways that nothing else will. If nothing ever lasted we should be denied that beauty.'[23]

The sewing machine, from its first appearance to the present day, embodies powerful and conflicting messages, and was seen as an agent of both exploitation and hope. 'The hour of the machine had struck,' was Karl Marx's famous response in 1867 to the sewing machine in the context of his analysis of the effect of mechanization and factories on labour and capital. He saw it as the 'decisively revolutionary machine, the machine which attacks in an equal degree all the innumerable branches of this sphere of production, such as dressmaking, tailoring, shoe-making, sewing, hat-making and so on'. On the grounds that the sewing machine tended to 'compel the concentration, under one roof and one management, of previously separated branches of a trade' and the resultant factory system depressed the wages of handicraft and other outworkers and prioritized cheaper labour, Marx thought the centralized use of the sewing machine was ultimately responsible for the 'fearful increase in death from starvation during the last ten years in London'. He noted that girls and women, cheaper to employ, were the preferred factory operatives of sewing machines, a tendency seen on a global scale today.[24] Marx's critique was matched by growing public concerns about working conditions in the sweated trades alongside the emergence of the sewing machine. In Britain, Thomas Hood's well-known 1843 poem 'The Song of the Shirt', in which the overworked sickly seamstress is represented as sewing her own shroud, raised awareness of exploitation rife in the dressmaking trade. By contrast, other poems then followed in praise of the sewing machine across the second half of the nineteenth century. They aped Hood's rhythms and structure – for example, in one case, Hood's 'Stitch! Stitch! Stitch!' became 'Click! Click! Click!' – to promote a misplaced optimism that the machine would spare seamstresses the drudgery of the past.

It is often assumed that the sewing machine was utterly and rapidly transformative in superseding hand sewing. In fact, there was plenty the machine could *not* do. Close examination of a commercially produced 1860s hoop crinoline in a private collection reveals that two different machines – chain-stitch and lock-stitch – were used, plus another tool was required to press the metal hoops' closures in place. Several yards of hand stitching were also necessary to assemble and attach the supporting tapes and belt. The combination of hand and machine stitching is commonly found in late Victorian women's garments where bodice linings or curved sleeves required the hand, not the machine. One commentator noted in 1907, 'The sewing machine has taken away much of the drudgery of home sewing, but its use does not lessen the need of skill in handwork. No machine can finish ends of belts, collars, sew on trimming, fastenings, and like work and the finish has much to do with the general appearance of a garment.'[25] This remains true today, in high-end men's and womenswear. The mechanization of sewing had the unintended consequence of valorizing hand sewing when greater finesse is needed.

As anyone who uses a domestic sewing machine knows, the contrast between hand sewing and machine sewing is in some respects blurred. The machine is no use without the hands of its operator. The sewing robot has yet to arrive, though they are working on it. Even pre-computerized machines bristle with knobs and levers; they need two hands to fill the bobbins and thread up the machine, to adjust the tension and length of the stitches, to feed and guide the cloth being stitched, to sew curves or to pivot on the needle, and then to finish off and release. Any number of special attachments may be used for different purposes, each with its own little intricacies of fitting and using well. All this handwork must combine with the operator's foot to control the power. Pre-electric machines allowed the user to manage the work in progress with two hands if it was also powered by two feet on a treadle, but only one hand on models where the other had to turn the drive wheel. In all cases the machines require continuous coordination with the body of the user, at close proximity. The ornamentation seen on so many surviving antique cast-iron black machines like my little 'Silent' model often shows the signs of wear caused by the constant contact with their user's hand and arm, evidence of the machine–body partnership. Not always a harmonious marriage, it's common to see surviving first-generation machine-sewn garments that betray a machinist's poor control of thread tension, signs of panic as the stitches wobble round a curve or seams failing when single-thread chain stitches unravel. The machine, then and now, has always demanded the fullest attention of its operator or it can indeed become a feral beast. Today's domestic sewing machines can power along faster than their Victorian ancestors and offer a much bigger repertoire of stitch types at the press of a button, but in exchange they have lost some durability and character along with the inlays and decal ornamentation. These said 'sewing machine' for so long that modern stick-ons can be added now to emulate the traditional appearance.

There is something about the sewing machine that attracts loyalty. It is common to hear women speak of fond memories of their sewing machines, their first one particularly so, rather in the way some people reminisce about their first car. But what is it about the machines old and new that can generate the emotional attachment so frequently expressed? As one Canadian recalled of the 1940s: 'The first sewing machine I had was a treadle one . . . I dearly loved that machine.'[26] For many women, myself included, when the first sewing machine is given for their coming of age, it represents a new independence, a rite of passage. Perhaps more than any other sewing aid, the durable sewing machine can be a long-term presence, and, given as a present on engagement or marriage as it commonly was, it was a part of its owner's role in family life. It became a visible investment in future home-making. In many homes, the machine had to be paid for in instalments over time, which was not to be taken lightly and made its presence felt in the family budget for some years. Irene told me in 1995 how she had recurrent anxiety dreams about paying the instalments due on a second-hand Jones sewing machine she acquired in the early 1930s. Not a good start, but she went on to use the machine regularly for over four and a half decades before she sold it. In the aftermath of the Second World War, Elsie in Portsmouth, England, was for two years on the waiting list for a new Singer, a gift from her fiancé. It eventually arrived when Elsie was 26 and she had an electric motor added to this 'very heavy' machine. Its indestructability meant that she taught her teenage daughter to sew on it and continued to use it herself for another half-century. For many women, their sewing machine in this period was the only labour-saving device in their house, another reason to treasure it. In addition to years of service, old sewing machines have often been passed down through a family and come with the stories of the past that families tell about themselves. They retain their freight of memory and affection, which make deep bonds between past and present. Susan, another Singer owner, feels a close connection between her childhood and her machine:

> I have a huge sentimental attachment to my great-aunt's sewing machine, which must be a hundred years old. She was a much-loved relative with whom I stayed as a child. I have never forgotten the joy of waking up in her house to the sight of sunlight on pretty chintz and faded rose-coloured rugs . . . The fact that she made those chintz curtains on what is now my sewing machine is almost unbearably poignant.

Outside domestic traditions, the sewing machine may offer an escape from family life or work. It empowers those who enjoy making as a matter of choice at a private level, adding to a sense of machine as companion to the user on their personal creative journey. When Anne was a busy junior hospital doctor in residence in London she was often on call. Her portable sewing machine, bought on a whim, gave her much needed quiet moments to make things when her duties allowed. The sewing machine can be a means of communication and gift making. When recruited during the COVID-19 pandemic, it allowed makers everywhere to express their altruism as they rushed to put their foot on the pedal to make PPE at home to supplement supplies to health workers. The machine joined key 'Pandemic Objects' for a recent exhibition of the same name organized by the Victoria and Albert Museum, London. In the words of curator Becky Knott, the 'scale of the pandemic has left many people – particularly those who are not already frontline workers – feeling helpless; the sewing machine has become an avenue by which ordinary people can make a significant contribution to this global emergency or simply find solace in the act of making'.[27] It is often not entirely a female preserve: in many homes the sewing machine connects men and women when it is given by a husband to his wife, and is sometimes mended and maintained by him. Paul remembers sewing well enough as a young boy on his mother's industrial machine to contribute to her paid home work, and by the age of ten he was competent in servicing and repairing it. A contestant in the 2022 TV series *The Great British Sewing Bee*, Cristian, who grew up near Transylvania, was given a sewing machine by his parents when he turned eighteen.[28] These days men are buying and using sewing machines in big enough numbers to spark the nickname 'sew bro'.

The sewing machine is often a treasured machine that corresponds to Bachelard's 'dimension of intimacy' in its nooks and crannies. Barbara recalls: 'My mother's Frister & Rossmann cabinet sewing machine was a fixture of my childhood. I loved playing with the bobbins which lived in a dear little set of drawers inside the door and was fascinated by the wondrous gold sphinx which decorated its black body.' Helen Howes is an expert on old sewing machines and repairs them too. She has found birth certificates, cash, letters of condolence and 1920s birthday cards tucked inside them in good states of preservation. In fact, she told me she has never encountered an old machine that does not have some sort of non-sewing item stowed inside its drawer or box. These discoveries are a reminder of the machine as a convenient and private space, the equivalent of the Georgian workbox used to stow little keepsakes or other personal items alongside a sewing kit.[29] Entwined with everyday life over time for many reasons, it is no surprise that the sewing machine holds a special place among the tools of sewing.

In a good number of machine-stitching projects, no matter how carefully planned, even those following a familiar pattern, there comes a time when personal judgement and adjustment are required and only a hand tool will do. The more trial and error and intuition there is in a project, and in the mind of the maker, the more likely a hand tool is to be involved. It can be a tiny one. When asked to name a favourite, Ingrid echoed others when she said, 'Best tool ever? The un-picker – I have quite a few of them.' The hand-held seam unpicker or ripper, also called a thread snipper, is a midget compared to the heft of the sewing machine. While the sewing machine is a maker, stitching fabrics together, the artful little seam ripper has the opposite purpose: it cuts the stitches open and unravels seams, it unmakes. Yet by undoing the work of the needle, ultimately the seam ripper allows corrections or improvements, so it too is on the maker's side.

However big or small, simple or complex their sewing tools, the maker needs a repertoire of hand skills and understanding of materials and processes to put them to best use. Expertise and satisfaction are dependent on that. The 'dimension of intimacy' can be inward-looking, even meditative. We might also wonder if the familiarity of loyal tools held close in making hands has a steadying effect and contributes to mental well-being, as does the process of stitching itself. At the same time our tools connect us to the wider world.

5

Fruits of Our Work

The world is awash with manufactured stuff. Ready-made textile goods proliferate from toys to cushions to furnishing to garments and accessories; they are on offer everywhere in shops and at any time on the Internet. Making them at home with your own hands may seem superfluous. Yet people with busy lives still find what it takes to sew things. Men and women, young and old, sew at home either for their own personal use or for family, friends, neighbours and charity. They may have enjoyed doing it for years or they may be novices, they may be sewing addicts or – to stretch an analogy – may incline to more episodic needle use, and their sewing practices will almost certainly ebb and flow somewhat over their lives as circumstances change or new skills and tastes emerge. Despite all their differences, all those who participated in both my projects were united in knowing that sewing matters to them, a finding amply confirmed in other studies as well. But what are they making? Looking more closely at the fruits of their labour can also uncover some more about why they do it and what they think about spending their time in this way.

Taking a long view of stitching at home, it is easy to imagine practical sewing going on by lamplight in every home in the past, a cosy practice we have somehow left behind. By 1840, with

Queen Victoria (herself a capable needlewoman) just a couple of years into her reign, the anonymous 'A Lady', author of a ground-breaking instructional book on the benefits of cutting out and sewing skills for making clothes and furnishings at home, noted sadly that her book was motivated by the fact that gentrywomen and girls were often 'mere novices' in such matters and the poor were 'in total ignorance'.[1] Allowing for some exaggeration on her part, she was not alone in her concerns. In the Victorian period plain sewing certainly went on extensively – it was taught in all schools, although commentators bemoaned falling standards – but it was already being eroded in homes by external factors such as the cheapness of dressmakers' labour, the expanding availability of ready-made basic clothing in new varieties of cheaper cotton and more paid employment for women and girls outside the domestic sphere. Nor should we assume that those women and girls who did sew at home were all skilled at it or enjoyed it. Home sewing has a diverse and uneven history: for some it was a solace or necessity, for others a task to be dropped as soon as circumstances or wage packets allowed.

Today, not surprisingly, personal life events experienced by individual makers still have a direct impact on the sewing they do over time. Some drop out altogether, or switch to or combine with other needle crafts, or move in and out of stitching as their circumstances alter. Others sew because they always have and can't imagine life without it. 'Come what may, I expect I'll sew until I can't see,' says retired Andrea, whose motivation is still strong after a lifetime of stitching clothes, banners, quilts and bags. In the USA, Lauren describes her sewing as 'a lifelong companion'. They represent many sewing loyalists who have stitched all their lives. It will take a lot to stop them now.

Today, like much unpaid work traditionally associated with women at home, making clothing and other stitched items is not much celebrated in public. Because it's done in private homes, it's not really a measurable activity. It is even harder to know what it means to those who do it. But when a survey undertaken across fifteen European countries (including the UK) between 2008 and 2015 asked men and women how they spent their time, it showed that across Europe a good deal of needlework was happening per participating household. Women spent more time than men on unpaid household and family care and upkeep activities in general. More specifically, it comes as no surprise that time spent on handicraft and needlework activities of all kinds – knitting, embroidery, making curtains and new clothes, and using a sewing machine – and care of textiles, were also sharply divided between men and women. National and generational differences in these activities were significant too. Across the board, more older women tended to undertake these activities than those of working age. Across the different countries more young women undertook these activities than young men, though not as much as older women.[2]

We probably see these variations in gender and age echoed in our own local experience, but the dipstick findings of this survey, while indicative, inevitably mask important elements. Missing from statistics is the passion of people who take up sewing as newcomers. Nor can the numbers capture the instructive or other affective ripple effects sewing may have on other people who know or see a stitcher in action at first hand or on the Internet. The story is further complicated by the fact that stitching projects undertaken at home vary over time, because they are inevitably affected in part by social trends. For example, online sewing communities have emerged to support people wanting to join the greater visibility of gender fluidity in clothing and personal styling, since sewing at home can be the way forward for those not well served by ready-to-wear. The u.s. group Sewqueer believes that 'sewing, clothing, and making are inherently political' through connections to global economies, through community and by 'self-presentation' that lets people assert their 'genders and take up space'.³ There is no doubt that sewing at home increases in response to economic trends. Eithne Farry, journalist and author of two books on making fun and thrifty DIY clothes, noted that in 2008, in anticipation of that year's recession, the UK retailer Argos reported that sales of selected sewing machines were up by 50 per cent on the previous year. Writing about her own experience, Farry knew what might lie behind these statistics. 'The first dress I made didn't have anything so technical as a zip, and if you looked closely, the hem was crooked, but every time I wore it I had a dizzy sense of accomplishment.'⁴ Positive experiences like this are behind a lot of what happened in 2020 as well. When lockdowns began in the COVID-19 pandemic there was another rise in sewing and other crafts measurable through retail sales. Hobbycraft, the UK's biggest retailer across all handicrafts, reported a 200 per cent boom in online sales during that time. Sewing sits alongside new crafts trends in handmade home decor and knitting and crochet remain as popular as ever.⁵

A significant factor at play here is the current expansion of appreciation among experts and the public alike of the mental and physical health benefits of making things in general, something confirmed by reports of the restorative effects of sewing on mental well-being during COVID-19 lockdowns. At the same time, there is growing public concern about the ethical and environmental downsides of the textile industry and fast fashion. It would be unwise to predict what lies ahead for those manufacturers selling in our already economically battered and shrinking high streets where a cheap and once seemingly inexhaustible abundance of ready-mades now looks a tad more vulnerable. Among Rachel Hart's customers at Raystitch, her stylish haberdashery and fabric shop in central London, which also runs classes, younger sewers are now less interested in saving money and more in styling garments to the realities of their physique.[6] They want the fun of making and wearing something unique to themselves. The tyranny of the perfect fit has retreated. Less likely to conform, they can also outwit that co-tyrant, slenderness, because they are more interested in the quality and character of the fabric than looking like a fashion model. Numerous small independent paper pattern companies such as Tilly and the Buttons, Merchant & Mills and Paper Theory are responding around the world to this new taste with simpler, relaxed and less daunting styles frequently coupled with tutorials for beginners or returners and an interest in sustainability. They are a challenge to the old-established paper pattern companies. This is surely an example of what is meant by 'a different kind of love affair with "stuff" – a long-term relationship of appreciation, slow pleasures, care and respect'.[7]

The Great British Sewing Bee on the BBC is a useful barometer for the popularity of sewing. It has been a UK favourite since 2013, frequently ranking top or second in national weekly viewing figures. Audiences averaging over 6 million each week watch a group of amateur sewers, male and female, compete in different timed challenges: sewing to a pattern, transforming old clothing into something new to wear, creating something made-to-measure to be modelled live on the show.[8] Contestants have diverse ethnic and economic backgrounds, ages, motives and jobs, including home maker, charity worker, teacher, engineer, retired shopkeeper, nurse, cleaner, mechanic, doctor, student and jewellery designer, yet it is telling that despite this diversity their biographies often reveal they were inspired by relatives who sew. The show has been credited with reassuring boys and men that it's OK to sew. The same show format is popular in other countries around the world. Competitors are judged by professionals, leading to one overall winner. Charismatic presenters and amateurs from all walks of life bring viewers practical instruction mixed with inspiration and an entertaining dose of competitive tension. Some viewers think sewing against the clock distorts the realities of the making process, but one self-taught stitcher told me it was 'a revelation'. It showed her that 'everyone makes mistakes and, you know what, often they can be fixed! I also learned about equipment and saw that you could convert patterns and upcycle old clothing. I began to truly enjoy sewing and gained enough confidence to experiment a little.'

Proficiency or pleasure in sewing of any kind might seem strangled at birth if it is no longer rated as a dedicated part of children's education. But this is far from the whole story. As we saw in Chapter Two, learning to sew is not confined to schools: it happens in families, friendship circles and classes run by individuals or shops. In the Internet age it can happen almost anywhere, and the self-taught and latecomers often go on to become intrepid stitchers. Sewing in schools may have declined, undoubtedly with a long-term impact yet to be fully realized, but it seems that today there are plenty of newcomers, youngsters and men who pick up a needle with enthusiasm and swell the ranks of home stitchers. 'The first time you put your own work on your body feels like magic, it's wildly addicting,' says Jonathan Simanjuntak, a young American 'sew-bro' who makes his own clothes.[9] It is clear that stitching men are on the increase and 'ready to take on challenges', according to Rachel Hart. She also notes that social media has become a 'massive' part of making sewing 'cool' for newcomers and, in her experience, sewing was increasing significantly even before the 2020 pandemic.[10]

The arrival of the gender-neutral term 'sewist' (neatly replacing 'sewer', sometimes a tricky homograph) hasn't entirely displaced the association of sewing with women still embedded in the terms 'seamstress' and 'dressmaker'. It is also obvious that the ever-broader reach of home sewing embraces experienced stitchers as well as novices who might feel marginalized for personal reasons, but now find themselves welcomed with open arms by the plentiful upbeat blogs and websites run by stitching groups. Lots share the goal of the U.S. Sewcialists: 'to build community and make everyone feel welcome. We support crafting as an inclusive and welcoming space for people of all ages, abilities, ethnicities, genders, orientations and sizes.'[11] In the UK Danielle, in her early twenties, exemplifies the new sense of virtual belonging. She enjoys the 'Instagram sewing community', which brings her 'a lot of inspiration'. Many, like Danielle, learn new techniques from each other on Instagram and post their 'makes' to share with other people round the world. There can be no doubt from these and other viewpoints that today sewing at home matters to large numbers of people across the world, although quantitively they and their output elude precise tallies. Ultimately what matters is that the true human and practical value of sewing and its place in people's lives are recognized. Qualitatively, this becomes clearer when reasons for home sewing are considered.

From the nineteenth to the mid-twentieth century keeping up appearances formed a particularly powerful social driver for sewing, although it is less talked about today. Appearances in clothing and domestic interiors served then to convey respectability and commitment to certain values and underpinned access to public life, civic events, outings, employment and credit. A key element in the endeavour to make the grade was needlework. Sewing at home could often achieve the otherwise unaffordable, disguise the worst failings and in extremis keep shirts on the backs of the breadwinners. Home sewing was sometimes an act of desperation. 'I have taken things off my own back and made my children things. Necessity is the mother of invention.'[12] Plain items could still be fabricated at less expense than buying ready-made but there were also other parallel motives. Sarah Gordon, writing on that period in the USA, concludes that some home stitchers wanted to disguise their poverty or ethnic differences, but others wanted to defy these limitations. 'Sewing was a sea of contradictions and understandings of women's work and roles. The same skills that aimed to create an ideal housekeeper, wife, and mother also promised sexual attraction and artistic satisfaction, masked class difference, and allowed for personal interpretations of modesty and style.' She cites some African American women of the period as sewing to 'match or even surpass white standards of propriety' and in other cases making items that referred to their ethnic origins.[13]

In the past, the rising presence of fashion trends promoted by ever more prolific fashion printed media and the dubious quality and unpredictably sized ready-to-wear, often in flammable or flimsy materials, could constitute a trap of false economy for the poor, but also incentivized home sewing for all social classes. An American editor echoed advice all too familiar to previous and subsequent generations when she stressed in 1913 the merit of home dressmaking for women of 'modest means' in terms of fashion and value. 'Fashion changes so rapidly that it requires one with a ready and clever needle . . . to keep up with its dictates.' She described ready-made garments as 'generally gotten up to catch the eye, much trimmed, but of inferior quality and workmanship'. Buying ready-mades was easy but 'in the long run extravagant' when making clothes at home could use 'better material, better workmanship' and not least achieve 'a better style' and more individuality.[14]

For Jo, born in 1926 in London, sewing was so much part of her family upbringing and her time as a domestic science student that she was twenty years old before she owned her first ready-made dress. She told me in 1995 that she was in no doubt that her subsequent sewing for her home and children made a 'tremendous amount of difference' to their household budget. 'I mean either we wouldn't have had the clothes or the things that I made or we would not have had so many or we would have had to wait a lot longer for them.' For some, like Jo, substantial savings are made. Jenny recalls: 'I made all the curtains for our new house except for one window which must have saved us a fortune.' Sewing for necessity's sake is not without other rewards: process can matter as much as outcome, as Lucy says: 'I sewed quite prolifically as a student nurse in the early 1970s as I was poor, and fabrics were still relatively cheap compared with the price of ready-made clothes. So my motivation was partly to save money but also the satisfaction of the creative process.'

Today thrift is not necessarily a motivation. Ready-mades proliferate, fabric is more expensive and earning money outside the home is often a more pressing use of women's time. Changes in the relative value of their time coupled with tensions that can arise between paid work outside the home and unpaid work in the home all affect stitching at home more than ever. But in a further twist, with recent experiences in the pandemic and more demands within the workplace, those very tensions have alerted people to a need for a kinder life–work balance. In this context, sewing is now recast as a restorative activity, bringing some calm into lives lived at pace in an uncertain world. It is possible that fast fashion will raise its prices as it scrambles to outlaw the unsustainable practices that made it cheap in the first place, something fashion insiders warn will happen, which once again could foreground home sewing as a means to save money. Surveying common reasons why their members sew, the online group Seamwork has found that a wish for sustainability now features among other well-established reasons, such as meeting personal tastes, loving fabrics and creativity and feeling connected to other makers.[15] On the other hand, expanding clothing rental services may tempt consumers into a cycle of novelties in which they feel more detached from the experience of making anything or caring for it themselves.

Some of the fundamentals involved in home sewing are evidenced in a rare study of a skirt being made by an 'avid seamstress' in 2008. It set out to calculate 'how we spend time, energy, and money' and echoes the comments above made in 1913. The experienced maker in question already owned the necessary equipment, new fabric for the skirt cost $35, and, including time spent shopping for the fabric, the skirt was completed in about five hours. Skirts were available to buy ready-made in nearby shops for less money, so why did the maker spend her time in this way? She made it because she could choose fabric to her own taste and probably of better quality than shop-bought skirts at the same price, choose the exact garment shape and details, and ensure it fitted her perfectly and chimed with her wardrobe style. The skirt project confirmed that sewing 'requires time, effort, money, and skill' but concluded, for that particular maker, it was 'a pleasurable process with a gratifying result'.[16] Her skirt making was not driven by economizing but by the enjoyment unique to making something. A recent comparison by an online sewing community of the costs of making or buying a selection of women's garments showed just how many variables are involved. The cost of a homemade dress depends, among other factors, on whether or not you price in the cost of your own sewing time and use cheap or expensive fabric. The price tag on a dress in a shop also reflects the quality of the fabric but nowadays it presents another choice for aware consumers between a label that is made more costly because it cares about fair wages and sustainability and a cheaper one that does not. In the end, the calculation to make or buy is as much a matter of personal preference as simple arithmetic.[17]

A qualitative study of what sewing for leisure means to 78 women aged forty or under, geographically dispersed across North America, Europe and elsewhere, found recently that thrift was not a motive for them, confirming what we saw in Chapter Two, but other motives and personal rewards were powerful. 'Sewing for sewing's sake' – making clothes, toys, quilts for themselves and others – brought these women strong feelings of pride and accomplishment. It was calming because of repetitive hand movements and the 'downtime' it offered without stressful demands. They enjoyed the social interactions and the 'flow' and self-awareness they experienced when engaged in the craft.[18]

Responses about enjoying social interaction in real or online groups confirm sewing as not only a private pleasure but one with broader social significance that is probably driving a change in retailing. In one U.S. city, San Diego, a journalist reported the closure of older-style fabrics shops because they are failing to meet the changing needs of sewers, particularly among the increasing number of younger sewing enthusiasts. Male and female, they want to have quality garments they have made themselves. A sense of adventure prevails, and they are seeking more from a shop than just bales of cloth: they want more social contact, more sense of community with like-minded people of their age and the chance to access learning opportunities. These shifts are reflected elsewhere.[19]

But enthusiastic beginners may meet some bumps in the road. Amy Twigger Holroyd notes in her perceptive book *Folk Fashion: Understanding Homemade Clothes* that the meanings of all clothing are 'multiple, movable and potentially ambiguous'. She argues that homemade clothes heighten that ambiguity. Shop-bought clothes are part of a known system of value and identity, but meanings of home-made clothing are more 'difficult to place'. Their significance is hard to define; for some home-made is always best, for others it has a lingering stigma and an association with poverty.[20] Making clothes or other things at home is often admired, the knowhow seen as enviable. But there is a tricky course to navigate between sewing that satisfies the maker, for any number of reasons, and how their output may appear in the eyes of others. Both makers and onlookers are only too aware that if the results look even a tad 'home-made', admiration and praise can melt away. Hilary, a keen stitcher, feels 'pleased' with a compliment on what she's wearing 'especially if it is not known that I made it myself'. Despite those who share Eithne Farry's 'dizzy sense of accomplishment' even with a crooked hem, for some people a puckered seam or wonky zip is their equivalent of a baker's 'soggy bottom'. Another prolific and successful home sewer, Grace, says, 'I worked in investment banking and homemade clothes would have had me laughed out of town.' But what constitutes success can change over time as fashion itself changes. An ill-set sleeve would have ruined the meticulous tightness of an 1880 bodice although a 1920 flapper's frock could be technically much more forgiving. By the 1930s the tyranny of fit was back again and fit also meant conformity with fashion. A popular 1950s dressmaking book spoke for many amateur and professional makers pre- and post-war, declaring the classic conventions that a dress should be 'becoming' to the figure, emphasizing its 'good points', and concealing those that were 'less pleasing', or at least not draw attention to them. To achieve this at least sixteen different body measurements were required.[21] Times change and nowadays, while nobody would want to emphasize the bits they don't like, many home stitchers still revere a fine fit and are skilled enough to enjoy meeting its challenges in dresses, and the soft tailoring of suits, jackets and coats, but others happily turn to looser frocks or baggy trousers. The same differences now apply to household items: home stitchers can choose complex swags and heavy lined curtains or an easy waft of artless muslin at the window – it's all OK.

Of course, it is never effortless, even when sewing's mise en place is fully lined up: time and the right tools and fabric for a project. Poppy described the highs and lows:

Sewing can be (and mostly is) fantastically satisfying. It can also drive you crazy when things go wrong – jammed machines, tricky unpicking, cutting things wrong, making a fit error, sewing over a bit underneath your intended seam, accidently snipping into the body of your garment. I am not the tidiest sewist, so also pins on the floor, scissors going missing, pattern pieces misplaced.

Different stages, from conceptualization to completion of projects, appeal to different people. Some enjoy choosing fabrics or the making process more than the outcome. Gaye, a retired cartographer and illustrator, particularly enjoys 'the cutting and construction processes, opening a new pattern and placing the pieces on a new fabric gives me a thrill which cannot be hurried'. Hilary likes getting to the end. 'I do not enjoy finishing such as hemming and neatening seams etc., but I have a sense of satisfaction when it is done.' Heather is ambivalent: 'Once I'm done it feels a bit empty, though if it is something as a gift there is definite pleasure in that.'

It's another nice twist in the tale that a reasonable level of skill among those who make their own clothes and household items often makes them more discerning shoppers for ready-mades. In shops, they get ideas, inspect seams and feel fabrics; they are unimpressed by manufacturers' cost-cutting tricks but appreciative of quality when they meet it. Teenagers may have a different take on things. Making something to last is not the aim, more the urgent need for something to wear at the weekend. Novelty, speed and disposability are the markers of this approach. Alyson remembered going to parties on Saturdays when she bought fabric in the morning and made 'a long dress ready for the party that evening. I achieved that quite a few times, and a few of my friends did too.' Of course, grown women want to join the party as well and have told me they did the same. For Hilary it wasn't exactly for a party that she sewed in haste, after 'the craziest visit I made to Liberty' on the first day of their winter sale 'when very heavily pregnant. I then went home and made a nightdress from the lawn I had bought in time to wear it in the maternity ward 3 days later.'

There is an abundance of evidence that personal satisfaction is a real driver of sewing at home. It is often expressed directly and plainly and sometimes verging on rapture. Nobody who sews seems in any doubt about this. Whether a project is simple or complex, it is imbued for them with multiple possibilities. It involves occupying a particular room or space, assembling familiar tools, the tactility of fabrics, planning, manipulating paper patterns or improvising, measuring and cutting, solving problems, expanding skills, enjoying freedom of choice, feeling gratification at the end of it all. Sally spoke for many participants in my survey: 'I can't imagine a life without being able to sew ... it's so useful, versatile, satisfying.' Among the participants in *Our Sewing Stories*, sewing practices frequently emerge as a gift that keeps on giving well beyond the satisfactions of the making process themselves. They often acknowledged their sewing as forming connections and bonds with others, past and present, near and far. An American proud of her pioneer ancestors told me she gets 'a sense of inheritance from sewing, a connection to my past and my family history', something she values, and it was also an interest she shared with her mother 'from childhood right until she died aged 90 years'. Links like this are articulated as positive emotional experiences, brought to mind simply by the act of sewing. It becomes a kind of journey. The stitcher moves forward, advancing their project, and at the same time is touched by the past that lies behind them.

Other motivating pleasures of connection can come from outside the circle of family and friends when stitchers are part of wider communities of interest. Most famously in the quilting world there is a tradition of bringing quilters together in each other's homes or community spaces. When done in physical companionship alongside others, stitching of any kind, though requiring concentration, can quickly promote conversation and friendships. In pre-telephone, pre-railway times when life was more circumscribed for women, sociable sewing was an important way to consolidate or extend links with kin and neighbours. Today the Internet is a means to form virtual sewing communities.

The evident satisfactions of sewing for oneself are matched by the satisfactions of doing the same for other people. Only one participant in the *Our Sewing Stories* project said they sewed entirely for themselves. In keeping with others, one put it very simply: 'I love making things for other people.' Like almost any kind of making done freely for another person, sewing becomes an expressive process that can enrich relationships between people. In Philadelphia, the 'self-taught sewist' Michael Gardner has made several very glamorous birthday outfits and other fun garments for his young daughter. He celebrates his handiwork as bonding with his child in a way that also encourages her own creativity.[22] Becoming parents is typically a stage of life when home stitchers turn up the dial. Sewing in this setting becomes another important branch of provisioning and parenting and is often very gratifying – although small children don't usually mix well with sewing machines.

Jo told me in 1995 how she made her daughter a pair of flared trousers when they first came in, exactly as requested, in denim with stripes round the hems. 'I can remember standing in the bay window . . . watching her go down the street and knowing that she was thinking that she was really the cat's whiskers that morning.' Sewing for your children can be hard to schedule into a busy life, especially at the eleventh hour for an event at school or elsewhere. Sometimes it requires a certain amount of sacrifice. A touching story concerns four-year-old Jane's patchwork dress, now in a museum, made for an unexpected party in 1944. Despite wartime fabric limitations in force in Britain, working through the night her mother conjured up from scratch a pretty frock from odds and ends of cotton and silk in time for the party.[23] Such a task can be turned into a joint project. New Yorker Stella enjoys all the stages of making original Halloween and other costumes for her daughters. 'It's fun to imagine the costumes with my girls, to go to the fabric store with them to pick things out and design costumes as we go . . . Of course, reality doesn't always line up with imagination, but overall my girls have been pleased.' Part of her satisfaction stems from following in the footsteps of her own mother, who did the same for her brother and herself when they were children. Amy told me that her sewing is strongly motivated by the need to make bespoke clothing that meets the precise preferences and capabilities of her autistic daughter, whose learning differences also shape her approach to what she can wear. She also invested a lot of effort into making her own wedding dress and her daughter's bridesmaid's dress for a ceremony held in between COVID-19 lockdowns. 'At a time when the world was turning on its head it was a commitment to the future and an optimistic act, showing myself and my daughter that life would go on.' The dial goes up again with the arrival of the next generation. Making things at home for an extending circle of youngsters carries significant emotional weight. It is a practice that embodies a very particular sense of connection, continuity and intergenerational family identity. It is bound up with memories and feelings about home and the physical legacy of sewn artefacts. Ingrid's pushing herself: she told me she's making quilts for 'five great-nieces and -nephews'.

For many women, sewing a wedding dress or a bridesmaid's dress for their daughter, friend or even themselves is one of their truly memorable satisfactions, a high point that's certainly not stress-free for those that venture to do it but delightful when it works out well. A woman's entry into marriage has long been associated with textiles, from a 'bottom drawer' stocked with items in preparation for running a household to dowries and marriage chests for more elite brides, bulging with personal clothing and household linen viewed as economically valuable and long-lived assets. Making a dress seems like today's variant on these ritualized preparations. It wraps the bride in a bespoke gown made and invested with care and love, sending her off confidently to face her big day and all those cameras. For Elaine, her daughter's wedding dress 'was the best thing I have ever made', a response echoed by other women who have done the same. The intricate and intimate processes involved in the making of these special dresses can also form powerful memories. Claire Wilcox writes in her memoir that her mother made most of her daughter's clothes, and was often unable to speak while she fitted them 'because she had pins in her mouth'. The last thing she made for her was her wedding outfit, 'based in a roundabout way, on the designs of a famous couturier, a poet of fashion. Now, when I look at his designs, I think of my mother, and of her inching around me on her knees, and the clothes she made just for me.'[24]

Families can be geographically separated sometimes over great distances and making things for far-flung loved ones is one way to maintain bonds and express affection. The making represents emotional attachment in the face of physical detachment; it is an investment of time and care on the maker's part, recognized by the recipient, if not immediately by a child, then hopefully in retrospect. Susan thought of one special gift she made as a kind of material testimony to her deeply felt bond. She found it tough in COVID-19 lockdown to be separated from her pregnant daughter 'but making a bear for the baby gave me a sense of connection and purpose . . . it is proof that I was thinking about him throughout those long weeks.' The sewing self is seldom isolated or adrift from others. The sewer's focus is on the project in hand, but their thoughts can turn outwards. We know that most individuals are anchored in, and responsive to, family, friends and an underlying need of communality that comes in various overlapping forms such as work, neighbourhood, sport, faith, activism and so on. Stitchers and crafters seem generous by nature. Some are prolific gift-makers and it can start in childhood. 'The first things I made as a child were small gifts for family, often in felt – needle cases, pincushions, bookmarks,' says Grace, who continues to make for others.

In Western societies we normally acquire a commodity through a utilitarian transaction. Things are bought and sold without much – if any – attachment between the parties concerned, and the relationship between them ceases when the transaction is completed. But unlike a commodity transaction, although framed differently in different societies, broadly speaking gifts are messages used to mediate social relations. They bring an expectation or even an obligation of reciprocity. What is involved in fabricating rather than buying something intended as a gift? That gift signifies the maker's time, their work, their materials, their intentions, their focus that led up to the gift. These components of making have particular significance in our time-poor, high-speed First World lives. Terry counts her time as part of her giving. Regardless of the utility of what she makes, 'it is good to send something personal, a gift of free time devoted to sewing.' For the maker, the stitched gift has been planned in *their* minds, turned and turned over in *their* hands, made with *their* attentiveness to the future recipient as well as to the making. The gift now in the recipient's hands is a vessel for the maker's feelings embedded in it. Sometimes we recognize all of that; we understand the artefact *is* in some senses its maker and feel touched and grateful. Sometimes the gift is unwanted, or not well made, or out of sync with our tastes, but surely, we should *never* let on. Shouldn't we match the maker-giver's kindness with the courtesy of a white lie, and, after all, who doesn't know how to tell such a lie when it's needed? Claire, who teaches short sewing courses near London, says her students love to make needlework gifts but only give them to people they consider 'sew-worthy'. In this finely calibrated giving, recipients must be the kind of people who appreciate the time and effort expended, not those who think homemade things are 'naff'. A survey of sewers found that some get a sense of external validation when they make successful gifts, or otherwise show their finished pieces, adding to their sense of achievement.[25] A stitched gift can fulfil a pressing need and repay a debt of gratitude at the same time, as one woman explained to me:

> One of the best things I have made was a cotton voile nightie for my mother who was suffering badly with the heat in a care home shortly before she died. She wanted to save it for best but I insisted that she put it on immediately and wear it as much as possible to be as comfortable as possible. This she did, and I was so glad to have been able to do this for her, after everything that she had taught me in the past.

In another form of giving, stitching with a compassionate and charitable needle for strangers is a generous thread running through generations of women and girls, and men too, voluntarily committing their time and skill directly or indirectly to meet the needs of others. With their work, altruistic sewers try to alleviate the fallout of war, poverty and other crises, squaring up to urgent demands that never go away. Thankfully these gallant needleworkers are prepared to carry on sewing for people they may never meet. They sew primarily in the spirit of benevolence but can gain the never-to-be-underestimated recompense of feeling useful. A crop of work may stem from an individual, sometimes immense amounts, but commonly also from group and community collaboration, giving shared support and validation for those who support others. If ever stitchers rose to meet an urgent need, it was during the COVID-19 pandemic, in this case aided by the Internet and social media to create informal groups with common goals. In the pandemic many people rallied, alone or in groups across the world, to sew scrubs for health workers and masks for everyone who needed them, including family and friends.

When people thread up in the spirit of altruism, they can be proud of a long lineage behind them, a theme which deserves an entire book to itself. Sewing for the troops has often been prodigious and shaped semi-formally by official and semi-official bodies. There are more permanent organizations that have grown out of addressing immediate needs. A group of influential friends started making garments for an orphanage in 1882, from which the London Needlework Guild was formed in 1892. Two years later it was producing more than 52,000 garments annually for distribution to charitable causes. This body later became Queen Mary's Needlework Guild, in its heyday famous for a Herculean war effort during the First World War and its aftermath, making over 15 million clothing and surgical items. But the guild's prayer about 'the work of our hands and hearts' will resonate with the hopes of many of all faiths and no faith who stitch for others in need: 'so that each garment may carry to the wearer not only decency and warmth, but courage, comfort, and hope for brighter days'.[26] It may be more common these days to contribute directly or indirectly by giving our second-hand clothing to charity shops or buying from them, or donating cash to such causes. Keen stitchers often buy clothes or furnishings from charity shops to cannibalize for fabric or upcycle.

Sewing to alleviate poverty in the past, although often motivated by humanitarianism, was never simple. As Vivienne Richmond points out about nineteenth-century England, 'what surfaces repeatedly, even amongst the most well-meaning, is their utter incomprehension of the poor's circumstances, needs and desires.'[27] Bazaars selling all manner of craft and needlework to raise money were popular in the Victorian period, right across the Empire and in the USA, aimed at customers with cash to spare for good causes and time to enjoy an outing. Visitors were fortified by the 'busiest' stall of all – the 'very remunerative' refreshment stall, as one author advised. Work for sale ranged from decorative pen wipers to tobacco pouches, quilts and foot warmers, employing all kinds of needlework, knitting, crochet, embroidery, netting and tatting as well as leatherwork, basketry and canework. In 1875 a handbook advised how a 'committee of ladies' could band together and organize these events. The author commented that they were 'a great feature of the present age' and admitted that so common were such events that the pressure was on. 'Ingenuity and originality are severely taxed in the effort to produce something different from the ordinary monotonous line of pincushions, antimacassars, and tennis aprons.' Among the mass of attention-grabbing ornate novelties, the author also promoted the idea of a stall for selling clothes made especially for giving directly to 'the poor'. Social class being what it was, the stall could not 'of course present the attractive appearance common to the others, but the usefulness of the articles displayed' would raise significant sums as well as providing for the poor when donated to them by the stall's customers. Doubtless the impoverished recipients found the adult garments and children's and babies' clothes such as nightdresses, pinafores, dresses, socks, caps and mittens a good deal more welcome than a cigar stand ornamented with shells or a dozen menu cards prettily gummed with autumn leaves.[28]

The work of hands and hearts has never been solely the domain of women of means. There was a strong working-class solidarity and fellowship to be had through making for others, as shown in the old tradition in northwest England of communities holding large-scale Whit Walks. These usually required the participating girls to wear new white clothes and in old age in 1981 Florence Atherton recalled her dressmaker mother's acts of kindness. Raising a big family, 'living a hard life sewing' for her own family and to earn a living, her mother still found the time and resources to make 'the poor children sets of frocks and knickers to walk in so they wouldn't feel out of it'.[29] Florence's mother put her skills into acts of neighbourly kindness. Others sew in the spirit of charity to raise money for the needs of people they don't know or teach sewing to refugees to aid self-reliance, language skills and community relations. All of the many variants of sewing for others known and unknown connects us one with another and forms a valued component of many sewing lives today. Working from home alone during lockdown, dressmaker Cathy describes how making for others brings its own gratifications. 'I definitely felt alive when making PPE for the community, I worked long hours giving my time for free, knowing I was helping in a small way was so rewarding. My daughter also helped me during this time, which was a fantastic bonus as it gave us time together.'

Things stitched at home, like any artefacts, have a variable afterlife, sometimes with consequences the maker could never imagine. Professionally made garments can take on a stardom of their own by personal association, such as Princess Diana's glamorous frocks, but stardust can also settle on amateur needlework items, although they may be unexceptional in their day in either technique or fabric. More or less impromptu, Geri Halliwell's sister famously selected a ready-made printed Union Jack tea towel and sewed it to the front of an expensive barely-there LBD for Geri's performance at the 1997 Brit awards when she was a member of the highly successful girl group the Spice Girls. That improvised dress quickly became a celebrated artefact in its own right: it was sold at auction in 1998, raising £36,200 for a children's cancer charity. It even has its own Wikipedia entry, according to which in 2010 the frock was voted top of an online poll to find the ten most iconic dresses of the past fifty years. Some home sewing projects move more slowly, of course. One such was started when Jane Austen, one of the world's best-loved authors, sat down with her mother and sister to make an intricate patchwork coverlet somewhere around 1815. It has thousands of pieces joined with about twelve stitches per inch. At Jane's death in 1817 it remained in her family, known only to a few, but eventually by 1950 it was put on display in her former home where it had been made. Seventy years later, in 2020, it was formally donated to what in the meantime had become Jane Austen's House, an independent museum in Chawton, Hampshire, where it remains as a treasured object.[30] The speedy impromptu Union Jack dress of 1997 contrasts with the painstakingly executed and slow Georgian coverlet that took years to emerge into the limelight, but both are now celebrated by global fanbases. Both were homemade, using readily available materials, but while one, a solo work, became a commodity for sale almost overnight, the other was made by a team and transformed at a leisurely pace into an inalienable object in a museum collection for all to enjoy but none to buy. They illustrate extremes in the diverse and unpredictable afterlife of things made at home and point to the general question of what becomes of what is stitched at home and how we dispose of such things. Is it easier to say goodbye to a ready-made item than one you made at home for yourself?

Homemade clothes have another form of afterlife within family photographs and memory itself. Showing me a black-and-white photograph of her teenage self eating an ice cream at the seaside in 1940, 55 years later in 1995 Elsie could recall the dress she was wearing that day made for her by her sister, 'lovely woollen material in a heather shade . . . (with) little buttons . . . in striped taffeta' to match the 'striped cuffs' on the puffed sleeves. 'I used to love that dress.' Elsie went on to become a skilled dressmaker herself, making clothes for her daughter and granddaughter and teaching them to sew well too.

Elsie was not alone in the precision of her recollections. It is striking how well the most minute details of home-sewn items are preserved in the memories of the participants even by those at very advanced ages, with or without the prompt of a photograph. These recollected garments became autobiographical in their telling. They filled a cherished place within their life stories, as an aide-memoire for linked events or to recall personal relationships. My 1995 project was my first step towards trying to recover something of home dressmaking's then overlooked history, and many of the participants are now dead but their tape-recorded voices preserve their recollections. The vivid manner in which long-gone frocks were described to me was an affecting experience for the participants and for me. Sometimes there were tears. These women taught me through their stories how sewing for oneself and others could really matter, how deeply it was embedded in these women's lives. This informed my subsequent research, so those remembered things continue as yet another form of legacy. The recent *Our Sewing Stories* project undertaken in 2020–22 has reinforced, 25 years on, how sewing, memory and emotions are still inextricably entwined. Now in her seventies, Carol describes how she remembers her childhood dresses. 'I find that I can remember my dresses not only by the look of them (especially if prompted by an old photo) but also I can still "feel" the fabric in my mind.'

A final story about memory and afterlife gives us a child's-eye view of the stand-out experience a frock can be, including its later reincarnation. Hattie Gordon wrote a moving account of her mother making her, aged six, a smocked frock in dusky pink floral Liberty Tana lawn. 'I still recall the fizzing excitement I felt about this dress. It looked like the kind of frock a girl could have adventures in, both real and imaginary . . . it was well loved and worn for several years. It was my party dress, my summer frock, my dress to wear for school photographs, to cycle in – it was a dress for anything and everything.' On her mother's death, the teenager Hattie found it preserved among her mother's own clothes and recognized what she calls 'the emotive pull' of the homemade frock, which holds memories of her mother, and its role as 'evidence' of her mothering. Not having a daughter of her own, the adult Gordon dispatched the dress to her nine-year-old niece in Australia, where the dress now has 'a second life' and provides a potent multi-generational connection between the niece, the grandmother she never knew and her aunt in the UK. Gordon feels that, 'in some ephemeral way, it fleetingly shrinks the thousands of miles between our families'.[31]

Sewing is about change and continuity. The number of people who sew will fluctuate as the world and their lives in it keep changing. But there are many constants. Alone and not alone as they plan and progress their projects, they freely speak of an introspective realm of calm and memory coupled with feeling connected to other people in a network of sewing past

and present, real and virtual. Their sewing bonds them directly
to their kith and kin; they become creative and useful at the same
time; what they do is full of tangible and intangible rewards.
Of course there are temporary frustrations, compromises and
disappointments, but still they speak of their sewing as a 'feel-
good' practice. Through my encounters with these makers, I
have come to think of them as possessing a kind of courage and
inventiveness by which they define their own domain as they
sew. Their own values and ways of being are evident, fashioned
by their own efforts. And how they sew – it seems there is almost
nothing ready-made that somebody somewhere can't replicate
at home with more fun and satisfaction than a shop can ever
provide. The inventory is remarkable, whether it's clothes for
women, men and children they know, strangers, the homeless, or
curtains, blinds and more curtains, cushion covers, bags, quilts,
dolls' clothes, soft toys, play tents, umpteen badges for Scouts,
Brexit mourning armbands for UK Remainers, covers for camper-
van seats, printers and bird cages, protest banners, pennants and
flags – even pouches for orphaned baby kangaroos. It seems there
is no end in sight.

6

The Business of the Needle

In rural Uganda, Georgina stations her sewing machine by her door at home to face the road. She bought the machine with a $55 loan from a financial empowerment initiative started by and for women in her village. Her business is mostly repairing children's torn clothes and she earns $1.40 a day. When we think of those who sew for income, no two human stories are alike. In Georgina's case, her machine work has brought her greater self-reliance and confidence with new ambitions to design and make clothes with local fabric for her community.[1] Stitching as commerce, whether by individuals like Georgina or multinational clothing brands, presents a murky landscape with bad weather, but with sunny spots too. Exploited labour forces, opaque supply chains, fast fashion and environmental damage mark the lows. The highs are marked by imaginative designers, makers, legislators, sustainability certification organizations, campaigners, researchers, journalists, charities and projects like Georgina's all pushing for positive change and those fashion brands which work with serious intent towards that end. Over a vast and varied landscape, the weather forecast is improving. Slowly.

All of us travel in one part or another of this landscape of making when we use the vast output made by people paid to stitch – our clothes, trainers, car seats, backpacks, even our cat's bed – to name just an infinitesimal fraction of what leaves factories and workrooms round the globe. Our dependence on the workers who sew them is incalculable. The focus in this chapter is on the people who make our garments in this labour-intensive manufacturing sector. People and planet are inseparable, and textiles and clothing together constitute one of the world's biggest industries with one of the largest environmental impacts. The tens of millions of people involved underline why we should know more and care about this largely invisible workforce.[2] Everything about this industry, the first to globalize, is on a vast scale. Worldwide, 100 billion items of clothing are made annually, equating to 62 million metric tons of clothing, and if this pattern continues, by 2029 this will have risen to 102 million tons.[3]

Anyone who has made themselves a garment will understand that the workforce sewing these vast numbers of garments is doing skilled work that should be acknowledged as such. Jade Halbert, a UK academic, set out to make a dress for herself for the first time, a project that was 'fun' but also a steep learning curve in more ways than one.

> I'm more convinced now than ever before that making clothes is not, by any definition, low-skilled work. It is engineering with cloth and, from first cut to final stitch, it is a process that demands meticulous attention to detail and sustained concentration. The people who make our clothes, in factories, workrooms or living rooms, are deserving of our deepest admiration.[4]

But when the garments we buy for ourselves are made at a great distance, in unknown places, it surely contributes to disengagement from the processes and people involved. Out of sight, out of mind, and ethics can be undermined by distance. Even when our garments are made in factories closer to home, a consumer at the point of purchase online or in a shop may feel little meaningful connection with the people who sewed them, let alone the 'deepest admiration' they deserve.

Not only are the numbers of people employed in the garment trades so vast, and the amount of clothing produced so jaw-dropping, but the diversity in the businesses that make clothes complexifies the landscape even more. There are giant brands with multiple retail outlets round the world, tiny experimental start-ups, charitable projects, sole traders, elite haute couture houses, labels focused on sustainability, traditional bespoke menswear outfitters. Some businesses are low-profile, turning out standardized workwear and uniforms at scale, and for others cutting-edge fashion design is the *raison d'être*. There is also variety in the degree to which clothing companies and brands keep manufacturing in-house or outsource it, often in lengthy supply chains obscured across multiple processes in different countries. H&M is a big player in clothing production and retailing, based in Sweden but operating worldwide, and their supply chains show what can be involved. It is a classic fast fashion model, that is, a system in which cheap clothing is made with minimal time lag between design, manufacture and supply, resulting in multiple style changes each year not confined to traditional seasons. Behind their garments are 'approximately 750 suppliers that manufacture products for its eight global brands in around 1,400 factories across 41 countries, which are sold in around 5,000 stores in 75 markets and across 52 markets via its online shop'. It is used by the United Nations Alliance for Sustainable Fashion as an example of why it is so difficult to measure environmental impacts and trace conditions for workers in the industry.[5] Brands have generated major problems for themselves in any journey ahead towards sustainability and social justice.

Asking what it is like to earn a living wholly or partly by sewing has no single answer. There are too many variables. Many practical factors shape an employee's experience over and above the size of their wage packet and the hours they work: the immediate environment where they spend their time, as factory or smaller workroom operatives or as homeworkers; whether they sew by hand or machine or both; the quality of the fabrics they handle; the ergonomics of their workstations; the reliability of the machinery; if they make samples or long-runs; the garment construction and finishing standards required of them; whether or not the elements of construction are divided up repetitively, or if the worker assembles a whole garment. All these elements contribute to what sewing for money is really like. Some people like the regularity and companionship of work in a factory; others hate monotony or regimented pressure on their productivity, in extreme cases achieved by degrading supervisory practices. Others balance the risks of self-employment with the flexibility it can offer. Some people, especially women in developing countries or immigrants in more developed countries, have little or no choice about the mode of work available to them. Of critical importance for all garment workers everywhere is the degree to which they are protected by effective legislation for their pay and conditions, including health and safety, and if these are audited in a timely and convincing way. Unfortunately, it is common knowledge that the garment industry round the world all too often fails its workers on these counts. As consumers, we should remember that whatever their tasks, the people who make our clothes still want the dignity, meaning and fundamental sense of achievement that work can offer. This is true of any work anywhere, whatever our job. 'Almost everyone wants to feel she is getting something accomplished.'[6]

It is estimated that there are at least 60 to 75 million people employed in apparel manufacture worldwide, 75 per cent of whom are located in the Asia Pacific region where China, Bangladesh and Vietnam are among the world's top clothing exporters. Eighty per cent of garment workers globally are women, mostly women of colour.[7] These workers are often already disadvantaged, with little choice about where or how they work. Human rights violations, including sexual abuse, are common in the sector. As women, they often work as carers for their families alongside waged work, making their lives even tougher. If they are internal or external migrants, they may be cut off from their normal support networks. One of the reasons the number of workers involved in the industry globally is an estimate is that supply chains in garment manufacturing typically involve sub-contracting, 'often several layers deep'.[8] Increasingly intermediary labour contractors are used, often in countries without clear audit trails, and so those at the end of the long chain, such as homeworkers, sometimes have little or no presence in official figures. The span of these shadowy areas is huge, as in the case of India, where an estimated 5 million homeworkers are engaged in the garment and textile supply chains.[9]

The term 'precarious employment' was coined to describe this kind of work.[10] It is important to stress that not all garment workers experience hardship. There are plenty round the world who are grateful for work they enjoy, but countless others endure unacceptable conditions because they are caught up in a global race to the bottom where, at worst, child and forced labour are used. The Clean Clothes Campaign is a global network committed to assuring the rights of garment and sportswear workers. It notes that the 'dominant business model pits country against country, and supplier against supplier'. Nowadays clothing manufacturers often can't even set their own charges. Instead, it is their customers, the big fashion brands, who have 'the freedom to pick and choose from low-cost and low-wage economies and in these markets, brands can dictate prices, quantity, and quality, with little consideration for the impact on supplier factories and their workers'.[11] Commenting on the UK, one fashion editor wrote: 'For decades the fashion industry chased the cheapest needle round the world, abandoning British manufacturing in the process.'[12] One consequence underlining the outsourcing of manufacturing overseas is that of the 500,000 people employed in the UK in fashion-related jobs, the vast majority are employed in retail and wholesale, rather than manufacturing. Although the number of manufacturing businesses is starting to creep up after long decline, largely thanks to small- and medium-sized enterprises (SMEs), skills shortages are a concern, and most people working across all three sectors are situated in London despite sizable employment areas elsewhere.[13] In the USA 90 per cent of all clothing sold is imported.[14] The uncomfortable reality is that many developed countries, in chasing the cheapest needle, have in effect also outsourced the social and environmental damage it currently causes. To make matters worse, the same countries, after importing their clothing, then discard it frequently after only light use.

Andrew Brookes observes that the relentless consumption of fashion in wealthier nations is at such a rate that it not only perpetuates the drive to the bottom in terms of garment workers' pay and conditions, but also produces a major waste-disposal problem. This is often 'solved' by dumping immense quantities of second-hand clothing on developing nations, posing major problems for their own home garment manufacturing. Brookes argues for more than individual acts of ethical consumption, which is anyway often only feasible for better-off consumers. He describes the need for cooperation across the whole fashion system itself as the only eventual route to sustainable and just clothing.[15] One solution being pushed hard is the idea of a circular textile economy, in which materials used in discarded clothing are reformed to make into new clothes, thereby reducing land-fill. It would also reduce leading brands' infamous practice of incinerating unsold goods to protect the impact and value of their incoming new styles. The many proponents of this circular economy, such as the Ellen MacArthur Foundation, argue that this could be achieved by a combination of the power of designers, science and technology, manufacturers, retailers and consumers.

Thinking differently about the production of garments also presents challenges on a global scale. There is some debate today in the West about the benefits of repatriating the industry, or reshoring as it is sometimes known, to shorten supply lines, reduce transport costs and control quality, but there are also concerns about skills shortages in the West after such a long period of sending the work East. Younger people in the West are not racing to get jobs in the commercial garment sector and those who formerly had the skills and experience are at or approaching retirement age. There is anyway seldom a single place of origin for a garment, so where is 'home' in this global jigsaw? Where was the garment conceived or designed and was that in-house or freelance? The base, market profile and heritage of the brand that generated it might be rooted elsewhere. The constituent raw and finished materials were probably derived from, and processed in, other countries. The people who cut and stitched the garment together were also likely to be far-flung. In all, reshoring is a convoluted matter for clothing companies to weigh up. Their decisions will undoubtedly have repercussions for their workers everywhere.[16]

Around the world the poor employment terms and dangerous working conditions of garment workers are all too well known, but holding to account those responsible is no easy task because of the scale of the industry and its presence in so many countries with different regulatory frameworks. Deep change is unlikely without consistent international cooperation on the part of workers and legislators. Nevertheless, there are active research and lobbying groups who shed light on these issues and their reports keep up the pressure for change. For example, drawing attention to human rights abuse in clothing manufacturing for famous German fashion brands in workplaces in Ukraine, Serbia, Croatia and Bulgaria, the Clean Clothes Campaign, part of Labour behind the Label, underlined that significant exploitation occurs in Europe too.[17] As I write, fast fashion manufacturers based in Leicester, England, working primarily for Boohoo and Pretty Little Thing, are seldom out of the news over their abusive and illegal employment practices. These include paying wages below the national minimum, failing to protect workers during the COVID-19 pandemic and even threatening to fire those with symptoms if they didn't show up to work. There have also been 'numerous allegations of links to modern slavery and trafficking'.[18] There are global guidelines for responsible business and due diligence practices already.[19] But compliance is hard to track and malpractice continues.

Looking at the full lifespan of garments, our actions as consumers directly affect their environmental impact through how long we keep them in use, how we wash them and how we dispose of them.[20] In the UK alone an estimated £140 million worth of clothing is thrown into landfill or incineration every year, or 336,000 tonnes. It is said that annually New York landfills an amount of clothing that is 'the equivalent of over 440 Statues of Liberty'.[21] Globally clothing goes to landfill at the rate of a rubbish truck every second.[22] These numbers surely show that the items sewn by all those workers round the world seem to be of little importance to many of those who buy them. Why do so many consumers of fashion buy so much? Is it because clothes can be so cheap? Do we enjoy the buzz of shopping more than the clothes themselves? In the UK, there are thought to be 118 items of clothing in the average person's wardrobe, of which over a quarter will not have been worn in the preceding year.[23] Individuals will no doubt have different reasons for this. It was a salutary exercise to ponder my own wardrobe, already in need of a rethink, and face some tricky questions about what stays, what goes and why: something needs to shift within me as much as in my cupboards. If we wish to change our attitudes and habits to develop more ethical consumption and stem the irrational level of global and personal waste, we may need more information to make a start on finding the best ways to maintain the clothes we want and dispose of our unwanted clothes responsibly and reduce consumption thereafter. Several organizations exist to help people do just that at a practical level.[24] The mind is focused by learning how little of the price you paid for a T-shirt went to the person who actually made it.[25]

Efforts are underway to help consumers and everyone else involved to better understand the systemic issues across the clothing industry as a whole. Many argue that tracking the claims made by individual brands about treatment of workers and their progress on environmental issues needs transparency across their entire operation, verified by trusted third-party assessors, to improve consumer confidence and increase understanding of how fashion actually works and how it could work. There are now apps that show clothing brands' sustainability records, designed to make clothes shopping a more informed experience that can advance consumer power. Ordinary citizens participate internationally alongside industry figures in the Who Makes My Clothes campaign, seeking respect and fair wages for garment workforces everywhere. A recent survey of consumer thinking in the UK on these matters found that over half of respondents said fair pay for workers was 'the most important aspect of sustainability' for them. The report concluded that any brand not taking effective action on ethical standards will inevitably begin to feel the impact on their profits.[26] These kinds of conversations are much more evident in the public domain than ever before, giving some cause for optimism that exploited garment workers may eventually benefit from consumer awareness and various manifestations of fashion activism.

There are now more examples of corporate change reaching beyond the 'greenwash' and 'greenwish' that undermine consumer trust, making the values they and their customers wish to steer by more explicit. In the USA the Eileen Fisher brand, founded in 1984, is often cited as a model of good practice and transparency across its operations, including workers' rights. In the UK Stella McCartney has flown the flag for transparency and sustainability at the high end of the market and at least one popular UK brand of lower-priced fashion now publishes on its website the names and addresses of all its manufacturing facilities and the gender and size of the workforces there. Some fashion brands have obtained B Corp certification, which shows that they can verify good practice in all their business activities. Specialist businesses now exist that work to inform and support others looking for transparency in their supply chain, including their suppliers' suppliers. The Sedex Members Ethical Trade Audit (SMETA) is an example of a social audit used by all kinds of businesses across the world that want to achieve responsible human and environmental practices across all their activities. Yet however laudable these efforts are, it will take national legislation and international agreements, now emerging, to give shape to lasting and radical change.[27] An important example is the international effort across the sector to try to ensure the 2013 Rana Plaza disaster in Dhaka, Bangladesh, would not be repeated. A poorly constructed building with five garment factories inside collapsed and killed 1,333 people, injuring thousands more. It was the worst death toll – although by no means the only one – occasioned by a tragedy in garment factories in that country. It resulted in a legally binding accord committing over 220 companies to better safety standards and is believed to have been responsible for producing safer conditions 'for millions of Bangladeshi garment workers'. The original five-year accord was renewed recently.[28] So there are some positive steps on behalf of workers, but it remains true that fashion is now a major problem for all of us: consumers; designers, textile and clothing producers and the workforce at factory and workshop level; and of course legislators and activists. One fashion journalist has spelled it out. 'Everyone in fashion knows that they need to get back on the right side of history, and fast.' Garment workers and those they clothe are entitled to ask when fashion will 'find its conscience'.[29]

The rollcall of challenges for garment workers, and, by implication, all of us, is nothing new. The current situation of workers would be recognized by their counterparts over many generations past. It is a common misconception that in the past clothing was mostly made at home by householders for their own use, but this is in fact very wide of the mark. The historian Beverly Lemire has studied the ready-made clothing trades before and after industrialization in the seventeenth and eighteenth centuries when they 'assumed new and larger prominence as a source of commercial wealth, as source of varied consumer products and as an employer of labour'. A hierarchy formed of financiers, manufacturers, middle men, petty shopkeepers and artisans. 'Collectively they enlarged the production of apparel to an unprecedented degree.' From the earliest days of this development in Britain and elsewhere, the seamstresses whose work underpinned it all were at the bottom of the economic heap. And there it seems they have remained ever since. Lemire notes that at the time the great expansion of clothing manufacturing as a whole 'drew less attention than perhaps any other occupational sector'.[30] And so those stitching girls and women were sealed into even deeper obscurity. It is worth noting that this expansion took place within the development of sweated labour practices in other industries too. Ever since, it seems to take bad news to focus public attention on those who sew the clothes we wear each and every day.

However, the Victorian seamstress became visible as a common trope in literature, the visual arts and the rhetoric of social reformers. Richard Redgrave's 1846 painting *The Sempstress*, a version of which is now in London's Tate Britain, gave reformers an apt image of a weary young woman sewing in an attic as dawn breaks. Redgrave sought to render her as an innocent victim in need of public sympathy in contrast to a popular view that such women easily strayed into prostitution. The Victorian seamstress came to symbolize the moral tensions between the new consumerist aspirations of the age and the shadowy hinterland of production. Customers who ordered their bespoke gowns from their dressmakers at short notice were often oblivious of the conditions in which exploited seamstresses toiled to sew these complex garments, a situation that reformers campaigned to change.[31] In the case of ready-mades constructed in sweatshops and factories, calls to improve working terms and conditions for the makers of garments became more vociferous in industrialized countries over the nineteenth century. In the USA in this period, there was increasing public awareness of conditions for garment workers after the shocking Triangle Shirtwaist Factory fire in 1911 in New York killed 146 people – a steep death toll directly attributable to management's decision to lock exit doors in an effort to reduce theft and stop workers taking breaks.[32] Those who died were mostly immigrant women making women's blouses, and the tragedy became a rallying point for unionization there.

In 1909 in London a report based on a year's door-to-door research shone a light on the experiences of the female workers in the various men's and women's clothing trades across London. It investigated conditions from upmarket bespoke West End establishments to the cheapest wholesale manufacturing and outwork. It was an eye-opener for the researchers involved. They noted that the 'essential virtues of the woman worker – her patience, her industry, her marked sense of fair play – stand out very clearly'. But in exchange for all their hours of work they got 'a very small share in the joys, the comforts or the beauties of life'. The authors admitted they themselves felt 'oppressed by the intolerable weight of human burdens' and reported that 'horribly sad facts remain impressed upon the memories of those who have been active in this investigation.'[33] They noted similar findings from research conducted in Germany. The practices and labour conditions particularly of sweatshops have been always difficult to control and improve, notwithstanding efforts to do so. In Edwardian London, despite some workers' protection provided by law, the inspector was never welcome, and in one case evaded altogether by simply putting the poorly paid indoor hands working 'very late' at the back of the building and keeping the front of it unlit. In that workplace, 'no worker dares look at the copy of the Factory Act displayed in the work-room for the address of the inspector for fear of being suspected if the inspector came.'[34] Conditions were doubly difficult to monitor when outwork or home-based labour was the norm. 'A young woman machined and pressed a coat and skirt of black cloth for 8d. The skirt had five double-stitched seams and a band of lining with four rows of stitching at the hem . . . The making of these two garments took nearly a day.' She had to supply the cotton thread and do it all by a foot-powered sewing machine. After rent and living expenses she would have little left over, and even this meagre rate of 8d, could decrease without notice, or vanish entirely during the trade's slacker months.[35]

When factory work was sometimes accused at this time of undermining traditional femininity, sewing jobs were also defended by some commentators partly on the grounds that the skills gained helped women to be better homemakers. Subdivision of labour on different parts of a garment was possible in menswear, which changed less often, but it was disruptive in womenswear because of the swift variations needed to keep up with style changes. In womenswear, workers could make a whole garment from start to finish. 'This has the triple advantage that the work is far less monotonous, that when out of employment a girl will find it a good deal easier to find a new position to suit her, and that if she gets married, or for any other reason gives up working, she will be well equipped to make the family clothes at home.'[36] This particular view from the 1920s sustained the Victorian belief characterized by Vivienne Richmond as 'the pervasiveness and endurance of the notion that needlework formed the very core of working-class femininity'.[37] Coupled with the idea that stitching is somehow natural for women, the same notion still shapes many assumptions today in the terms and conditions offered to women sewing in workshops and factories round the world. It has a very long shadow cast across generations of workers.

Around the world today there are men and women who sew garments for basic survival. They work at home, whether it's to pay the rent or buy food, fuel, schoolbooks or medicine. In Afghanistan's Pawan province, two orphaned, unschooled and brotherless sisters, now adults, explained in August 2021 how they dreaded the return of the Taliban. They are already shunned by their 'conservative community' because they have no male guardian and, at the time of the interview, they therefore had nowhere to which to flee, but despite their huge disadvantages they have managed to support themselves financially by sewing in their dilapidated home. But their monthly income, the equivalent of £55, was fast drying up in the face of the Taliban's advance.[38] In such settings, sewing for even a meagre living is motivated by powerful aspirations and fears. Lifting yourself and your family out of poverty, striving for some measure of self-reliance, healthcare and education, makes sewing a real investment in future quality of life. Sewing often features in poverty alleviation projects in some of the world's poorest nations because it is flexible, relatively low-cost to set up and organize and, when successful, can be transformative. A sewing machine can come via micro loans or donations. Basic sewing can be taught quite quickly when learners are well motivated and the work can be conducted at home alongside other domestic work, cutting out the need for rent or travel. Fatin Abu Dhaka, living in Gaza, once provided with a new sewing machine, an iron and some cloth, was quick to make use of it. 'At the end of the first month, I made more than $200 and was able to buy food for my family as well as buying more fabric for the project.' Enabled to improve her family income, she thought of employing another woman. 'This woman . . . was supporting another big family. I'm very happy to have become a productive woman in my community and my self-confidence has increased.'[39] It is striking how often a sewing machine is the mother of empowerment. It doesn't fix social injustice or cure the systemic causes of poverty, but it can offer an effective and dignified lifeline to those in most need.

A world away from the sisters in fear of the Taliban and from the lives of Georgina in Uganda and Fatin in Gaza, in Paris there are garment workers at the top of an exclusive tree. Parisian haute couture needleworkers construct fashion pieces for ultra-wealthy and international clients at prices that would transform the lives of whole villages elsewhere. A day dress might cost thousands of euros, with the most elaborate gowns costing up to €1 million, and behind the scenes the makers, the *petites-mains*, are a uniquely skilled and trained workforce. This old-established trade is governed by French legislation because it carries such reputational and cultural capital. The Chambre Syndicale de la Couture was first formed in 1868 and today still meets to approve membership of this elite group of businesses.[40] To be eligible to use the term haute couture (literally 'high-level dressmaking'), a business must showcase a minimum of 25 of its own original designs twice a year and also produce one-off made-to-order pieces for private clients, fitted and made in its own workrooms. These companies use their global names to promote or license other luxury products, including ready-to-wear, important when haute couture can be loss-making. They may now be owned by huge conglomerates such as LVMH (Louis Vuitton Moët Hennessy). Many people find these luxury brands unacceptable for numerous reasons, others aspire to them, but from whatever standpoint, what they regard as their underlying and priceless haute couture status rests on their own in-house creative flair and technical prowess. And no matter how talented the designers, nothing is realizable without the sewing skills of the backroom workers.

There are probably no stitches more consistently excellent than those still called for in haute couture. In a single large establishment like the House of Dior in the heyday of post-Second World War fashion in Paris, in-house workers numbered in the hundreds. Today Dior are said to have sixty 'artisans' working on women's couture. Following the same organizational principles established under the founder, Christian Dior (1905–1957), they work in specialist departments under supervision of the *premières* to the highest standards of their various crafts – tailoring for more structured items and soft dressmaking – within the context of the seasonal collections. They progress each garment on its journey from design to the initial toile or prototype to the shows, each outfit requiring multiple adjustments and representing hundreds of hours of labour. When at last the levels of perfection and finish required in the garments for a classic Dior fashion collection were sufficient to satisfy even the demands of the founding *grand couturier* himself and Mme Marguerite, his *directrice technique*, they would exclaim: 'It's impossible to believe that they are the work of human hands!'[41] Those needle-workers who worked by hand with the soft fabrics in the 'flou' workrooms, making blouses, skirts and dresses, were described by Dior as having *doigts de fées* – fairy fingers.[42]

It is said that there used to be upwards of 20,000 clients for this class of clothing. Now the number is estimated at 4,000, but they have deep pockets and, somewhat counter-intuitively, are said to be getting younger. 'Thousands of hours of exacting embellishment, a schedule of fittings and wait times of up to 12 months for a single dress: the old-world traditions of haute couture, at first glance, do not appear to speak to our express age of three hours from click to collect. Yet the percentage of Millennial couture clients worldwide is growing, and fast.'[43] Today, the number of haute couture houses based in the city, around twenty, is significantly fewer than in the past, with correspondingly fewer *petites-mains*, estimated today at about 2,200. Their standards of needlecraft, though now on a reduced scale, are still the Everest of stitching.

In that golden age of bespoke clothing, London also had a reputation for making fine garments for women. The Incorporated Society of London Fashion Designers was founded in 1942 to further promote London couture and other fashion design. Part of its remit was to develop 'standards of skilled workmanship'. No matter how grand a fashion house seemed, clothing royalty and film stars, its success always came down to the quality of the hands in the workrooms. English designer Hardy Amies knew which side his bread was buttered when he wrote in the 1950s: 'A girl in the workroom who is making a good buttonhole is surely as near God as a designer. I sometimes think nearer.' But after twenty years of success, by the 1960s the society was out of step with developments and ceased to function in 1970, although London's reputation for fashion continued in evolved forms.[44]

The long-established bespoke tailoring trade for men remains one of London's clothing gems, conjured up in the place name Savile Row. Bespoke work of this kind is found around the world, for example in Hong Kong, and has international investors, but wherever it is situated, it faces challenging circumstances. Industrialized mass production led to the erosion of slower traditional hand and needle skills and between the world wars, this was already worrying top-end bespoke or master tailors. Not only were men starting to enjoy less restrictive informal garments that sidelined traditional tailoring techniques, but cheaper factory-produced suits for men were threatening to overwhelm the bespoke trade. In the USA it was estimated that by 1928 probably 10 per cent of menswear was custom-made.[45] These developments left traditional tailors feeling undervalued and concerned that their patient and esoteric craft based on age-old needle skills was at risk. The British trade weekly *Tailor and Cutter* hit back the following year with a heartfelt defence of the 'invisible' craft. 'Of no work under the sun is the general public so ignorant as tailoring . . . All the cunning and knowledge of generations of craftsmen is embodied in a suit.' Their words still ring true.

> Think of the innumerable and unsuspected details hidden away in the interior of a coat; the stays, tackings, padding, stitches, the puffs and pleats . . . the multitudinous but evanescent basting stitches . . . The working of a buttonhole may be a bit of art; the sewing on of a button be full of life or as dead as a doornail.[46]

The piece is lyrical about the handiwork involved, from meticulous measurements of all the dimensions of the customer's unique body form to cutting quality cloth accordingly, itself a specialist skill, and through to the final construction stages using subtly tempered combinations of stitching, pressing and fitting. Only the accomplished tailor, as he forms and curves the suit, 'knows when to sew tightly or when to pull his hand slackly, how to work fullness in, and smooth it out'. The writer in 1929 probably didn't anticipate that more women are now training and succeeding in these once mostly male workrooms. Superior fabrics, hand skills and the time involved improve the fit and comfort of the garments and also lead to a final price which can be thousands of pounds for a fully bespoke suit. But there are enough appreciative customers with big wallets for such workmanship to survive. The durability of the best cloth combined with the best tailoring craft gives such garments great durability, so some customers view them as an investment. Over the years since the *Tailor and Cutter* bemoaned off-the-peg suits as a threat to bespoke making, the improved technology and quality of factory-sewn suiting for men can also now produce real value for money, although it seems workplace conventions are changing, and suits of all sorts are now becoming less obligatory in certain situations.

In search of smaller manufacturing alternatives that bypass fast fashion and focus on other values, I visited the workrooms of two very different businesses. First, Old Town is a clothing business in the UK founded thirty years ago by Will Brown and Marie Willey. Working to Will's designs, they produce about seventy garments a week – coats, jackets, shirts, trousers, dresses – based now on eighteen patterns, made up by a small team of local outworkers sewing in their own homes. A pattern cutter comes in for two days a week. The working space is correspondingly modest, almost homely, reached by a steep wooden staircase in an unpretentious little Georgian building nestled in a back street in Holt, a charming town in Norfolk. Natural light comes through the windows. The workroom walls are lined with pattern pieces hanging on traditional pattern hooks, shelves are filled with button and thread boxes and some rolls of cloth lean against a corner, all in subdued colours. Will's 'old friend' lies on the workbench – a wooden yardstick marked in inches and centimetres that has been in continuous use for forty years, adding to the rather timeless feel of the room. There's a 1970s sewing machine by the window and a steam iron. In a corner, Will's buttonhole machine canters through the equivalent of twenty minutes of handwork in twenty seconds; otherwise work proceeds at a human pace in a quiet professional atmosphere. This is a place to savour flow and skill. There's no smoke and mirrors here, no change for change's sake, yet it's all absolutely *du jour*. It could not be further from the clamour of factory machinery churning out a frenzy of fast fashion and the garments and fabrics could hardly be less glitzy. It has proved a lasting business model in its own niche market.

Steered with design intelligence and a sure grasp of social trends, the clothes that leave this workroom are finely tuned to customers' lives and aspirations. Durable fabrics are favoured, such as stout cottons, Yorkshire wool, Italian linen, corduroy and canvas; most are plain, with occasionally some geometric prints in a limited palette, nothing loud. Customers can be very loyal, some of them still enjoy wearing the same long-lasting garments they bought when the business first started. Garments are made to order with sleeves and legs to length, and delivery takes six to eight weeks, so nothing's grabbed off the rail. Anyway, in this context, a bit of delayed gratification has its pleasures. The business works on deceptively simple principles. It provides a limited range of garments designed to evoke workwear and an apparently timeless aesthetic, but cleverly tweaked over the years to stay in tune with the zeitgeist. 'You have to change to stay the same,' says Will. For customers, 70 per cent of whom were men at the time of my visit, this is an unfussy easy-to-read wardrobe that is also comfortable and reliable. Most customers are urban professionals often in creative jobs. Their choice of the Old Town look, suggestive of those artisans and manual workers seen in Edwardian photographs, gives them an air of grounded seriousness. It has been said that these are old-style 'working class clothes for middle-class people'. As with any good design realized by makers with fluent expertise, it was a pleasure to feel welcome and witness this workroom in action.

Second, I visited Cathy, a local dressmaker working single-handed in her own home. In the UK between the two world wars, local dressmakers working in their own right like Cathy were numerous. Their numbers were swollen by the thousands more employed in the workshops of department stores and other retailers, and together in big centres they could match or out-number those who worked in wholesale factory manufacturing. 'It may safely be said that in every town with a population of 200,000 or more there are at least 1,000 dressmakers employed by retailers or private customers.'[47] There is so much sewing 'in the blood' that many of these past dressmakers are still 'alive' in the family memories of their descendants today, who often say they feel a connection to them when they sew. The retail clothing trade has changed, manufacturing jobs have gone or changed, yet on the sunnier side of the landscape of sewing and commerce, among all the alternatives to fast fashion, one of the oldest has survived for generations and continues to meet needs today – the dressmaker like Cathy, with a neighbourhood cli-entele known by word of mouth or minimal local advertising. 'Your sewing skills are like money in the bank,' commented the go-to American sewing writer Mary Brooks Picken in 1961. She confirmed the enduring association of the sewing machine ever since its invention with a woman's opportunity for profit, as a kind of insurance, as well as for pleasure and domestic economy. Learning to sew well would mean a woman could always pay her way, come what may.[48]

Today as well as in the past, teaching adults and children to sew provides a way to earn money full- or part-time and of course sewing at home remains, as it always was, a flexible way to bring extra cash into the household. Participants in *Our Sewing*

Stories have put their skills to work at home for money in various temporary or longer-term ways, at different stages of their lives, often crafting homeware as well as garments, making customized dolls or soft toys, curtains, finishing factory-made glove seams at home as a schoolgirl to save some money up, or providing replica costumes for museums and selling small items on Etsy. In Sharon's case she has combined teaching with running her own business crafting 'heirloom' pieces such as quilts and cushions that combine sewing and embroidery. When happy customers around the world send her photos of her pieces in situ, she enjoys feeling part of those families. From when she first came to London from the Caribbean aged seventeen, Ludvinia was always a dressmaker at home for family and friends, including for special occasions and making suits for men, work she continued even when she became a tutor at a private fashion academy in London where she had trained. Kay's sewing journey has taken her from being a sixteen-year-old factory machinist making blouses for a retail chain – 'hard work, exhausting and tedious' – to running her own shop with a curtain and soft furnishing service via the alterations workroom of a department store and tutoring part-time at a local college. Some fans of sewing are very willing to sew at home to generate cash for charity or school fundraisers but dislike taking on more ambitious quantities of sewing on their own behalf, especially repetitive sewing to meet deadlines; several participants said they stopped when customers weren't willing to pay the true cost in fabric and time.

In her darkly comic novel *The Dressmaker* set in her native Liverpool, Beryl Bainbridge describes Nellie the dressmaker as 'in her element' when she sat at home at her Singer sewing machine. She captures the significance her trade had for Nellie and what it meant for her self-respect despite the limitations of her thwarted life. 'She wasn't like some, plying her needle for the sake of the money, though that was important: it was the security the dressmaking gave her – a feeling that she knew something, that she was skilled, handling her materials with knowledge; she wasn't a flibbertigibbet like some she could mention.' As far as I know, and hope, no real-life dressmaker has ever put her sewing skills to such sinister use as Nellie eventually does. Nevertheless, underpinning her fiction, Bainbridge understood the value of knowing 'something' for those real women whose hard lives she saw around her in the working-class communities of Liverpool. Her words echo what real-life dressmakers say. Self-respect runs deep, heard in many accounts of sewing for others past and present, and it should not be underestimated.[49]

When I visited Cathy, I learned how a rural seamstress trading alone can sustain a modest living in the UK today. Her village has a population of fewer than six hundred people yet provides over twenty returning customers. In total she has well over two hundred more names on her books, not all regulars, drawn from a 40-mile radius. For established customers who move away, she sometimes provides a postal service. She has a small workroom in her garden but no showroom. Some time is set aside each week for fittings. At the heart of her work, and the satisfaction it gives her, are the higher qualifications she holds in clothing technology and pattern cutting, so her fortunate customers, if they wish, can have pattern blocks cut for them for an exact fit. She has built these skills on a lifetime of sewing, starting even before she went to primary school; she recalls getting her 'first red tin sewing machine aged five years. It had a bobbin, so did real sewing.' Her mother sewed for the family and her four aunts sewed in factories, and with a tailor for an uncle Cathy is another example of someone with sewing 'in the blood'. She prefers to guide customers' choice of fabric and supply it herself, to avoid the problem of customers arriving with inferior or unsuitable ones which, when made up, could reflect badly on her workmanship. This is part of retaining control of her standards and workflow.

As I sat in her workroom, Cathy was upgrading a man's colourful ready-made party shirt with more elaborate buttons. There were jeans in the queue for alterations and a custom-made wedding dress awaiting some last-minute alterations for a bride who had lost weight before her big day. Repairs and alterations are becoming more common, perhaps a response to economic conditions. Although Cathy's customers bring all kinds of work year-round, there are seasons too; after a busy spring and summer of making dresses for weddings and cruise holidays, there will be August alterations to school uniforms. In the autumn curtains and blinds are made as people spruce up homes and party dresses are ordered for Christmas; then, making school prom dresses is a substantial part of the business from February onwards. Cathy was motivated by her determination to be self-reliant with flexible working hours when left as a single mother with two small children some years ago. She owns her own home and choses an unpretentious debt-free lifestyle: 'Everything I have I own.' Her lifestyle allows involvement in her immediate community such as teaching girl guides to sew, making PPE for local doctors and hospitals during the COVID-19 pandemic and even making a replacement flag for the village church tower. It is a career she would recommend to anyone with a passion for it, but not for anyone who wants to get rich. It can be lonely too, but she gets great satisfaction from the transformations she achieves for happy customers, especially with one-off prom dresses and bridalwear.

The challenges and satisfactions of working as a dressmaker in these circumstances today tallied closely with descriptions shared with me of a similar business in the interwar years, particularly in making wedding dresses. Planning a wedding dress, Cathy advises brides, often to their surprise, to take the time of year and even time of day of the ceremony into consideration because of the changeability of the human body. Her observations resonate with those made to me in 1995 by Evelyn, a retired dressmaker who first set up in business on her own account in Southampton in 1927, aged 22:

> it made a very interesting job because there were never two bodies alike . . . a woman's body in particular is never two days alike, it's always altering, you might think you got absolutely perfect one week and she'd come in the next week and put her wedding dress on and she'd either gone in or gone out a bit . . . it's not an easy job, not an easy job, and dressmaking is not an easy job if you do it properly.

Like Cathy now, Evelyn also enjoyed the successful completion of these important dresses. Cathy knows a dressmaker's need for tact, 'you need to choose your words wisely,' but Evelyn had rather less diplomatic thoughts. Hanging the wedding dresses up 'all ready to go home', she would think 'oh, they'll never look as lovely as that again . . . because the girls were all shapes and sizes, you get big fat ones and little thin ones.' Cathy and Evelyn alike rightly expressed pride in their work, although their customers might not understand all that it involves. But Evelyn didn't mince her words: 'The one thing I did hate: somebody'd come to see me and say, "Will you run me up a dress?" I'd say "I've never run up a dress in my life." That was degrading. You made it properly . . . I think they respected me.'

Hearing the stories of sewing lives reveals many continuities and satisfactions on the part of all those individuals who choose to sit at their sewing machines to earn their crust and find it a positive experience. At the same time, what lies on the darker side of the landscape can seem intractable, needing systemic solutions beyond the scope of individual consumers. However, we can empower ourselves to make a personal contribution to the solutions or at least we can try not to make matters worse. If we remember the exploitation at the heart of fast fashion or the high level of skills often present in well-made clothes, we bring the workers into focus. We might not change the system, but we can change attitudes, our own and perhaps those of others. There can be difficult facts to absorb, making us uncomfortable as consumers of clothing and citizens of Planet Earth, but there are also reasons for optimism. If, where we can, we only select clothes that are durable and sustainable, if we buy if we can afford it from ethical brands with transparent records on workers' rights, then that will propel change down the line. We can vote with our wallets. If we wear the clothes these workers made for longer, wash them sparingly, dispose of them thoughtfully, then our actions will also directly benefit the planet. In this context, less really is more, and kinder. To be thoughtful when considering the workers who make our clothes can connect us more to their lives and enhance our appreciation of what we wear.

7

The Alternative Stitch

A needle can be a tool for public activism or an agent of personal change. It is both for some people. In practice, if we make a decision to change ourselves in one way, change often follows in another. To voice their values in public, people might sew a protest banner and take to the streets to campaign for a cause dear to them. At a personal level, sewing folk might design, make or adapt their own clothes to assert an alternative image for themselves and bypass commercial fashion. There is a close association too between sewing, mental health and personal resilience. The world over, the needle is used with great effect in countless acts of dissent or transformation big and small.

Sewing for change and well-being in these various ways invites enquiry about the role and status of stitching in the construction and communication of alternative realities. In this context, when a person applies their needle to promote a difference or claim a position, it becomes a kind of declarative sewing, an engagement with the world around them that involves not only the stitcher themselves but those who witness, and may be affected by, their practices and artefacts. If sewing is used to call attention to wrongs or injustices in the hope of making a society a fairer and more inclusive place or giving an individual a better life, then it follows that we should also think about the ethical dimensions of sewing. What would the ethics of sewing look like?

To begin in the public arena – accepting that our public and private selves are not wholly distinct – when stitching is done with intent to make a direct material statement or public protest it constitutes a (normally) peaceful encounter with the world. It is in pursuit of altering that world for cultural or political reasons. Subverting traditional expectations of needlework as a domestic and apolitical practice, activist stitchers generate an unorthodox narrative. It is a tactic deployed internationally by groups and individuals to generate stitch-led manifestations of alternative viewpoints and identities, and resistance. Shifting needlework into the public sphere in this way gives more opportunities for more such stories to be told to more people. Worrying over whether needlework of this kind is an art or craft is irrelevant in situations where participants and audiences experience stitching as an accessible and persuasive medium for exploring issues of public interest. These might be human rights, political violence, equality and diversity, building community, the climate crisis. Call it what we will, there is a clear trend in inserting the needle into civic conversations, a process supported by curators and conservators who put the resulting textile pieces on show and ensure their survival.

The documentation and display of 'conflict textiles' is one such example. These seemingly modest pieces of narrative sewing made by victims of conflict serve as powerful testimonies of human suffering otherwise unevidenced. At the opposite end of the scale, weighing 54 tons, with almost 50,000 panels, the USA's AIDS memorial quilt began life in the 1980s. It has expanded over time and now commemorates more than 105,000 people lost to AIDS. It has been exhibited in part or whole on numerous occasions, another manifestation of a commonplace needlecraft reconfigured by many hands to build a formidable public monument. These are acts of remembrance that claim a space for people and histories that may be marginalized in official records.[1]

Some take up their needle in defence of cultural identities and preserving favoured practices that they feel may be obliterated or forgotten, for example, by diaspora. Anella James was an accomplished exponent of her country's 'freehand' dressmaking method when she came from Jamaica to live in Britain in 1961. She continued to practise this way of making garments without paper patterns despite its difference to the British pattern-based convention, asserting her own Jamaican 'aesthetic-self and by extension a collective identity'.[2] Sewing, like other activities that can embody components of homeland such as cooking or gardening, holds individual and cultural memories and offers a sense of belonging and agency for migrants.

Whatever form it takes, stitching for change, like constructive or affirmative activism of any kind, draws its strengths from an engagement with the activist's head *and* heart. Activist stitching, or craftivism as Sarah Corbett has called it, is a labour of love, not a pastime. 'Being the change we wish to see in the world doesn't come easily . . . virtue requires thought . . . We need to work hard to make moral thinking and actions become second nature to us.'[3] Activism can, and perhaps should, change the activist. It is certainly not for the complacent. Stitching activists can look back on an impressive past and their imagination and commitment today continues an evolving practice.

Activists who deploy their needles face an obdurate cultural legacy rooted in the belief that working with a needle constitutes a form of oppression of women and girls, part of restrictive domesticity, firmly the opposite of any kind of push against the status quo. The same view regards the resulting sewn artefacts themselves as things of limited significance. This reading of needlework past and present may be persistent, but it can be turned on its head by more maker-centred thinking. A study of the Women's Christian Temperance Union (1874 to now) in the USA is an example of reading through a different lens and serves to make the case, still applicable today, that working with a needle has all manner of potential. Its authors argue that the products these campaigning women founders sewed to raise funds and public awareness, including quilts and banners, can be seen as outcomes of 'conventional femininity'. But looked at another way, at the same time they were 'ones where a woman's skills are directed towards new audiences and serve new purposes in situations where the stitching, and perhaps the stitchers as well, are imbued with new cultural values'. From this more inclusive perspective, their needlework became 'a vehicle through which women have constructed discourses of their own, ones offering a broader range of positions from which to engage dominant culture'. To continue with this perspective, it is clear that 'needlework activities can be viewed as providing a rhetorical space in which women could reflect, a space in which to stitch not only a seam but also a self.' That such situations are 'rife with possibility' is just as true today as it was then.[4] And it is not just women's needlework that has rhetorical as well as practical potential. For example, today when men sew and explore making their own clothes, they create a rhetorical space that challenges gender stereotyping and what that might mean to them and the people around them.

Another hurdle to recognizing plain stitching's potential for activism is that the best-known and most cited examples of needle activism feature embroidery, such as Judy Chicago's mixed media *Dinner Party* (1974–9), a ground-breaking, defiant work on a vast scale made by many hands and now installed in the Brooklyn Museum, New York. It includes 39 elaborately embroidered runners in its celebration of individual women from antiquity to recent times. Yet however radical and arresting such work undoubtedly is, embroidery, pictorial or otherwise, has never been the full extent of women's needlework. Of course, needlework procedures of different kinds, whether embroidery, knitting, crochet or others, are overlapping practices: all of them are domestic needlecrafts also used in activist work and often practised by the same people. Yet plain sewing's equal potential in its own right for voicing dissent is usually overlooked and needs to be underlined.

When we foreground the story of plain stitching and its work in voicing those 'new cultural values', its presence as an expressive medium emerges. Sewing for yourself alone or collectively with others can form new memories and narratives, forming an intentional countercurrent to the tide of the dominant culture, politics or commercial fashion, allowing practitioners the means to create a personal counter-memory or a more public 'counter narrative' for themselves.[5] Whether or not Rozsika Parker was right that embroidering was a repressive part of women's education and lives, what she also famously said about embroidery's potential as a 'naturally revolutionary art' may equally be applied to plain sewing. Even when limited to needle and thread as their only available expressive practice, 'women have nevertheless sewn a subversive stitch.'[6] Among those women who chafed against the restrictions of domesticity in early modern Europe, and felt it silenced their voices, there were some who argued that they had as much right to express themselves publicly as authors with a pen as with a needle, that is, to write as freely as men did. There was significant debate at the time about the suitability of the use of the pen or the needle in women's lives that lingered on into the nineteenth century.[7]

Activist or rhetorical sewing in overtly political circles was evident in the campaigns in Britain for votes for women in the decade before the First World War, particularly Millicent Fawcett's National Union of Women's Suffrage Societies (NUWSS) and Emmeline Pankhurst's Women's Social and Political Union (WSPU). They were sharply divided over direct action militancy. But, in common with the Christian Women's Temperance Union in the USA, they were united in their grasp of the importance of their image. No matter how effective their behind-the-scenes networking and fundraising was, it had to be matched by getting themselves in the public eye. As well as posters and publications, they did this with needle skills familiar to women, making a visual impact through massed banners, pennants, costumes and sashes to create spectacular pageants, parades and demonstrations. Parker argues that in their banners their use of embroidery alongside the more respected medium of paint in these very prominent pieces showed traditional feminine needlework as a strength and as not the only medium available to them.[8] But the substantial constructional plain needlework that went into these important much-photographed public displays needs to be recognized. In the UK the founder of the Artists' Suffrage League was asked, 'Can we make the banner ourselves?' (There were professional banner-makers in business at the time.) Mary Lowndes's reply was practical, comparing the task to domestic skills. 'If you want a new pair of winter curtains for your dining-room, can you make them yourself, so that they shall hang straight and true and the linings not be puckered? If you can, I think you can make the banner.'[9] A surviving 'Votes for Women' banner made by London's Peckham branch of the Women's Freedom League in about 1908 is thought to be of home-made construction using offcuts from curtaining or clothes. It speaks of the needlework capability and economy then well known in many homes being redeployed ingeniously in the service of their challenging cause. The shield-shaped banner exemplifies how plain constructional sewing could give a voice to a powerful demand that really mattered to its makers. It took some courage to carry it aloft in often hostile public spaces and spell out to the government and the world in appliqué letters: 'Votes for Women This Session'.[10]

Wearing your heart on your sleeve in a street march is one form of expression but making your own everyday clothing into a potent form of communication and dissent also has a long tradition. This proved, and still proves, challenging because of the monolithic fashion industry and all its allies. Alluring and frustrating in equal measure, fashion's homogenized products smother difference as much as they offer novelty. It's a challenge that many sewing amateurs are conscious of today, and, as we will see later, one they meet with creative flair. It can come as a surprise, and perhaps an inspiration to today's fast fashion sceptics who sew in search of expressing their values in slower or more personal alternatives, to realize for how long and with what passion women and men, as vocal individuals or groups, have campaigned *against* fashion and its effects on makers and users and *for* more comfortable and more lasting styles. Over the last three hundred years or more, the expanding imperatives of capital and the mechanized mass production of textiles and clothing took hold, twinned with growth in the retail trade and fashion press. Opposition to these forces arose in different quarters in the industrializing countries that were driving such developments, fuelled by concerns about health, aesthetics and the exploitation of labour.

Organized efforts or activism to liberate clothing from extremes of fashion echoed, and often overlapped with, the journey towards female suffrage and reached a peak in the later nineteenth and early twentieth centuries. Jean-Jacques Rousseau was a precursor when he argued in 1762 that young girls should be taught to find and stick to a simple style of dress that suited them. 'The love of fashion is contrary to good taste.' Children needed physical activity, proved, he thought, by boys liking best the 'plainest and most comfortable clothes' because they gave them most physical liberty.[11] In the nineteenth century Karl Marx and Friedrich Engels provided radical analyses of capitalism and its consequences for working people, giving broader context to the shocking realities of textile and fashion production and consumption and revealing the appalling conditions in manufacturing centres. Thomas Hood's 1843 'The Song of the Shirt', published anonymously in the London magazine *Punch*, opened many customers' eyes to exploitation happening behind the scenes in the dressmaking and millinery trades.

Inventive practical alternatives to the fashion system came from all directions. The ardent American campaigner for temperance and women's rights Amelia Bloomer (1818–1894) also advocated female sartorial freedoms, as did many others, and on her lecture tours she wore loose Turkish-style trousers that showed beneath her shortened skirt. She was not quite the first to wear them, but they soon became known as 'Bloomers', and hundreds of women wrote asking for patterns so they could make them for themselves, such was the attraction of the ease of movement they offered. Bloomer and her colleagues eventually returned to conventional dress partly because the level of ridicule aimed at bloomers distracted from what they saw as the more essential aims of their work.[12]

It was evident that a head of steam was building up around these complex and interwoven issues. In Britain the Rational Dress Society were creative in their promotion of less restrictive forms of dress, and supported the idea of making bifurcated garments for women. Their campaign included the presentation of more liberating garments at the International Health Exhibition of 1884, hosted at the vast Albert Hall in London. The Healthy and Artistic Dress Union (1890–1906?), supported by some leading UK artists of the time, spelled out its twin philosophies by its name. By its extensive promotional activities, it hoped to evolve for the better the dress of both men and women. In the USA and UK and across Europe, the lively dress reform movement at this time produced an abundance of publications on these topics. One shared concern was the acceptance of clothing that recognized the realities of the human form instead of reshaping it. The American Annie Jenness Miller (1859–1935) advocated evolutionary improvement rather than revolutionary reform in women's dress, arguing it should be more natural in shape and comfortable and coupled with physical exercise for women to arrive at 'the triumph of utility and beauty'. She made a business of her ideas. Her publications and lectures were popular, and she included patterns to be made up at home such as those for pregnant women and babies in one of her publications, based on the assumption that mothers-to-be enjoyed sewing their newborn's clothing. She also patented garments for sale ready-made. To our eyes today, many of her designs and suggestions are not what we would understand as 'natural' in shape or style, but her career indicates a significant appetite at grass-roots level for clothing that was easier to make and wear.[13] In general, the principles of simpler dress valued by so many campaigners would help dressmakers and home sewers more readily achieve good results. In the UK it chimed with a taste for what became known as 'artistic' dress and home decor, including a taste for Japanese style, perhaps best known through the London shop Liberty, founded by Arthur Liberty in 1875. Still trading today, it is often seen by home sewers as a hotspot for fine fabrics.

The Arts and Crafts designer, author and early socialist William Morris (1834–1896) was deeply troubled by the woeful conditions of his day in which manual workers lived and laboured and also by what he saw as the shoddy design and quality of many of the goods they were condemned to make in relentless profit-before-people manufacturing. Many people today stand by Morris's famous 'golden rule that will fit everybody', 'Do not have anything in your house that you do not know to be useful or believe to be beautiful.'[14] Further he expounded: 'Never have anything which is not good and sound in workmanship.' On the matter of dress, he was equally forthright in extending this philosophy. Morris called for simplicity, grace and beauty in clothing and at the heart of his plea for change was the question of freedom of choice. In one much quoted lecture he said, 'I beg of you fervently, do not allow yourselves to be upholstered like armchairs, but drape your-selves like women.' This appeal to women was made at a time when there were dressmakers trading in every community and at every price point ready to produce whatever was required and the take-up of domestic sewing machines was increasing, so responding to Morris didn't mean customers had to wait for ready-mades that might or might not fit this philosophy.[15]

There were other voices registering concerns that seem only too familiar today. One of the most analytical conscientious objectors to fashion was Charlotte Perkins Gilman (1860–1935), the American feminist, novelist, essayist and sociologist. She pro-moted the idea in 1915 of a new regime in womenswear, spelling things out from women's perspective. Among the abundance of books, pamphlets, articles, lectures and exhibitions campaigning for clothing change over this period, her clarity still hits the mark today. She regarded clothing as 'a social tissue' and observed that the 'more solitary we live, the less we think of clothing; the more we crowd and mingle in "society", the more we think of it,' an experience many found familiar during the recent lockdowns. Gilman rejected the 'excessive production' of fashion by 'bloated enterprises' profiting from rapid changes of style that she called 'our perpetual cyclone of new fashions'. To Gilman, fashion in this unthinking form did not serve the best interests of either workers in the trade or customers. The alternative 'equilibrium' she advocated would include women having such a 'keen sense of economy, that we shall not be willing to buy poor garments, or to throw away good ones. We shall become so proud of our own skill in selection or construction that we shall boast: "I have worn this six years!" instead of our present silly pride in "the very latest."' Over a hundred years later her sentiments still resonate strongly with the thinking of many consumers and individual makers and continue to reflect motives for much home sewing of clothing today.[16]

When men exercise choice to make their own clothes, as plenty do these days, or wear shorts in the city, they too follow in the footsteps of earlier campaigners. At the tail end of organized campaigning came the Men's Dress Reform Party, which was active in the UK and internationally between 1929 and 1941. Their close links with the New Health Society and the Sunlight League indicate the direction of their thinking. They stood for sandals, shorts and open-necked shirts and loosening up male garb in general for wearing in town as well as at leisure. Many of their prototype suits and 'blouses' in art silk and other soft materials could be made at home, while more traditional thicker materials needed to be shaped by trained tailors. Like earlier groups, they espoused art and health together in clothing, but unlike some of their predecessors, their campaigning was aimed at specific targets, such as the BBC Promenade Orchestra, which conceded that its musicians could wear soft shirts. Seaside local authorities heeded their demands for swimming 'slips', or briefs for men, instead of more cumbersome torso-covering swimsuits on public beaches. If a wartime bomb hadn't hit their London office, who knows where they might have led men's clothing over time. Looking at menswear today, the sartorial aims of their activism seem to have been largely realized, although they were often ridiculed at the time. 'The dull, unimaginative, conventional, stuffy, non-creative, unproductive nincompoops, whose palsied minds would destroy health, efficiency and freedom, by their sneers and jeers have utterly failed to crush the movement for men's dress reform.' All too easily their ideas embraced not just health but eugenics; nevertheless they were in the vanguard of the relaxation of modern menswear.[17]

In practice, all the while, many people continued living out their avoidance of conventional fashion in their daily lives, much as they do today, making or selecting clothes that expressed different values. Religious communities, both male and female, have stuck to this for centuries with garments to indicate separation not just from fashion but from worldly ways in general. Quakers in the past were renowned for their unshowy clothing, as are the Amish today. In the Muslim world, covering the body and face has many regional variants in the expression of privacy, piety or reputation, a kind of social space negotiated through apparel, which is sometimes contested or politicized and often subject to misunderstandings by non-Muslims. Some of these forms relate to earlier pre-Islamic practices illustrating the enduring use of clothing to wrap the body rather than reveal or mould it as Western fashion does today.

The reforming zeal of the organized anti-fashionistas and their disdain for profits, patriarchy or gender differences is one thing but not everybody wants to look different, and fashion offers them an element of social cohesion. Difference can be awkward or uncomfortable although for others it is a matter of pride. Many feel that fashion offers individuality, self-expression or group identity, even though it is today on a vast scale. As a child of late capitalism at its most globalized and homogenizing, it is far more complex than earlier objectors could have imagined. 'Fashion *speaks* capitalism,' as Elizabeth Wilson puts it, arguing that it is the ambiguities of fashion that make us love and hate it.[18] Those ambiguities are regarded by some not as neutral but damaging. Defining fashion as a 'regime of domination', Otto von Busch expands on the idea of 'fashion supremacy' as 'an intrinsic part of today's social life', a system that requires pro-active behaviour to escape. 'What makes fashion supremacy so deceitful is the imagination that cheap and accessible fashion is a form of democracy, a system governed by and for the people.' To challenge this, he calls for constructive 'disarmament' in which 'other values that build courage and self-esteem beyond consumerism need to be embraced and practised.'[19] Those who are sewing for change in political or personal terms, banners or frocks, are already generating their own proactive escape routes to express different values.

Context is everything. Nobody sews in a vacuum: they sew within the real world as they find it. They clothe themselves within or against the prevailing value systems embodied in the products generated by textile and clothing manufacturers and the monetized fashion structures of retailing. There are changes of emphasis in today's concerns, but there are also fundamental similarities with earlier efforts. Morris and others urged a respect for the natural world and for workers. He warned of the grave injustices they suffered, but nobody from that previous generation of reformers and activists could have foreseen the scale of the environmental and climate crises now facing us, in which the disturbing realities of global production of textiles and dress are deeply implicated. The real world of textiles can be shocking: for instance, the production of textiles emits more greenhouse gas every year than all shipping and international flights put together.

The slogan 'fashion shouldn't cost the earth' is well known and the movement towards more self-aware and ethical consumption is growing round the world. These facts motivate many people to sew for themselves. Unsustainable pressures on the environment are global and systemic; nevertheless individuals can and do stitch their own values into their responses. They engage with these particular issues through their own practice and their own choices, such as using cloth made from natural fibres and finding second-hand sources for it, eschewing fast fashion in favour of slower garment construction at home. With the capability to be active makers, amateur stitchers can react in practical ways if they choose, making clothes of their own that follow fashion or modify it, or opt for another aesthetic altogether. At the same time, they gain insight into the marketplace:

> When you have a better understanding of how the things you own are made, you have so much more respect for them. Even if you only make one pair of jeans, the next time you go to buy a pair you'll think so much harder about the work and care that went into that product . . . It's made me look at other areas of my life, too: can I build my own bed? My own kitchen table? Being self-sufficient is a really good feeling.[20]

Today there's a belief among the stitching community that making your own clothes can register a particular form of validity or sincerity. Not usually associated with activism, yet in reality performing a kind of body activism, people of diverse body shapes, gender or disablement use needle skills to make their own garments. They do this to assert their enjoyment of comfort and style, and to reject standardized fashion goods still designed to fit slender bodies, seemingly oblivious to the realities of physical diversity. Their steps towards personal change and self-expression should be recognized as equally radical and challenging as other more public or collective forms of activism. Stitchers can find deeper gratification in making their own clothes than shopping for ready-mades. With making comes the acquisition and development of skills, and there are plenty of opportunities to sew in the company of real or virtual groups, and to share a fellowship and conviviality. They can savour choice in fabrics and style. If their body shape conforms to industry norms, they can use commercial paper patterns in the knowledge that the resulting garment will fit or only require modest adjustments. Many teach themselves the skill of pattern cutting in order to make a lasting resource for making garments precisely adapted to their needs. But there are others with more restricted options, because paper patterns often fail to take their body shapes or aspirations into account. When people wish to resist insidious bias against them, such as racism or sexism, stitching garments for themselves can provide more control over their appearance and help create a visible statement about their selfhood or values. It gives some resilience against negative feelings caused by unsatisfactory consumption of ready-mades and offers a satisfying sense of accomplishment. The manifesto of the online 'private' sewing community called Seamwork emphasizes the wider matters that sewing can engage with, echoing the stance of other such virtual communities: 'Instead of easy, we choose creativity. It's a path that challenges us and forces us to slow down. It causes us to question what we truly need. It also brings us a deep sense of gratification, pride, and joy.' In common with other such groups, there is an emphasis on connectedness and greater autonomy than the marketplace offers. 'It is a way to infuse creativity deeply into our everyday lives and feel connected to who we are and our impact on the world.'[21]

The mental benefits of sewing to construct something and express an identity are described time and again by those who have experienced them. There is also plentiful evidence of sewing in extreme situations where the stakes are high and benefits include even sanity itself. There are remarkable accounts of sewing that took place in Second World War internment camps, in prisons and mental hospitals, which are often vital as statements of personal or group identity demonstrating the psychological benefits of craft for people in confinement. Details of how this can emerge in hostile environments are recounted in *Khiam*, a documentary film made between 2000 and 2007 by two Lebanese film-makers. They used the testimony of six people who survived years of incarceration in a notorious detention centre in that country to show how these men and women individually and collectively risked their lives in order to be makers. They gathered various random discarded materials in secret and experimented tenaciously with them until they contrived a functional needle, including efforts with dried orange stems, the teeth of a comb, plastic and wire. Then they generated threads and eventually they could sew to mend their clothes and craft small items. This high-risk activity, potentially punishable by torture and solitary confinement in horrendous conditions, was about self-respect or identity. It was also a form of escape. Their fortitude enabled them 'to obliterate, in a mere instant, and through processes of making, the effect of confinement'.[22] The story these prisoners told of sewing in such an appalling setting, and those related by other confined people, is wholly unlike most people's experience of sewing, in which freedom of the individual and freedom of their practice are taken for granted. Nevertheless, they share the fundamental urge to communicate something of their real selves, to use the voice given by making and sewing to speak and reach out beyond the limits of their immediate circumstances.

There are sewing practices today that derive from mental and physical dissatisfactions and discomfort with fashion, even a sense of alienation, and generate what is in effect a form of activism, reflecting Otto von Busch's call for 'other values that build courage and self-esteem beyond consumerism'. One experienced stitcher has several motives for sewing her own clothes, including the fact she is above average height, but she also values how her sewing skills offer an informal means of exchange outside conventional markets: she has sewn stage outfits for a musician friend who in turn is teaching her to sing.[23] When standard sizing in ready-to-wear or dressmaking patterns don't even offer anything in your actual dimensions or only lacklustre products and you turn to making your own clothes, a new world opens up. Tierney, a Canadian, gained more than better-fitting clothes as she learned to sew them; she gained insights about her own self. Her comments on that sewing journey match what other sewers formerly demoralized by ready-to-wear have experienced:

I've come to be very familiar with my body shape, and it's normalized my body to me. Yes, it's outside the average. All bodies are outside the norm one way or another. I have learned how to adjust patterns so that they fit the body I have and make it look and feel good. The self-loathing I used to feel when I went shopping and couldn't find anything to fit has been replaced by equanimity. So those jeans look awful. That's not a problem with me, it's a problem with the jeans because the manufacturer

didn't have my body in mind when they created them –
and why would they, they've never met me.[24]

Many people sew with a radical view of their own bodies.
They don't want to conform to body conventions and are
determined to gain a greater sense of ownership of their own
appearance. Doing this in supportive fellowship, such as sharing ideas and skill about pattern adjustments, is even better. A
good example of this approach is the Curvy Sewing Collective in
the USA, which has almost 25,000 members online. It caters for
'plus-sized, curvy, pear-shaped, and extravagantly buxom, just
to name a few'. They want to avoid 'sizist pigeon-holing' and
reject 'body shaming' and any kind of 'negativity'. This collective
exemplifies how a sewing community can feel safe for its members
and they in turn can make garments that make them feel safe
in everyday life – 'we celebrate the female shape in all its varied,
beautiful glory.'[25] One of their contributors writes, 'Sewing is
my hobby, therapy, and way of participating in a like-minded
community. It is also my way to have clothes that are a better fit
for my figure, preferences, and personality than anything ready-
to-wear seems to offer. Sewing challenges, grows, and soothes
me, usually all at once.'

In a slender-centric Western fashion system, a recent shift to
what some identify as fat pride has been liberating for victims
of fatphobia, but it has not banished implicit and explicit fat-
shaming practices, which see large people as unruly or deviant and
underline the importance of safe places as represented by CSC.
By enabling the assertion of personal tastes, groups that offer a
haven for sewists to control what they make and wear give them
a chance to disarm what they dislike about the fashion system.

There are of course plenty of instances when the commerce of fashion quickly monetizes these aspirations, as when commercial pattern producers catch up with this kind of assertive self-help and improve their styles for larger sizes.

For those whose non-binary, trans or other gender fluidity is central to their identity, finding a visual language that speaks more precisely for them may cut across the deeply entrenched gender norms in personal appearance that prevail the world over. Sharing resources and skills to meet their needs, sewing for themselves, can help construct the look they want. Their search for a sartorial equivalence to new ways of thinking and being is again a form of activism. Perhaps this is also evidence of delight in authentic original or adaptive styles without fashion designers, a shared energy that expresses diversity. Adaptation of men's shirts, for instance, is taught on sewing sites and blogs as a way to achieve an androgynous look for female-shaped bodies, occupying a space between conventional male and female style.[26]

For wheelchair users the failure of mainstream fashion to consider their clothing needs is currently getting more attention from designers but still presents ongoing problems. Those whose conditions require them to be seated all day can find conventional garment shapes uncomfortable and lumpy, with openings, seams, pockets or waistbands set in the wrong place. Garment styles designed to fit and move on a standing and walking body can multiply restriction if they ride or bulk up when confined to a chair. It is also often assumed that disabled seated people have no interest in style. 'Products are often created without consulting the disabled clientele they seek to serve,' is the view from the Open Style Lab in New York, a not-for-profit organization dedicated to making style available to everyone 'regardless of their cognitive or physical abilities'. They report a 'severe disconnect between how the able-bodied perceive accessibility needs, and what disabled individuals actually need'.[27] Seeking to bring style and relief to this user group and reclaim a sense of individuality requires awareness of the range of body forms and capabilities they represent. Clothing for the bedridden or dementia sufferers, even hospital gowns, can all be constructed more sensitively. Long-overdue changes are emerging from a number of individual designers and organizations. For some, adaptive sewing of existing garments can be successful. Designing from scratch is another approach.[28] These projects can bring real improvement in comfort and pleasure to those whose everyday lives benefit. Garment design and making deserve a bigger part in public conversation about disability and ageing.

Sewing your own clothes with attitude, taking a stand to change the sartorial status quo and sewing as direct activism is a fluid process and it is in the nature of these endeavours that there are no fixed manifestos, universal labels or particularly useful distinctions to make. But one name that has stuck internationally is 'craftivism'. It neatly amalgamates the words 'craft' and 'activism', although it means rather different things to different practitioners. The term is credited to Betsy Greer in the USA, who first articulated it in her 2008 book *Knitting for Good! A Guide to Creating Personal, Social, and Political Change Stitch by Stitch*. What do craftivists do? A well-known approach nowadays sees groups of loosely affiliated participants use a variety of techniques and materials, including knitting, crotchet, felting and working with paper, as well as fabric and sewing, to make often small artefacts. They then wear them or insert them into public spaces, or actually make them there. Their purpose is to draw attention to their concerns or to what they may wish to celebrate. Their message is often enhanced by putting their pieces in incongruous, random or provocative locations such as on statues, lamp posts, postboxes or shops. Despite their impermanence, precisely because they harness familiar techniques and everyday materials in unexpected settings, the makers' interventions have surprise on their side, yet their messages are still readily understood.

Because craftivism is a broad church, there are differences of approach to it. Slow craftivism is advocated by the UK's Sarah Corbett, who seeks to promote environmental issues and social justice through non-aggressive, non-judgemental, kind and mindful means. Her Craftivist Collective's motto is 'Changing the world one stitch at a time.' The benefits of this carefully planned approach were demonstrated when, in conjunction with a shareholder campaigning group, Corbett led an effective craftivist campaign to encourage one of the UK's biggest retailers to become a Living Wage Employer. The work, which included giving personalized stitched messages on handkerchiefs to individual board members at their AGM, moved the company's debate forward and drew attention to consumer concerns. Crucial to understanding this kind of work are the benefits it brings to the person engaged in the making process itself, even before their finished work reaches the public domain, or, in some cases, when the making takes place in public. Corbett argues lucidly for what she calls 'gentle' craftivism, an approach and state of mind that she has exemplified in her own output and in the workshops she runs.[29]

Sewing as part of professional art practice is another dimension of the needle's significance in working to create change and dialogue and is not confined to hand sewing. British quilter Sara

Impey, while she is grounded in traditional quilting, uses her 'sewing machine as a pen' to create what she calls 'stitched essays'. She writes her own content 'directly on to the fabric with lettering that covers the whole surface and is an integral part of the design. The technique of free-machine stitching – one letter at a time – enables me to write stitched essays of several hundred words and comment on social and political issues or (my favourite topic) thoughts about sewing in general . . . These days the writing and the subject matter are as important to me as the design and the process.'[30]

Textile or fibre artists working in the expanding and international field of stitch-based practice, sometimes called socially engaged practice, aim to de-stigmatize or raise awareness of public issues and create projects and events in a variety of traditional and non-traditional settings. This kind of work is marked out by its expansive public reach and participatory activities. Sewing can be deployed to help kindle or rekindle a sense of local or national community, a social equivalent of the surgeon's healing suture. The 2021 Violet Protest in the USA, a 'friendly protest' organized by fibre artist Ann Morton, generated thousands of small, stitched pieces blending the binary blue and red colours of Democrats and Republicans to symbolize a 'common hope for unity'. Made by over two hundred people in all fifty states at a time of political tensions, these were sent to every Washington legislator to express 'collective voices' trusting 'in the power of making to hold our homes, our lives, and even our country together'. It is calculated the stitching represented 75,000 hours of work, a fair measure of their commitment to their cause.[31]

Other projects focus on diverse and hard-to-reach groups of people for whom they offer fresh means of expression, cohesion and communalities from which they may otherwise feel excluded. Drop-in open-access sessions located in public spaces and outcomes such as physical or digital exhibitions increase the visibility of these stitched projects in the wider community and offer a further degree of public engagement and recognition. Based in Manchester, England, the textile artist Lynn Setterington has led numerous projects that exemplify this field of work. Her related *Scaffolding for Life* and *Safety Net* engaged with the construction industry to draw attention to the higher-than-average suicide rate among its workers. For instance, the banners bearing the message 'There is no health without mental health' were made by many hands, including those of youngsters from a local mental health charity, and then displayed by construction workers at their sites.[32] The Social Justice Sewing Academy founded in California is another example of aiming to put stitched work designed by people from marginalized communities into public spaces, in this case to remember and draw attention to victims of violence and social injustice.[33] Many such endeavours have significant impacts on participants and their locality but like much work of this kind they can be transitory. They may depend on the energy of a single founding individual; they are not easy to organize and are often underfunded within a cultural context that has frequently undervalued stitching as a form of expression.

The multiple benefits of this field of stitched work are acknowledged widely but can present challenges on the ground for artists, organizers and participants alike, particularly when the issues touch on lived experiences that are normally unspoken and require respect and some form of protective boundaries. In these settings, collaborative sewing workshops are creative but may also have the potential to disturb participants. The UK's Stitching Together network acknowledges that these practices are unlike individual or friendship group stitching and that to reach their full potential their design and operation require care. It is a sign of the vitality of this area that the network's research and resulting good practice guidelines have been co-funded by universities and a prestigious national research council. Alongside other work to establish principles in socially practised art, it specifically situates stitching as a contributor to the expanding and multi-disciplinary arts and health field.[34] In common with the craftivism articulated, for example, by Greer and Corbett, socially engaged practice, though led by a professional artist, if happening in group settings, can accommodate all levels of skill. It welcomes absolute beginners or strangers to art in the belief that the process of making is as valuable in its own right as the results it produces.

Stitched activism, like craft itself, may seem a tranquil place, associated with authenticity, sustainability and individuality, screened from the social and environmental exploitation that shape so much of the mass marketplace. When it becomes a public and socially engaged practice, it is often perceived as part of liberal and socially progressive politics in a different setting. But craft turns out to be a highly contested place with plenty of makers, critics and academics disputing these perceptions as simplistic. It is argued, for example, that this kind of activism can't solve the bigger problems of consumerism, that monetized craft appropriated by profit-driven forces can't be counter-cultural (the evolution of Etsy is often cited as an example), that industrial goods get promoted with the language of artisanship in a kind of 'craftwash' and that community-based social engagement projects are doing the social work that is more properly the responsibility of the state.[35]

Sally is now in her fifties. She has sewn on and off since she was a child and feels life would be poorer without it. Today her interest in sewing has expanded into a sense of greater personal agency and a heightened appreciation of the context in which she sews.

> I've always loved sewing and I love being able to make things. I am enormously glad that I can because now I am more fully aware of the environmental and ethical impacts of our clothing industry. I feel lucky to have the skills to opt out. For me this is political. I am increasingly motivated to talk about this more publicly and to try and inspire others to learn.

Sewing people who think in this way might not define themselves as ethical, but their practice can be seen as such in several ways. They are mindful of others in generating gifts or acts of charity. Amateur stitchers may be campaigners and activists who use their time and needle skills to command attention to urgent social issues. They tend to be allergic to waste – they like to reuse, mend and recycle, as we'll see in the next chapter – so in these ways they are conscious of other people and other needs, careful with finite resources, mindful of the planet. For older people, these are well-anchored habits, as lifelong stitcher Elizabeth told me. 'Today the need to counteract the throw-away culture is more important than ever and is almost second nature to a war baby like myself.' Chloe, at half Elizabeth's age, connects to sewing like many of her generation when she explains how 'environmental sustainability and social justice' are important to her and how they affect her sewing practices. 'When I do buy new, I try to buy from an ethical brand, which I can't always afford to do, so I buy less and try to make more.' Unlike consumers who only buy ready-mades, the maker with a needle has another set of options. The former may be aware of the social and environmental problems embodied in clothing and want control over what they purchase and wear, and act ethically in other spheres, but the practical agency and greater independence of the one who sews is immediate. They choose a different space.

The global players of design, manufacturing and retailing are walking, not always willingly, towards a new future of greater responsibility for people and planet. At home, alone or in fellowship, stitchers are already ahead of the game, busy using their needles to subvert old practices, to resist market platitudes and slow their pace of consumption, to sew with fabrics that do not harm the environment and clothe their actual bodies, not the body shapes determined by the fashion trade. They sew to overcome obstacles. They want to be in touch with their own inner and outer realities, engage with the pleasures of making and enjoy the world they inhabit in a different way. They want to represent themselves, as bodies and citizens, as they feel themselves to be, and their works of public activism – stitch-based defiance and protest – have good reason to continue.

8

Into the Fray

Mending is more important than it seems. It is an intervention undertaken to extend the useful life of stuff and it is also a practice with cultural and social significance. You would never guess that, given how hidden from view and hidden from history it is. But if we look more closely at mending, through a sewing lens, we see it is an act of transformation that embodies a cluster of motives and aspirations. People who mend their clothes and household textiles might do so because they want them to last longer – they are trying to get better value for their money, or they may aspire to slower and more sustainable consumption habits in general. Some people mend their things because they simply don't want to part with them for sentimental or emotional reasons. Others have discovered the soothing mental-health benefits of using their needle to darn and repair, especially as a consciously unhurried activity. If we think about mending alongside remaking, recycling, upcycling, and repair in general, together they can be a form of agency every bit as creative and ingenious as making from scratch.

After being hidden for so long, then seemingly irrelevant in the age of fast cheap clothing, repair and recovery and remaking practices are enjoying new attention and status today, celebrated as both an economy and a craft that brings its own pleasures. If the number of new how-to mending books are anything to go by, it appeals to big audiences. As well as retailers catering to the trend, the enlarged conversation includes craftspeople and academics who recognize that repair has far-reaching implications. As Anna König puts it, mending doesn't fix our relationships to things, 'it opens up a kind of dialogue in which the consumer becomes an active agent in their material lives.'[1]

To quote from John Taylor's famous 1631 poem 'The Praise of the Needle', the 'Needle (though it be but small and slender),/ Yet it is both a maker and a mender'. So it has been for centuries, though beneath the notice of mainstream history. However, there are four lines in Taylor's poem that sound a warning bell and remind us of an all too familiar attitude. Despite his lengthy praise of needlework, he reveals an underlying bid, common enough then and now, to marginalize women's voices. Taylor was clearly averse to women who used their needlework time together for bonding, collaborating and talking.

> It will increase their peace, enlarge their store,
> To use their tongues lesse, and their Needles more.
> The Needles sharpnesse, profit yeelds, and pleasure,
> But sharpnesse of the tongue, bites out of measure.[2]

Sewing is attracting younger people and more rookie stitchers than ever before. Menders join makers now in an intergenerational activity and they don't want to keep quiet. From sewing on replacement buttons to turning old jeans into skirts, bags or cushions, replacing defunct zips, patching tears or revitalizing second-hand and vintage garments, people are sharing ideas and advice about mending and reusing in all kinds of settings and media. It signals a growth in awareness of what's in our homes and wardrobes, who we are as consumers and the surrounding worldwide problems in clothing and textile production. In this context, mending has become thoughtful, expressive and political. Taylor might approve of new enthusiasm for needlework, but he wouldn't approve of all this talking and, heaven forbid, critical thinking.

Individuals engaged with repairing their things are in effect not only rescuing their possessions from the bin but asserting their own values, defining on their own terms what kind of consumer they really want to be. Their activities map directly onto the dilemmas of twenty-first-century consumerism in economies built on the model of perpetual growth. But readiness to transition to more aware lifestyles on the part of individuals and households is in the air, be it more self-provisioning or reduction in the use of plastics. Repair cafés can be found in towns and cities around the world; there are currently over 2,500 of them.[3] The popularity of the BBC TV series *The Repair Shop* echoes this shift in sensibility allied with consumer frustration with rapid obsolescence, clutter and waste in these challenging economic and environmental times. The programme regularly has over 6 million viewers. It recognizes the desire to cherish items of sentimental value and at the same time to savour the display of the craft and care involved in extending the life of things. But its message has wider implications. By understanding more about craft makers and the processes of making, we are 'becoming more respectful of the intelligence that is embodied in making', and are on the way to building what have been called 'communities of respect'.[4] The intelligence embodied in mending, a species of making, deserves the same respect.

Mending fabric well has long been thought an art form in its own right. One best-selling Victorian manual of needlework was in no doubt about the merits of repair. 'How best to disguise and repair the wear and tear of use or accident is quite as valuable an art, as that of making new things.'[5] Use and accident come in many forms and methods of mending fabric do too, each suited to particular problems. The different properties of modern manmade fabrics have not always made this easier, although they are often more durable and less prone to wear and tear than traditional ones. The Victorian manual assumed that the aim was to disguise the mend so well that it became invisible, an aspiration for generations of menders before and since. But many modern-day menders embrace visible mending, so there's more choice.

Darning shadows the original structure of the weave and is a versatile cure. It is the method of drawing split or ripped edges together or reinforcing threadbare fabric by sewing over or replacing damaged or worn threads, a kind of reweaving to fill or cover damage. In the past, and often still today, this was done as unobtrusively as possible by matching the colour and thread of the original piece. Arguably the peak of darning achievement was intricate darning to repair cloth with complex weave structures, such as damask or twill, and also woven patterns such as checks. This can be seen still in darning samplers that survive from the past in which the darner has precisely replicated the weave. I am lucky enough to have one which has twenty different examples of the finest intricacy, each the size of a large postage stamp, worked in different coloured threads and arranged attractively around the central stitched identification: 'May 20th Sarah Mugridge 1798.'

Sarah named herself as the maker of this exquisite but not unusual piece, no doubt with some pride. Perhaps it formed a testimonial to show a potential employer her skill in what amounted to elaborate but invisible mending of costly fabrics or an inventory of techniques she could call on in her own home.[6]

Such was the widespread practice of darning in most homes that many women in the past could frequently identify their own possessions by what seems almost signature mending, though probably not often as fine as Sarah's work. We can 'hear' this when a London court of law, as it often did, required victims of crime to identify their goods found in the possession of the accused. Bearing in mind the draconian punishments in the past for theft, this kind of testimony carried serious consequences for the defendant. Under oath, Ann Lough was confident in 1785 that she knew her own handiwork, something the courts regarded as normal testimony. 'One of the black cloaks I know particularly, by having a little darn of my own darning, I am quite sure of it.'[7] When challenged, Mary Pressy in 1795 was very firm about the importance of mending when the court doubted she would have bothered to repair such an old sheet: 'Old things must not be thrown away.'[8] Women who repaired personal and household linen for a living often did so in tandem with laundering them as well, and could be equally mending-literate, reunited as they were with their own work at each successive wash. Surrounded everyday by repaired clothes, they drew on intimate knowledge of their own handiwork, the memory particular to the practitioner herself. In 1853 Rosanna Dix identified cotton socks she had darned two months before. She even brought some of the same darning cotton with her to court to confirm the matter. Pride in her work led her to evaluate it at length: 'I can work a great deal better than this, but I did not think the socks were worth it – this other sock is mended much better – I work better sometimes than at other times – I did not finish mending the whole of this one, because somebody came for it   I mended all these places.'[9] Rosanna was justifying her uneven standards within the apparently urgent work she was paid to do and emphasizing that she would normally do 'better'. Her commentary indicates the same degree of engagement and specific kind of intelligence in mending as making new would require.

Patching is a method of repair that is normally done when the damage is too extensive for a darn to be adequate. Patches of all shapes can be applied in various ways on the outside or underside of the area to be covered. Thicker woven wool fabrics can be mended with a deliberately frayed patch of matching material darned round the edges into the original fabric, a painstaking process with almost invisible results. Iron-on patches that require no stitching have been popular since at least the 1940s, though they are best reinforced with stitches, and today invisible iron-on webbing is in common use for an almost instant firm fix for split seams or droopy hems that does not require a needle to be threaded. This is fast mending in both senses. Like darning, patching of all kinds is universal. Surviving garments worn by Thomas Jefferson (1743–1826), the third president of the United States, show patching alongside alterations. If this work was undertaken by his household's domestic seamstress, an enslaved woman called Betty Brown who lived in his household for sixty years, we can only guess at what went through her mind as she stitched.[10]

The full repertoire of fabric repair methods was put to use in households rich and poor, reflecting the realities of labour usually assigned to women. The London court records reveal not just the ingenuity involved but that the tasks were seldom finished. A bundle of stolen goods were identified by Elizabeth Brown in 1792 by details of their condition, 'a piece being put in the neck of the waistcoat, and the backs being one thing and the fronts another; the breeches were seated; the sheets, one patched, and one with a hole in it.'[111] Nowadays, our houses and wardrobes have changed but mending and techniques of preservation can be just as varied. A Londoner who has had a career sewing professionally for private clients still finds time for mending for herself: 'I repair whenever possible, I turn shirt collars, put elbow patches on sweaters, sew up moth holes a lot. I repair socks and jeans and replace zips. Many years ago when impoverished I made a duvet using the feathers from old counterpanes.'

The high visibility of fashion cycles and the dominant idea that fashion in use is a democratizing aspect of modern life and a means of group or self-identification seem to be unstoppable narratives, but they have always masked the numerous alternatives that co-exist with them. In fact, these have been far more important in the history of clothing and household economies than is usually acknowledged. Repair, reuse, adaptation, repurposing, all the processes seen today are a continuation of a deep-seated approach that has shaped consumption across time, geography and social class. Adaptive upcycling in past centuries often exemplified not only the skills and resources involved but the confidence that often underpinned such makeovers: one example, a luxury item now in the care of London's Victoria and Albert Museum, is a man's doublet and breeches dated 1635–40 made of beautifully quilted 'oyster' satin, also lined and sewn with silk. This sumptuous outfit is thought to have been conjured out of an earlier finely worked bedcover. The doublet was given twelve bows round the waist for added splendour, crowning a suit clearly intended for a man moving in elite social circles where such finery was appropriate. The bedcover-turned-suit moved from private bed chamber to public display, with continuing respect for the original fabric and needlecraft.[12] Even Queen Victoria's dressmaker frequently shortened the royal drawers and nightdress sleeves as Victoria's physical stature decreased strikingly in old age.[13]

The relatively high cost of textiles in the past as compared to the lower cost of labour is only part of the story. Superficially completely unlike, the stolen waistcoat identified by Elizabeth Brown, the bedcover-suit makeover and Victoria's economies complicate how we think about the motives and status of repair and repurposing in textiles. There may be more in common between the waistcoat, the suit and the drawers than meets the eye. They all point to an enduring philosophy of preservation that goes beyond simplistic definitions of wealth or poverty, haves and have-nots. It is a philosophy shared across social class connected to the notion of thrift as a way of marshalling and retaining household resources for longer-term benefit, even for the next generation's gain, and links with a sense of moderation as a virtue. We shouldn't overlook the sense of accomplishment enjoyed by those who improvised in these matters with such effective ingenuity. The way the stolen Georgian waistcoat was visibly pieced together – 'the backs being one thing and the fronts another' – would make it very attractive among all those who enjoy mending and remaking today, an illustration of both change and continuity in how these practices are valued.

In many cases necessity is the mother of invention. Elizabeth Custer (1842–1933), out west with her husband General George

Custer (1839–1876), far away from shops and tailors and although inexperienced at sewing for herself, spent several weeks making over one of his jackets to replace her own lost riding-habit bodice. At this time many army wives reused their husbands' cadet graduation jackets for their own riding habits, a form of domestic economy in challenging circumstances that kept the durable material in use, even across the gender divide.[14] Making over, like any sewing, can be a sociable activity and often an elaborate process that could benefit from another pair of experienced hands, something Elizabeth Custer and her like, past and present, could have used. The young poet Elizabeth Bishop (1911–1979) first met the older poet Marianne Moore (1887–1972) in 1934 in Brooklyn, where she lived with her mother. Moore herself said that her clothes were 'almost always hand-me-downs, sometimes very elegant ones from richer friends. These would be let out or, most frequently, let down.' On a visit to Moore's apartment, Bishop came across the poet and her mother

> occupied with the old-fashioned bit of sewing called 'making over.' They were making a pair of drawers that Marianne had worn at Bryn Mawr in 1908 into a petticoat or slip. The drawers were a beautiful garment, fine white batiste, with very full legs that must have come to below the knee, edged with lace and set with rows of 'insertion.' These I didn't see again in their metamorphosed state, but I did see and was sometimes consulted about other such projects.[15]

Resources are required before any mending or a 'metamorphosed state' can be achieved. Tools, thread, time. Materials have always come from almost anywhere. Marianne Moore's came from 'richer friends' as well as her own wardrobe. That old habit of hoarding comes in here. Eliza Jervoise (1770–1821), born and married into the English landed gentry, kept stuff in quantity. An inventory of her wardrobe taken on her death shows all manner of garment parts and pieces of cloth new and old amounting to almost 20 per cent of the items recorded, which were stored carefully in furniture alongside her clothes in boxes, cloth and paper.[16] These items represented a resource within a household where bills show recycling, mending and alterations took place frequently. A young stitcher in her twenties told me how she follows in this tradition today: 'I enjoy having clothes that are mended as it means I can keep them in my life for longer; when they eventually become too worn or damaged to continue using, I use them for material for other projects such as patchwork, dolls or other soft toys.' Like those who kept things in the past, looking stylish today can be part of the aim. Recruiting to their 'army of refashionistas', the UK organization WRAP promotes ways of getting 'new outfits from unloved garments' already owned. 'Getting creative with your clothes isn't just about saving cash: it can give you a fabulous style that nobody else can match.'[17]

When cloth is scarce more improvisation is needed. Joan Haslip started work in the sewing workrooms of the UK's John Lewis department store during the Second World War. 'At first, with materials being hard to come by, our work consisted mainly of adaptions to curtains from bombed buildings, in which you could find broken glass and some ingenious interlinings, to comply with blackout regulations. One I particularly remember consisted of flour sacks joined together with the name still clearly on them.'[18] Times change and more recently in a throwaway society there is ample choice.

> Charity shops can be a surprisingly good place to find interesting fabric . . . Look out for old linen tablecloths, vintage curtains, duvet covers and old-fashioned head-scarves with splashy flowers, quaint poodles or neat geometric patterns. The tablecloth can become a dress, the curtains can be made into bags with headscarf linings . . . It's a lovely way to recycle – instead of those pieces of fabric being wasted, you will have transformed them into covetable clothes and accessories.[19]

'Old things must not be thrown away,' said Mary Pressy in 1795. And in many homes now materials are kept for reuse. Janice, an academic and artist, described how she made herself a raw silk dress and matching hat to wear to her brother's wedding. It turned out to be the finale for her dressmaking, but fifty years later in 2021 some of the silk was still at work – incorporated into an artwork and some as a rag under the sink in her printing studio. Beatrice has made original bespoke shirts and other items as a part-time business at home in London for many years. 'More recently I have been hand sewing quilts from the mountain of remnants I have accumulated. I've had such fun arranging the colours together. I'm on my third quilt now.'

In Chapter Three hoarding was revealed to be part of something more complex than mere storage. Underlining this, it has been said that there is a form of keeping stuff in which possessions are accumulated 'in their fullness of shape and diversity, gilded with the patina of relationships'. In this scenario, familiar to people who sew, possessions are 'not being protected from use but preserved for use', without ever losing 'their rapport with the present'.[20] Elaine's sewing story is a perfect example of how sewing with care can serve to reconfigure a valued piece and embody human relationships. After describing her creation of her daughter's wedding dress as the best achievement of her sewing life, Elaine moved on to another special project –

> the Christening dress I made for my son's children from his wife's Harrods wedding dress – I had to brace myself to cut into the gorgeous silk taffeta . . . with a chiffon over skirt with shadow embroidery in a Celtic knot design (his wife is Irish). To date it has been worn by my five Irish grandchildren, four of their cousins and a friend's baby who is one of twins, so it's already a family heirloom.

Today vintage clothing is attracting attention. The word 'vintage' is usually understood to describe clothing over twenty years old, often second-hand but not always and not old enough to be considered antique or historical. It can fetch high prices when it bears well-known labels. In societies with an abundance of affordable new clothing, shopping for vintage and designer names is an elective option and often a conscious alternative clothing strategy. In some cases it can be an art form and a fun quest for wearable collectables, all helped by the recent growth in dedicated shops and online buying and selling sites. Vintage clothing may be designed and made to higher standards and with better materials than new fast fashion and can therefore lend itself better to adaptation. It also allows a more sustainable form of stylish statement wardrobe without purchasing new.

Obviously not all vintage garments are the same. When the late Queen Elizabeth's granddaughter Princess Beatrice married in 2020, she wore a borrowed vintage dress, not from a charity shop but nothing less than a silk and diamanté evening gown designed by royal couturier Sir Norman Hartnell for her grandmother in the early 1960s. The gown had been worn in public by the queen on several occasions. Shortened and with sleeves added, it was said to be chosen for its latest reincarnation as a suitably sustainable option and partly as a tribute to the queen, who also lent her own wedding tiara. Weddings, like christenings, are often occasions for the reappearance of treasured family things, worn with pride and more motivated by sentiment and tradition than thrift.

Stylish looks can be conjured up from charity-shop finds by enthusiasts with the nous to do it, but at the same time for countless people all over the world, second-hand, third-hand garments and beyond are the only available clothing options. Where there is some money to spare, used clothing can still be welcome, even if not destined for some sewing makeover. However, an aptitude for sewing allows the buyer to browse the second-hand market with a different eye, spotting how curtains or garments could be repaired, altered, embellished, transformed or cannibalized for materials for other purposes. Disconnected by time or context from known people, in a charity shop or car boot sale, these things are neutral. But anyone who has cleared a house after the death of a loved one well knows how hard this task can be because the familiarity, even a lingering perfume, can invest the things left behind with emotive power that complicates their future use or repurposing. Plenty of adventurous style-seekers welcome vintage and second-hand clothing as a kind of dressing-up box, a means of generating original fashions all their own motivated by a desire to exit the mainstream rather than by an aversion to fashion altogether. Research into the viability of a circular business model for clothing in the UK indicates there is significant public interest in getting clothes in second-hand or vintage form. Most second-hand items are bought from commercial retailers, which results in better garment longevity than buying new – 5.9 years compared to 4. Charity shops came next, followed by online resale sites.[21] With current rises in the cost of living, this market may expand. The circulation of used clothes and household textiles, whether purchased in cash transactions in street markets or second-hand shops or acquired informally outside the cash system, from relatives or neighbours or as perks of employment, has been critical in clothing strategies in times past. As a common practice today, it remains a significant other market, reducing consumption of new things, an incidental effect for some but a cornucopia of novelty and bargains for those who seek to live more sustainably.

When repair could be a relentless chore in the battle to maintain the textile resources of a pre-industrial household, the arrival of affordable ready-mades did not solve the problem. Ready-made clothing in the late nineteenth and early twentieth centuries was often made of cheap fabrics, frequently flammable, unreliably sized and poorly assembled. At that time, preventative mending or altering was recommended as a precaution for those of limited means, such as teachers or clerks and other white-collar working women who needed to look ship-shape despite being restricted to inferior-quality clothing in their scant wardrobes. It was sewing to the rescue.

Mending and altering are two branches of the great art of Needlework which no woman can afford to despise in these days of ready-made frocks and shop-bought costumes (suits). Turnings may be insufficient, buttons sewn on with too scant stitches, hooks and eyes trembling to fall off, but these deficiencies very easily can be put to right. A shop-bought costume that does not fit, however, is not cheap at any price. Learn, therefore, how to make alterations in the most common sense and practical fashion, and take preventative measures, before the garment is worn for the first time, to overcome the little deficiencies that we may expect to discover in the 'ready-mades.'[22]

Practical advice of this sort in books and magazines was in tune with other voices that sought to empower consumers who felt seduced by fashionable styles, urging them to avoid the trap of buying cheap goods that flattered to deceive. With needle and thread to hand they had an economical solution to the problem of how to look well on limited means.

Poor people stretched for even basic commodities in the past often wore sub-standard clothing or second-hand and hand-me-down items. Keeping such hard-used garments in use required more mending than better or newer ones did. Mending occupied wives and mothers endlessly, although it shouldn't be assumed they did it with enthusiasm or skill. It was more than likely that they learnt mending methods in their frequent plain sewing lessons at school, or, before compulsory schooling, at their mother's knee, but with families of their own it was applied in more challenging circumstances. Just before the First World War, a woman living in one of the poorest areas of London in one room with her working husband and four children said she mended her husband's clothes in the evening 'as soon as he gets them off'.[23] Without spare sets, mending kept the clothes of working sons and husbands in functional repair and underpinned their employment, a crucial contribution to household economy by wives and daughters. Mending was taught in schools for generations, frequently aimed at poor children to make them better stewards of their own future household resources but also to make them better domestic servants. They were needed in wealthier households where large quantities of clothing and household linen required constant upkeep, not least because rough laundry methods in the past inflicted more damage on the natural fibres and dyes then in use. The teaching of mending, alongside other plain sewing, was freighted with moral and religious values, as we saw in Chapter Two.

The UK's *Make-do and Mend* campaign (1942–5) was nationwide education of a very different character, a war effort to reduce the need for manufacturing new civilian clothing through the encouragement of domestic sewing. It was designed to extend the use of existing cloth and clothing by recycling, makeovers, renovations and repairs of all kinds. It was aimed at girls and women of all backgrounds and partly at boys' groups such as the Boy Scouts. The government promoted it by substantial advertising on the radio and in magazines, posters, leaflets and cinemas to back up thousands of local classes. Promotion and teaching on this scale certainly had an effect, utilizing existing skills and developing new ones among a population responsive to calls for patriotic action on the home front.[24] The campaign in general, and the linked advertising figure of Mrs Sew-and-Sew in particular, highlighted the preservation and reuse of cloth and clothing as never before. Some grumbled that it was yet again middle-class women telling working-class women how to do things they had always done, war or no war. It remains today as a folk memory rather than a habit, except for many of those raised as war babies or taught by mothers and grandmothers who never shed it. As time passed, mending slipped out of the school curriculum and, for many people, out of use. It's good to be reminded what this means.

> Remember that spare button. The fact that it's still sewn into new clothes speaks to a deeply rooted tradition of repair which fast fashion has only recently swept away on a tidal wave of cheap clothes. It reminds us what we know to be true: there's really no reason we should be throwing away so much perfectly good clothing for want of a small bit of stitching, or worse still, because it is declared to be out of season by an industry which demands exponentially increasing sales.[25]

Although substantial numbers of people today wouldn't know how to sew on that spare button, there is now no shortage of post-school informal ways to learn if they wished and to encounter other sustainable approaches to their clothing. Recent research in the UK found that 'over half of women and nearly a quarter of men expressed an interest in learning more about how to repair clothes.'[26] Looking around cities today, repair and alteration outlets are easy to find, often sited at dry cleaners, so there is always somewhere to get the work done by somebody else. Websites and blogs galore and a fresh generation of books by passionate menders and adapters represent a growing body of interest in DIY informed by environmental and other concerns. The new repair culture represents mending, recycling, altering and repurposing not as a chore but as creative and playful, and for many it has become a form of radical activism. For others, time-poor or daunted by making a whole new garment, or both, mending an old one can be a more immediate and fulfilling substitute. Mending and renovation as a starting point for needlecraft can bolster confidence in beginners. The variations in the standards of her darning pointed out by Rosanna Dix in 1853 and the fact that women in the past knew their own darning when they saw it can be attractive to menders engaged today in renovating their belongings. Some have taken variation to new extremes. 'It's okay if stitches aren't perfect. Like handwriting or illustration, each stitch has the signature and imprint of its maker . . . we want to embrace the handmade element . . . and recognize that our stitches were made by a human and not by a machine. These personal touches add intimacy, beauty, and even grace to a naturally aged garment.'[27] This is a changed view of what constitutes good repair or renovation. In the context of today's machine age, 'the handmade' is generally welcomed, and no doubt this view contributes to the popularity of the shift from discrete invisible to eye-catching visible mending that valorizes difference. Differences between the new repair and the original article and between the repairer's outfit and homogenized fashion are celebrated. Imperfections are a new kind of language. One commercial wool mending system sells its kits in bright colours intended to be seen. At a practical level, it has been estimated that repair, by the owner themselves or paid for, adds on average 1.3 years to the life of a garment. For some people it will add a lot more.[28]

Tom van Deijnen, a pioneering teacher of visible mending and known as Tom of Holland, sets great store by 'the relationship between (mended) item and user'. Travelling slowly in the opposite direction to fast throwaway fashion, he values the old tradition of preservation but wants to make it not just visible but expressive: 'My interest in using traditional techniques for creating and repairing textiles means that the acts of creating and mending are in constant conversation with each other.'[29] The popularity of visible mending combines with a strong emotional attachment to the article under repair and respect and even fascination for its ageing. Reversing the traditional preference for disguising repair, this kind of practice is uninhibited and varied, offering the chance for personalization. It is probably the first time this has been an acceptable proposition in the West. It fits well with Western enthusiasm for some traditional Asian textile recycling, renovation and reinforcement techniques that expose the layering, patching and stitching involved and add a conspicuous patina to the piece, such as Korean patchwork pojagi, Japanese boro and sashiko, or kantha work, a technique that originated in the Indian subcontinent, where the stitches often form the effect of wavelets. These old-established techniques were born of the necessity to keep even the most worn-out and damaged pieces of cloth in use by layering them together with stitching, giving haphazard surface effects. The results could be used for clothing, bedding or wrapping, all an outcome of a zero-waste approach. The techniques are now adopted in other countries as an alternative way of extending fabric life and also as a hobby involving meditative stitching, and are regarded as creative and attractive. Textile artist Claire Wellesley-Smith describes how with kantha 'the softness of the worn cloth and solidity created through the simple stitching feels comforting to touch'.[30] In this new context the appropriated technique is now a matter of choice for those who enjoy doing it and far removed from its roots in poverty and the associated stigma. Old surviving pieces worked in this way have become collectors' items, another signal of the esteem in which once-disparaged practices are now held.

Mending has been seen as women's work, but some men have always mended their own clothes, typically in men-only situations and *in extremis*. Sailors always knew how to mend the sails they depended on and repaired their own clothes at sea. There are countless scenarios when mending is vital. Injured in the Battle of Arnhem in 1944 when serving in the British army, Lieutenant Timothy Hall was admitted to hospital. There he darned the holes made in his battle smock by the mortar fragments that hit him, so he could keep it to wear as a prisoner of war, when it would be a valuable asset. It survives in a museum.[31] So boys and men can do it if they put their minds to it, and Tom van Deijnen is a reminder of that.

Looking at examples of hasty and botched mending on some historical garments in museum collections, it's hard not to conclude from them that mending was an unwelcome task. No doubt it felt as if there was just too much of it. Now it is gaining a following beyond sheer necessity because it can be seen as creative and sustainable, but it is still far from widespread and certainly not everybody's cup of tea, even when they are experienced makers and averse to waste. 'I regard mending as an unpleasurable chore,' Alyson explained. For her, fabric takes precedence. 'I try to recycle the fabric, either by making something else out of it or by giving it to fabric recycling.' Although Alyson has the necessary skills and does mend occasionally, her real enjoyment lies in the 'creativity of making something new which is much more exciting than mending.' Near my desk as an *aide-memoire* is an old suede wallet containing cards of stocking silks in different shades. On the outside are the words 'A stitch in time saves ladders,' a reminder that specific maintenance needs change over time as our wardrobes and attitudes shift. It contrasts with what today might be called visible unmending. Young women striding out today in their Doc Martens, shredded jeans or artfully patterned but conspicuously laddered tights delight in visible transgression. Historian Victoria Kelly has noted that 'it is only in a society in which nobody needs to be ragged that raggedness can be detached from shame, and used instead as an aesthetic strategy.'[32] In this case, the battered jeans and unmended tights become a personal stance against gender and consumerist norms, a kind of individualistic anti-repair manifesto.

Outside these trends, some people simply don't want to spend their time mending; life seems too pressured anyway. Fast fashion is made fast and used fast; its consumers don't expect or want durability. For these garments mending of any kind is inappropriate in many minds. It is a sad irony that immense quantities of the discarded synthetic fabrics used in fast fashion are more or less indestructible; for instance, it is thought that acrylics will take two hundred years to decay.

So why do repair and reuse retain their appeal today? It's a question that repays attention now that these practices are more in the public domain. What becomes clear is that they are often accompanied by renewed respect for the practical skills involved and the underlying values that drive a culture of preservation. It is also clear that there is a longevity to all this that pre-dates industrialization and even capitalism as we know it. When we recognize that these commonplace acts of maintenance are in effect a permanent feature of humanity's connection to cloth, today's practices and popularity look less transient, less modern, more embedded and more telling. But like all cultural practices, they shift over time and encounter resistance.

Preservation of stuff as a lived philosophy is exemplified, paradoxes and all, by the life of Edward Carpenter (1844–1929). He lived in an age of emerging awareness of women's rights and the related campaigns for clothing reform and at a time when throwaway fashion was hardly conceivable, but he has a contemporary relevance. Carpenter thought the multiple layers of cumbersome garments then in fashion were unnecessary for men or women. In his view, this superfluity increased the work of mending expected of women and at the same time hindered simpler ways of living. An Englishman of independent means, Carpenter was a charismatic radical free thinker, a sandal-wearing and sandal-making vegetarian, an early socialist and activist, a prolific writer, a political campaigner and pioneering sexual reformer. He is much admired still by present-day followers of his utopian ideals. For Carpenter it was precisely the rigidity of the domestic values of his bourgeois childhood that pushed him to alternative ways of thinking and living and into the realization that our relationship with stuff is complex. Carpenter has a particular relevance here due to his hands-on approach to what he called 'the simplification of life'. He would have embraced the new enthusiasm for more mindful consumption and his alternative lifestyle chimes with current ideas about the importance of restoring community and fellowship. When he moved to a 7-acre smallholding, he and his companions grew vegetables and fruit and kept chickens, a far cry from his own well-to-do urban upbringing. When Carpenter consciously adopted 'a more simple life and diet' sharing the life of rural workers, he came to realize for himself that 'bourgeois ideal of society', the mode of life he was raised in, 'cannot be kept up without perpetuating the slavery of woman'. He was thinking of all the provisioning and preparation of heavy meals and cleaning of over-furnished interiors, but also the maintenance of elaborate clothing. He regarded the endless darning of hosiery as 'another of the links in the chain which binds the women-folk down'. Having set out to simplify his own clothing, and do his own mending, he argued publicly for the health-giving properties of reducing the weight and number of garments and noted the savings in time that followed:

> who does not know the time which is spent, in any self-supporting household, in patching and mending the numerous garments worn, putting in fresh linings and renewing pockets? – time which might be largely saved if the number of garments was much reduced, and their construction altogether simplified from the beginning.

Carpenter's gay and politicized household was a magnet for aspiring socialists and passionate campaigners and did nothing by halves. His enthusiastic approach to waste would win him fans today, though his political radicalism may be understood less than his lifestyle. He didn't invent these particular tricks, but he enthusiastically cut up old hats and shoes to make ties for wall-climbing plants; old undergarments became bandages, then floor cloths. His lyrical account of his coat's life journey, written in 1866, is worth quoting at length as a hymn to recycling and what we would now recognize as an admirable carbon footprint:

When my coat has worn itself into an affectionate intimacy with my body, when it has served for Sunday best, and for weekdays, and got weather-stained out in the fields with sun and rain – then, faithful, it does not part from me, but getting itself cut up into shreds and patches descends to form a hearthrug for my feet. After that, when worn through, it goes into the kennel and keeps my dog warm, and so after lapse of years, retiring to the manure-heaps and passing out onto the land, returns to me in the form of potatoes for my dinner; or, being pastured by my sheep, reappears upon their backs as the material of new clothing. Thus it remains a friend to all time, grateful to me for not having despised and thrown it away when it first got behind the fashions.[33]

Carpenter's complex legacy remains somewhat elusive. A recent major biography concludes 'Now you see him: now you don't.'[34] Nevertheless, for anyone these days seeking to reconfigure their own habits, Carpenter's life, and in particular his pioneering critique and personal avoidance of materialism and over-consumption, might well provide some inspiration for makers and menders. He saw it as a step towards living freely and well, but also as an internal journey or 'an introspective psychological exploration'.[35]

It is striking how many writers today also describe their efforts to reshape their relationship with fashion and the contents of their wardrobes, of which repair is so often a part, as a form of journey and often arduous self-examination. Kate Fletcher observes that for many it 'seems almost impossible to take this psychic leap' out of the prevailing fashion system, to see beyond its unsustainable values and behaviours to alternative ones.[36] Is it even harder for women than men to distance themselves from fashion? Fashion's offspring, fast and ultra-fast fashion, were unknown to Carpenter but he would recognize the challenges they bring to a desire to preserve. However, in our Anthropocene age, preservation takes on an altogether more urgent and inclusive meaning that was unknown to previous generations. In this setting, mending has become a kind of metaphor – and perhaps it always has been. The context for repair and reuse of clothing includes some salutary statistics. In the UK, for example, it is estimated that 'four in five people own clothes that have not been worn because they no longer fit or need altering', all pointing to paradoxes of over-consumption and under-use.[37] So, the rationale for extending the life of garments by repair and renovation is emphasized yet again in this twenty-first century. It's fair to guess that much more repair work took place in homes in the past than today, but it has particular resonance now. It certainly matters to Pippa.

> I repair seams that have gone, I put on buttons. I do my best to repair clothing that have holes or wear. Often it's a simple job. I don't have the confidence to repair zips. I would take that to a repair shop. I like knowing I have beaten the throwaway culture! Every time I put a button on I think, yep, that's another item that has avoided the bin.

Aspiring to prolong the life of garments and household textiles is not confined to the personal sphere; the commercial sector is also gingerly putting its corporate toes in the water. The challenges are huge. The environmental cost of fabrics starts long before we buy them. Textile and clothing production have their own wastage problems at factory level, including deadstock, and our own usage of our clothes – washing, drying, significant shedding of micro-plastics in some instances, disposal all add to the environmental cost. Considerable technical progress has been made in recycling fabric by separating fibres out by mechanical, chemical and now thermal means, which allows them to be reused. State- and national-level legislation on cleaning up the textile and fashion industry already in the pipeline in the USA and Europe may hasten progress further, added to the green shoots of regulations on repairability of consumer goods. Some fashion brands, such as Cos, part of the global group H&M, and Levi's, one of the most instantly recognizable brands of denim clothing, now offer repair and buy-back services for their own pieces. They emphasize their progress in using recycled and recyclable fabrics. The latter actively promotes DIY repairs and repurposing projects online. These initiatives are one part of the corporate push to establish green and ethical credentials. It is difficult to measure their impact, but if the past is anything to go by, brands that offer repair services on their goods may simply monetize the process rather than build home repairability into the initial design brief, and thus far these initiatives apply more at the middle and upper end of the ready-made market. Ten years ago, Kate Fletcher and Lynda Grose, experts in fashion and sustainability, noted that the 'limitations of and possibilities for repair rarely, if ever influence the design of a new garment.' But if this changes, it is likely that smaller fashion businesses and indie designers will be the source of the creative solutions. Many fashion colleges round the world have research and teaching programmes committed to sustainability and many of their recent graduates are fired up for change. Fletcher and Grose believe that as fashion designers engage more with their wider social and cultural context, at a time when fashion's values are under scrutiny, they can take opportunities to 'widen design's sphere of influence'. They see fashion designers working in new ways 'as communicators, educators, facilitators, activists and entrepreneurs'.[38]

Efforts to change can be found all over the globe.

Breathing new life into discarded, torn or stained garments diverts, or delays, waste from being sent to landfill. The techniques involved in bringing a disused garment back to pristine condition are many and varied and have become the specialist territory of a growing body of designers who fuse thrift with creativity and embellishment . . . These pieces defy the general trend of downgrading the value placed on already-used materials, and are evidence that 'upcycling' – that is, *adding* value through thoughtful reclamation – is possible.[39]

But progress towards sustainability, often promoted through the idea of a circular economy, itself a contested model, remains achingly slow in textile production and finishing and in garment manufacture and distribution. These industries are fragmented, unregulated and lack shared science or methods and means of measuring or ensuring progress. Despite these hurdles, pressure to improve systems and products is being felt at management, board, shareholder and investor levels round the world, as well as at government level. How could it not be when consumer pressure is growing? In the UK alone, a recent report showed that a quarter of consumers surveyed said 'they think about sustainability all the time when shopping for fashion, and half sometimes think about it'. The same survey revealed that 54 per cent have made 'a conscious decision to be more sustainable when buying fashion.' Consumers are also starting to question sustainability levels in fashion packaging, with a third saying they 'have rejected a purchase because of unsustainable packaging'.[40] Nevertheless, there remains plenty of commercial greenwash. Consumers should beware of practices that simply swap social injustices and inequalities of one kind for another, amounting to tinkering around within the dominant fashion system. Yet, at the time of writing, the experience of COVID-19 and significant hikes in energy prices and the cost of living are piling on top of existing environmental and ethical concerns, all suggesting that a new age of critical consumer engagement and resistance may yet dawn. Fixing that torn sleeve is a repair with attitude. The thrift it represents is a philosophy and a statement of intent to fix bigger things. Is it too much to hope that future generations look back and see that repair as a symbolic step towards eventual global resilience?

All this can feel overwhelming, yet menders, renovators and recyclers at an individual level are finding creative and transforma-tive responses which won't solve those problems in need of systemic change, but do offer new language and new perspec-tives that open up spaces for us all. Menders and makers are tapping into a different way of living in the world. Their localized agency can reflect broader issues and their micro changes can help to build bigger ones for themselves or others. In her book *Mending Matters*, Katrina Rodabaugh coined the word 'mend-fulness' for her approach. She describes 'mending on a personal level of mending habits, mending false beliefs, and mending torn denim while simultaneously mending my relationship to the fashion industry'.[41] Collective Mending Sessions, for example, founded by American artist Catherine Reinhart, is an ongoing project that aims to connect people and communities through slow sewing group sessions engaged in the repair of abandoned textiles, another metaphor for mending as socially aware connectivity.[42] Quilt artist Sara Impey redeployed a friend's gift of 'a length of old mattress ticking', acquired at a boot sale and kept unused for fifteen years. 'The design was a striking red and white stripe and I stitched a text on to the stripes speculating how and why a utilitarian piece of fabric like this hadn't been thrown away and, more broadly, why we hang on to textiles that we recall from childhood or that have a special meaning for us. I called it "Social Fabric".'[43] Repairing clothes in various ways is like making clothes: it connects the stitcher to those who taught them and to previous generations. For young Jay, using old tools is part of the experience. 'Almost all of my tools and materials are second-hand or recycled; this is very important to me. This does reflect my wider attitude to life.' Textile conservators, of course, have always understood the necessity for slow and careful stitching as a route to prolonging the life of vulnerable historical pieces and the human stories they embody.

Latter-day thrift as practised in everyday repair, recycling and upcycling is not only about saving money. Indeed, for anyone who equates their time with money, it doesn't make economic sense. In the dictionary, 'thrift' has historic links back to the word 'thrive', an echo of the well-being that menders as well as makers report when they've extended the useful life of their possessions and made things in the first place. When the material world is in miniature form it can be engrossing – think doll's houses, pocket gadgets – and darning, to take just one form of repair, occupies a little cosmos of its own. The essential material properties of the damaged cloth, its yarn and its construction, come into close visual and haptic focus, needing almost microscopic attentiveness. It is likely that improvisation is called for, itself a mini-adventure in creativity. The intimate field of work involved in mending of this kind can be as enthralling as the larger task of making in the first place. The stillness and problem-solving required may be sufficient rewards in themselves, providing some restorative mental space, and respite from concerns in the world beyond. Cloth eventually succumbs to wear, damage and degradation, but the care, time and thought invested in making it last longer, regardless of standards of the work, are what give mending its twin utilitarian and personal value.

Is mending a kind of healing of ourselves as well as our things? Pulling things back together instead of letting them tear apart, delaying their decay or death, repairing things to restart their useful life, even reimagining a new purpose and future for them: these may all chime with a deeper human need to endure. Mending is hope and optimism, even when it is a chore, because it is for life and not against it. While budget, self-sufficiency, resistance to over-consumption and environmental sustainability may all come into play when we recycle, darn or patch, we may also be mustering the means to preserve emotion and memory, to maintain attachments, for instance, through saving a much-loved garment that has been part of our life for a long time. Human resilience takes many mental and physical forms. Stitching to mend and re-create is one of them.

REFERENCES

Introduction

1 Laurel Thatcher Ulrich, *The Age of Homespun: Objects and Stories in the Creation of an American Myth* (New York, 2010), p. 414.
2 Frank R. Wilson, *The Hand: How Its Use Shapes the Brain, Language, and Human Culture* (New York, 1999), p. 277.
3 Tim Ingold, *Making: Anthropology, Archaeology, Art and Architecture* (Abingdon, 2013), p. 122.
4 Mary Schoeser, *Textiles: The Art of Mankind* (London, 2012), p. 11.
5 Maureen Daly Goggin, introduction to *Women and the Material Culture of Needlework and Textiles, 1750–1950*, ed. Goggin and Beth Fowkes Tobin (Abingdon, 2009), p. 3.

1 Hands, Hearts and Needles

1 Jane Munro, 'Hands at Work', in *The Human Touch: Making Art, Leaving Traces*, ed. Elenor Ling, Suzanne Reynolds and Jane Munro (Cambridge, 2020), p. 38.
2 David Gauntlett, *Making Is Connecting: The Social Power of Creativity, from Craft and Knitting to Digital Everything* (Cambridge, 2018), pp. 32–3. Gauntlett includes computers and online practices as potential tools for beneficial creativity.
3 Amy Twigger Holroyd, *Folk Fashion* (London, 2019), p. 186.
4 Gauntlett, *Making Is Connecting*, p. 33.
5 WHO Europe, *Health Evidence Network Synthesis Report 67: What Is the Evidence on the Role of the Arts in Improving Health and Well-Being? A Scoping Review*, 2019, https://apps.who.int. See also briefings on research into craft and its benefits on 'Research and Policy', www.craftscouncil.org.uk, accessed 5 January 2023.

6 Frank R. Wilson, *The Hand: How Its Use Shapes the Brain, Language, and Human Culture* (New York, 1999), pp. 208–9.

7 Raymond Tallis, *The Hand: A Philosophical Inquiry into Human Being* (Edinburgh, 2003), p. 286.

8 Sara Impey, 'Negative Space, Positive Time', studio quilt, cotton, 93 × 74 cm, International Quilt Museum, Lincoln, Nebraska, USA, object no. 2017.089.0004, www.internationalquiltmuseum.org, accessed 5 January 2023.

9 Tallis, *The Hand*, p. 229.

10 Ibid., p. 222.

11 Peter Korn, *Why We Make Things and Why It Matters: The Education of a Craftsman* (London, 2017), p. 124.

12 Tallis, *The Hand*, pp. 178–9.

13 Raymond Tallis, *Michelangelo's Finger: An Exploration of Everyday Transcendence* (London 2010), p. 122.

14 Richard Sennett, *The Craftsman* (London, 2008), p. 230.

15 Ibid., p. 9.

16 David Pye, *The Nature and Art of Workmanship* (London, 1995), p. 92.

17 Sherry Turkle, *Evocative Objects: Things We Think With* (Cambridge, MA, 2011), p. 5.

18 'fc254', 'Kent's PhD Quilt', https://blogs.kent.ac.uk, 1 May 2019.

19 Ken Robinson and Lou Aronica, *Finding Your Element: How to Discover Your Talents and Passions and Transform Your Life* (London, 2014), p. 193.

20 Sarah Gilbert and Catherine Green, *Vaxxers: The Inside Story of the Oxford AstraZeneca Vaccine and the Race Against the Virus* (London, 2021), pp. 261–2.

21 *The Ladies' Work-table Book* (New York, 1844), p. vii.

22 Mrs Warren, *How I Managed My House on Two Hundred Pounds a Year* (London, 1864), p. 85.

23 James Edward Austen-Leigh, *A Memoir of Jane Austen* [1871] (Oxford, 1926), p. 98.

24 *The Diaries of Sarah Hurst, 1759–1762: Life and Love in 18th Century Horsham*, transcribed by Barbara Hurst, ed. Susan C. Djabri (Horsham, 2003), p. 127.

25 Bridget Long, '"Regular Progressive Work Occupies My Mind Best": Needlework as a Source of Entertainment, Consolation and Reflection', *Textile*, XIV/2 (2016), pp. 176–87.

26 Flora Klickmann, ed., *The Cult of the Needle* (London, 1914), p. 51.

27 Etka Kaul, personal communication; she also maintains a website: www.ektakaul.com.

28 The Quilters' Guild, '10 reasons why your New Year's resolution should be to do more sewing . . .', www.quiltersguild.org.uk, 5 January 2023.

29 Deb Taylor, 'Social Prescribing Linked Me to Art Which Saved My Life', www.england.nhs.uk, accessed 5 January 2023. For further research on social prescribing see also 'What Is Social Prescribing?', www.kingsfund.org.uk, accessed 5 January 2023. For more on the health benefits of knitting see www.stitchlinks.com, accessed 11 January 2023.

30 Matthew Crawford, *The World Beyond Your Head* (London, 2016), p. 8.

31 Marybeth Stalp, 'Quilt Rhymes with Guilt', in *Quilting: The Fabric of Everyday Life* (Oxford, 2007), pp. 95–109.

32 Crawford, *The World Beyond Your Head*, p. 21.

33 Ibid., p. 21.

34 See www.seamwork.com, accessed 5 January 2023.

35 Korn, *Why We Make Things and Why it Matters*, pp. 55, 49.

36 Crawford, *The World Beyond Your Head*, pp. 25–7.

2 Learning to Sew

1 Harriet Martineau, *Autobiography* [1877] (London, 1983), vol. 1, p. 26.

2 Mrs C. (born Hackney, 1902), oral history transcript, and *Children's Employment, 2nd Report*, Parliamentary Papers (London, 1864), quoted in Anna Davin, *Growing up Poor: Home, School and Street in London, 1870–1914* (London, 1996), pp. 192 and 196.

3 Chaney reminiscing on the podcast *Comfort Eating with Grace Dent*, Series 1, Episode 7, 27 July 2021, available at https://podcasts.apple.com.

4 Bridget Long, 'The Needle not the Spindle? Domestic Training at the London Asylum or House of Refuge for Orphan and Deserted Girls in the Eighteenth Century', *London Journal: A Review of Metropolitan Society Past and Present*, XLIV/1 (2019), pp. 37–53.

5 See Vivienne Richmond, *Clothing the Poor in Nineteenth-Century England* (Cambridge, 2013), for more on schooling and needlework generally in the period. See also Sarah A. Gordon, *'Make it Yourself': Home Sewing, Gender, and Culture, 1890–1930* (New York, 2009), on learning to sew, pp. 47–78.

6 Rev. John D. Glennie, *Hints from an Inspector of Schools: School Needlework Made Useful and School Reading Made Intelligent* (London, 1858), pp. 5, 15–16, 14.

7 Vivienne Richmond, *A Remedy for Rents: Darning Samplers and Other Needlework from the Whitelands College Collection*, exh. cat., Constance Howard Gallery (London, 2016).

8 British Heart Foundation, 'The Big Stitch Campaign', www.bhf.org.uk, 2017.

9 Radio interview cited by Matthew Weaver, 'Medical Students "Raised on Screens Lack Skills for Surgery"', *The Guardian*, 30 October 2018, www.theguardian.com.

10 Mike Rose, *The Mind at Work: Valuing the Intelligence of the American Worker* (New York, 2014), p. 166.

11 Frank R. Wilson, *The Hand: How Its Use Shapes the Brain, Language, and Human Culture* (New York, 1999), p. 296.

12 Mrs E. Griffith, preface to *A Manual of Plain Needlework* (London, 1932).

13 Claire Wilcox, *Patchwork: A Life amongst Clothes* (London, 2020), p. 161.

14 'We conducted a survey (using Google Surveys) and found that one in five Britons (21 per cent) took up sewing or embroidery during the 2020 COVID-19 pandemic. However, more men aged between 25–34 (23 per cent) were bitten by the sewing bug compared to women of the same age (21 per cent). In fact, sewing among younger men proved to be more appealing than getting into fitness (20 per cent), gardening (13 per cent), or even learning a new language (15 per cent).' Published at https://sewingcraft.brother.eu, 2021.

15 Personal communication with Rachel Hart, founder of Ray Stitch, London, 26 January 2021.

16 Sadhbh O'Sullivan, 'How Much It Actually Costs to Make Your Own Clothes', www.refinery29.com, 15 June 2022.

17 Sherry Schofield-Tomschin, 'Home Sewing: Motivational Changes in the Twentieth Century', in *The Culture of Sewing: Gender, Consumption and Home Dressmaking*, ed. Barbara Burman (Oxford, 1999), pp. 97–110.

18 Addie Martindale and Ellen McKinney, 'Why Do They Sew? Women's Motivations to Sew Clothing for Themselves', *Clothing and Textiles Research Journal*, XXXVIII/1 (2020), pp. 32–48.

19 Claire Mackaness, at www.beautifulthingshq.com, accessed 5 January 2022.

20 Martindale and McKinney, 'Why Do They Sew?'

21 Abby Glassenberg, 'Quilting Trends Survey Results 2020', www.craftindustryalliance.org, 19 June 2020.

22 Dr Jade Halbert, 'Making a Dress for the First Time Was Intimidating – and Brilliant', *i Newspaper*, https://inews.co.uk, 30 June 2020.

23 Roger Kneebone, *Expert: Understanding the Path to Mastery* (London, 2020), p. 65.

24 Jean-Sacha Barikumutima, 'Sewing a Better Future: How Vocational Training Turned Joselyne's Life Around', www.unicef. org, 30 July 2021

25 Peter Dormer, 'The Language and Practical Philosophy of Craft', in *The Culture of Craft: Status and Future*, ed. Dormer (Manchester, 1997), p. 219.

26 Sue Stuart-Smith, *The Well-Gardened Mind: Rediscovering Nature in the Modern World* (London, 2021), p. 65.

3 A Material World

1 For more about the origins and making of Harris tweed, see Victoria Finlay, *Fabric: The Hidden History of the Material World* (London, 2021), pp. 175–201.

2 Annette B. Weiner and Jane Schneider, eds, *Cloth and Human Experience* (Washington, DC, 1989), p. 2.

3 Claire Wilcox, *Patchwork: A Life amongst Clothes* (London, 2020), p. 129.

4 Guillermo de Osma, *Mariano Fortuny: His Life and Work* (London, 2015), p. 157.

5 Hilary Spurling, 'Material World: Matisse, His Art and His Textiles', in *Matisse, His Art and His Textiles: The Fabric of Dreams*, exh. cat., Royal Academy, London (2004), p. 23.

6 Ibid., pp. 15–16.

7 Marybeth C. Stalp, *Quilting: The Fabric of Everyday Life* (Oxford, 2007), p. 78.

8 *A Winter's Tale*, Act IV, scene 7. 'Lawn' was then a delicate linen, 'Cyprus' a lightweight gauzy cloth.

9 Clydebank Life Story Group, *Working Days: An Anthology* (Dumbarton, 2006), p. 4.

10 Hardy Amies, *Just So Far* (London, 1954), p. 63.
11 National Museums Scotland, African Commemorative Textiles Project with Edinburgh College of Art, 2016–17, www.nms.ac.uk.
12 Chapel Hill Zen Center, 'Taking the Precepts, Sewing Buddha's Robe', www.chzc.org, accessed 10 June 2022.
13 Celia Eddy, 'Paupers, Penitents and Potentates: An Investigation of the Symbolism and Meaning in Some Patchwork Garments', *Quilt Studies: The Journal of the British Quilt Study Group*, 21 (2020), pp. 8–35.
14 Natalie Rothstein, ed., *Barbara Johnson's Album of Fashions and Fabrics* (London, 1987).
15 Thomas Fuller, *Worthies of England* [1662], cited in Florence M. Montgomery, *Textiles in America, 1650–1870* (New York, 1984), p. xvi.
16 Colin Gale and Jasbir Kaur, *Fashion and Textiles: An Overview* (Oxford, 2004), pp. 35, 154.
17 Sven Beckert, *Empire of Cotton: A New History of Global Capitalism* (London, 2015), p. 431.
18 Freda Millett, *Up at Five: Voices of the Half-Timers in Oldham's Cotton Mills* (Oldham, 1997), pp. 35 and 27.
19 United States Department of Agriculture, Foreign Agricultural Service, *Cotton: World Markets and Trade*, www.fas.usda.gov, January 2023.
20 Akhtar Mohammad Makoii, '"People Are Broken": Afghans Describe First Day Under Full Taliban Control', *The Guardian*, 31 August 2021, www.theguardian.com.
21 Newlines Institute for Strategy and Policy, *The Uyghur Genocide: An Examination of China's Breaches of the 1948 Genocide Convention*, www.newlinesinstitute.org, March 2021.
22 UK Parliament Environmental Audit Committee, *Fixing Fashion: Clothing Consumption and Sustainability*, https://publications.parliament.uk, 19 February 2019; see also Cotton Campaign, 'Leading the Fight Against State-Imposed Forced Labor in the Cotton Fields of Turkmenistan', www.cottoncampaign.org, 1 February 2023.
23 Adam Sneyd, *Cotton* (Cambridge, 2016), p. 59.
24 Beckert, *Empire of Cotton*, p. 429.
25 European Environment Agency, *Textiles in Europe's Circular Economy*, www.eea.europa.eu, 2019.

26 Ibid. For more on fossil-fuel fibres and supply chains see Changing Markets Foundation, 'Dressed to Kill: Fashion Brands' Hidden Links to Russian Oil in a Time of War', http://changingmarkets. org, November 2022.

27 Will Grimond and Josie Warden, *Fast Fashion's Plastic Problem: Sustainability and Material Usage in Online Fashion*, Royal Society of Arts, 11 June 2021, www.thersa.org.

28 Rebecca Burgess with Courtney White, *Fibershed: Growing a Movement of Farmers, Fashion Activists, and Makers for a New Textile Economy* (White River, VT, 2019).

29 See www.stonycreekcolors.com, accessed 1 February 2023.

30 Textile Exchange, 'Organic Cotton Market Report', October 2022, www.textileexchange.org.

4 In the Gently Closed Box

1 Gaston Bachelard, *The Poetics of Space* [1958] (Boston, MA, 1969), pp. 83 and 85.

2 Ruth Schwartz Cowan, *More Work for Mother: The Ironies of Household Technology from the Open Hearth to the Microwave* (London, 1989), pp. 9–10.

3 Robert Scott-Moncrieff, ed., *Lady Grisell Baillie's Household Book, 1692–1733* (Edinburgh, 1911), p. 280.

4 *The Work-Box; or, Grand-Papa's Present* (London, 1828), pp. 7 and 3.

5 'A Lady', *The Workwoman's Guide* (London, 1840), p. 15.

6 Linda Baumgarten, *What Clothes Reveal: The Language of Clothing in Colonial and Federal America* (Williamsburg, VA, 2002), p. 213.

7 National Maritime Museum, Greenwich, London, sailor's housewife, object ID AAA2161.

8 Mary Brooks Picken, *Singer Sewing Book*, 3rd edn (London, 1961), p. 7.

9 See 'Organize Your Sewing Space in 60 Minutes or Less', www.allpeoplequilt.com, accessed 9 January 2023.

10 Mary Ann Kilner, *The Adventures of a Pincushion designed chiefly for the use of young ladies* (London, 1779–89?), no pagination.

11 Adam Smith, *An Inquiry into the Nature and Causes of the Wealth of Nations* (London, 1776), Book 1, Chapter 1: 'Of the Division of Labour', p. 6.

12 David Pye, *The Nature and Art of Workmanship* (London, 1995), pp. 28–9.
13 Averil Colby, *Patchwork* (London, 1976), p. 37.
14 Jill Oakes and Rick Riewe, *Our Boots: An Inuit Women's Art* (London, 1996), pp. 22–48.
15 Mary C. Baudry, 'Thimble and Thimble Ring Chronology', in *Findings: The Material Culture of Needlework and Sewing* (New Haven, CT, 2006), pp. 102–3.
16 Ibid., pp. 86–8.
17 Lynn Knight, *The Button Box: Lifting the Lid on Women's Lives* (London, 2016), p. 35.
18 Hilary Spurling, 'Material World: Matisse, His Art and His Textiles', in *Matisse, His Art and His Textiles: The Fabric of Dreams*, exh. cat., Royal Academy (London, 2004), p. 17.
19 *Making Smart Clothes: Modern Methods in Cutting, Fitting and Finishing* (New York, 1931), p. 4.
20 Sarah Levitt, 'Clothing Production and the Sewing Machine', *Textile Society Magazine*, 9 (Spring 1988), pp. 2–13.
21 Charles Kent, *The Modern Seven Wonders of the World* (London, 1890), pp. 189 and 226.
22 Nicholas Oddy, 'A Beautiful Ornament in the Parlour or Boudoir: The Domestication of the Sewing Machine', in *The Culture of Sewing: Gender, Consumption and Home Dressmaking*, ed. Barbara Burman (Oxford, 1999), pp. 285–301.
23 Pye, *Nature and Art of Workmanship*, p. 84.
24 Karl Marx, *Capital: A Critique of Political Economy* [1867] (London, 1976), vol. I, pp. 601–3.
25 K. Watson, *The Library of Home Economics: A Complete Home-Study Course*, vol. X: *Textiles and Clothing* (Chicago, IL, 1907), p. 162.
26 Ruby, quoted in Marcia McLean, '"I dearly loved that machine": Women and the Objects of Home Sewing in the 1940s', in *Women and the Material Culture of Needlework and Textiles, 1750–1950*, ed. Maureen Daly Goggin and Beth Fowkes Tobin (Farnham, 2009), pp. 69–89.
27 Becky Knott, 'Pandemic Objects: Sewing Machine', www.vam.ac.uk, 20 May 2020.
28 The Great British Sewing Bee, 'The 2022 Sewers: Cristian', www.thegreatbritishsewingbee.co.uk, accessed 3 February 2023.
29 See www.helenhowes-sewingmachines.co.uk, accessed 3 February 2023.

5 Fruits of Our Work

1 'A Lady', *The Workwoman's Guide* (London, 1840), p. iv.
2 A 2010 overview of how people spend their time across Europe can be found at 'Harmonised European Time Use Surveys (HETUS) – Overview', https://ec.europa.eu, accessed 3 February 2023. Findings from an equivalent 2020 survey are not available at the time of writing.
3 See www.sewqueer.org, accessed 3 February 2023.
4 Eithne Farry, 'A Stitch in Time', *The Guardian*, 29 April 2008, www.theguardian.com.
5 Miles Brignall, 'Hobbycraft Reports 200% Boom in Online Sales since Start of Pandemic', *The Guardian*, 3 August 2020, www.theguardian.com. See also Alexandra Bradbury et al., *The Role of the Arts during the COVID-19 Pandemic*, www.artscouncil.org.uk, 31 August 2021.
6 Personal communication with Rachel Hart, founder of Ray Stitch, 26 February 2021.
7 Andrew Simms and Ruth Potts, *The New Materialism: How Our Relationship with the Material World Can Change for the Better*, November 2012, https://thenewmaterialism.org.
8 See 'The Great British Sewing Bee', www.bbc.co.uk, accessed 3 February 2023.
9 Nick Pope, 'Rise of the Sew Bro: Why Men Have Been Crafting Their Own Clothes Over Lockdown', *Esquire*, 18 August 2020, www.esquire.com.
10 Personal communication with Rachel Hart.
11 The Sewcialists, 'Our Mission', https://thesewcialists.com, accessed 3 February 2023.
12 E. Roberts, 'Women and the Domestic Economy, 1890–1970', in *Time, Family and Community: Perspectives on Family and Community History*, ed. Michael Drake (Oxford, 1994), pp. 139–40. Oral testimony from Mrs M.I.P., b. 1898.
13 Sarah A. Gordon, *'Make It Yourself': Home Sewing, Gender and Culture, 1890–1930* (New York, 2009), p. 42.
14 Clara E. Laughlin, ed., *Practical Home Dressmaker and Milliner* (New York, 1913), p. 3.
15 Seamwork, 'Why Do You Sew Your Own Clothes?', www.seamwork.com, 5 October 2022.
16 Gordon, *'Make It Yourself'*, pp. 145–6.

17 Seamwork, 'Is It Cheaper to Sew Your Own Clothes?', www. seamwork.com, 28 February 2022.

18 Naomi Alice Clarke, 'Exploring the Role of Sewing as a Leisure Activity for Those Aged 40 Years and Under', *Textile: Cloth and Culture*, XVIII/2 (2019), pp. 118–44.

19 Brittany Meiling, 'Home-Sewn Clothes Are Making a Comeback. But Is It Too Late for Dying Fabric Stores?', *San Diego Union-Tribune*, www.sandiegouniontribune.com, 31 January 2020.

20 Amy Twigger Holroyd, *Folk Fashion: Understanding Homemade Clothes* (London, 2019), pp. 91–2.

21 Dora Seton and Winifred Parker, *Essentials of Modern Dressmaking* (London, 1951), p. 7.

22 Michael Gardner, www.daddydressedmebymg.com, accessed 3 February 2021.

23 Party dress, 1944, UK, V&A Museum of Childhood, London, museum number MISC.265.1983.

24 Claire Wilcox, *Patchwork: A Life amongst Clothes* (London, 2020), pp. 159, 161.

25 Clarke, 'Exploring the Role of Sewing as a Leisure Activity', pp. 125–6.

26 Queen Mary's Needlework Guild, www.qmcg.org.uk, accessed 19 January 2021. Still under royal patronage, it is now known as Queen Mother's Clothing Guild in acknowledgement of the hands-on support of the mother of the late Queen Elizabeth II. Its members use a range of needlecrafts to make clothing and bedding, which it distributes along with new clothing to British charities helping vulnerable and homeless people of all ages. Knitted items now outnumber sewed ones by some margin among the members' contributions.

27 Vivienne Richmond, *Clothing the Poor in Nineteenth-Century England* (Cambridge, 2013), p. 298.

28 *The Lady's Bazaar & Fancy Fair Book* (London, 1875), pp. 13, 9, vi and 15.

29 Thea Thompson, *Edwardian Childhoods* (London, 1981), p. 108.

30 Linen and cotton patchwork coverlet, *c.* 1810, 262 ×232 cm, Jane Austen's House no. CHWJA:JAH153. Personal communication with Sophie Reynolds, Curator, Jane Austen's House, 14 April 2023, https://janeaustens.house.

31 Hattie Gordon, 'Mum Sewed Her Love and Care into My Liberty Print Frock', *The Guardian*, 28 November 2015, www. theguardian.com.

6 The Business of the Needle

1 Raising the Village, 'Tailor-Made Solutions to Eradicate Poverty', https://raisingthevillage.org, 8 April 2021. Equivalents given in U.S. dollars.
2 Clean Clothes Campaign, 'The Intersections of Environmental and Social Impacts of the Garment Industry (2022)', www.clean-clothes.org, August 2022.
3 World Bank, 'How Much Do Our Wardrobes Cost to the Environment?', www.worldbank.org, 23 September 2019.
4 Dr Jade Halbert, 'Making a Dress for the First Time Was Intimidating – and Brilliant', *i Newspaper*, https://inews.co.uk, 30 June 2020.
5 United Nations Alliance for Sustainable Fashion, 'Synthesis Report on United Nations System-Wide Initiatives Related to Fashion', www.unfashionalliance.org, October 2021, p. 4.
6 Barbara Garson, *All the Livelong Day: The Meaning and Demeaning of Routine Work* (Harmondsworth, 1994), p. x.
7 Clean Clothes Campaign, 'Out of the Shadows: A Spotlight on Exploitation', www.cleanclothes.org, 2020.
8 Clean Clothes Campaign, 'Bad Contracts', www.cleanclothes.org, accessed 11 January 2023.
9 Florence Bonnet, Françoise Carré, Martha Chen and Joann Vanek, 'Home-Based Workers in the World: A Statistical Profile', statistical brief no. 27 (January 2021), available online at www.wiego.org.
10 Garment Worker Diaries is a project channelling communication from garment workers around the world. It shares their stories for the purposes of informing industry and other decision-makers about what affects them. See https://workerdiaries.org, accessed 3 February 2023.
11 Clean Clothes Campaign, 'Out of the Shadows'.
12 Jess Cartner-Morley, 'Why the New Era of British Fashion Is All About the Factory', *The Guardian*, 14 August 2021, www.theguardian.com.
13 UK Fashion and Textile Association, 'Compendium of Industry Statistics and Analysis 2020', www.ukft.org, September 2021.
14 Kelsea Schumacher and Amanda L. Forster, 'Facilitating a Circular Economy for Textiles Workshop Report', p. 12, http://nlvpubs.nist.gov, accessed 2 February 2023.
15 Andrew Brooks, *Clothing Poverty: The Hidden World of Fast Fashion and Second-Hand Clothes* (London, 2015), pp. 241–6.

16 Arooj Rashid and Liz Barnes, 'Country of Origin: Reshoring Implication in the Context of the UK Fashion Industry', in *Reshoring of Manufacturing: Drivers, Opportunities, and Challenges* ed. Alessandra Vecchi (Cham, 2017), pp. 183–201. See also Dana Thomas, *Fashionopolis: The Price of Fast Fashion and the Future of Clothes* (London 2019), Chapter 5, 'Rightshoring', pp. 125–47.

17 Clean Clothes Campaign, 'Exploitation Made in Europe: Human Rights Abuse in Facilities Producing for German Fashion Brands in Ukraine, Serbia, Croatia and Bulgaria', www.cleanclothes.org, April 2022. See also the Clean Clothes Campaign Fashion Checker at https://fashionchecker.org, accessed 3 February 2023.

18 Labour Behind the Label, 'Boohoo and Covid-19', https://labourbehindthelabel.net, June 2020.

19 UN Guiding Principles on Business and Human Rights, *Due Diligence Guidance for Responsible Supply Chains in the Garment and Footwear Sector*, www.oecd.ilibrary.org, 7 March 2018.

20 UN Environment Programme, 'Sustainability and Circularity in the Textile Value Chain – Global Stocktaking', www.oneplanet-network.org, October 2020.

21 Ellen MacArthur Foundation, 'Who Should Be Responsible for Recycling Clothes?', https://ellenmacarthurfoundation.org, accessed 11 January 2023.

22 Martina Igini, '10 Stunning Fast Fashion Waste Statistics', www.earth.org, accessed 11 January 2023.

23 WRAP, 'Citizen Insights, Clothing Longevity and Circular Business Models Receptivity in the UK', www.wrap.org.uk, October 2022.

24 A good place to start is www.loveyourclothes.org.uk, a website run by WRAP (the Waste and Resources Action Programme), a climate action charity working globally to change the way things are produced, consumed and disposed of.

25 Clean Clothes Campaign, 'Poverty Wages', www.cleanclothes.org, accessed 3 February 2023.

26 Drapers, 'Sustainability and the Customer', www.drapersonline.com, 20 September 2022.

27 For a global context, see the UNDP, 'Sustainable Development Goals', www.undp.org, accessed 3 February 2023: a 'universal call to action to end poverty, protect the planet, and ensure that by 2030 all people enjoy peace and prosperity' with the recognition

that these goals are interdependent. These SDGs were adopted by the UN in 2015.

28 The International Accord for Health and Safety in the Textile and Garment Industry took effect on 1 September 2021. A similar new Accord for Pakistan is currently affirmed and under development, see 'Accord Steering Committee Member Brands Affirm Their Commitment to Pakistan Accord', https://internationalaccord. org, 23 January 2023.

29 Jess Cartner-Morley, 'Fashion Must Get on the Right Side of History', *The Guardian*, 17 September 2021, www.theguardian.com.

30 Beverly Lemire, '"In the hands of work women": English Markets, Cheap Clothing and Female Labour, 1650–1800', *Costume*, XXXIII (1999), pp. 23–35.

31 The London magazine *Punch* published a cartoon by John Tenniel that depicts a young woman at her dressmakers, admiring herself in her new ballgown but startled to see in the mirror the ghostly figure of a seamstress dying after her labours to sew it all in time. *Punch*, 4 July 1863. See also Christina Walkley, *The Ghost in the Looking Glass: The Victorian Seamstress* (London, 1981); and Beth Harris, ed., *Famine and Fashion: Needlewomen in the Nineteenth Century* (Abingdon, 2005).

32 Nichole M. Christian, 'A Landmark Of the Unspeakable: Honoring the Site Where 146 Died In the Triangle Shirtwaist Fire', *New York Times*, 26 March 2003, www.nytimes.com. See also Baruch College, 'Disasters: New York City (NYC) Triangle Shirtwaist Factory Fire – 1911', www.baruch.cuny.edu, accessed 3 February 2023.

33 Mrs Carl Meyer and Clementina Black, *Makers of Our Clothes: A Case for Trade Boards* (London, 1909), p. 11.

34 Ibid., p. 71.

35 Ibid., pp. 79–80.

36 S. P. Dobbs, *The Clothing Workers of Great Britain* (London, 1928), p. 28.

37 Vivienne Richmond, *Clothing the Poor in Nineteenth-Century England* (Cambridge, 2013), p. 97.

38 Lida Ahmadi, '"Nowhere to Go": Divorced Afghan Women in Peril as the Taliban Close In', *The Guardian*, 13 August 2021, www.guardian.com.

39 Islamic Relief Worldwide, 'Stories of Change', www.islamic-relief. org, accessed 11 January 2023.

40 Now called the Fédération de la Haute Couture et de la Mode, https://fhcm.paris, accessed 3 February 2023.

41 Christian Dior, *Dior by Dior: The Autobiography of Christian Dior* (London, 1958), p. 12.

42 Victoria and Albert Museum, 'Inside the World of Couture', www.vam.ac.uk, accessed 11 January 2023.

43 Divya Bala, 'How Millennials Have Become Couture's Biggest Client', *Vogue*, 11 July 2018, www.vogue.co.uk.

44 Hardy Amies, *Just So Far* (London, 1954), p. 256. See also Gavin Waddell, 'The Incorporated Society of London Fashion Designers: Its Impact on Post-War British Fashion', *Costume*, XXXV/1 (2001), pp. 92–115.

45 Paul H. Nystrom, *Economics of Fashion* (New York, 1928), p. 416.

46 *The Tailor and Cutter*, LXIV, 15 November 1929.

47 S. P. Dobbs, *The Clothing Workers of Great Britain* (London, 1928), p. 27.

48 Mary Brooks Picken, *Singer Sewing Book* (London, 1961), p. 2.

49 Beryl Bainbridge, *The Dressmaker* (London, 1974), p. 27.

7 The Alternative Stitch

1 CAIN Archive, 'Conflict Textiles', www.cain.ulster.ac.uk, accessed 11 January 2023. See also www.aidsmemorial.org, accessed 11 January 2023.

2 Carol Tulloch, 'There's No Place Like Home: Home Dressmaking and Creativity in the Jamaican Community of the 1940s to the 1960s', in *The Culture of Sewing: Gender, Consumption and Home Dressmaking*, ed. Barbara Burman (Oxford, 1999), pp. 111–25.

3 Sarah Corbett, *How to Be a Craftivist: The Gentle Art of Protest* (London, 2017), p. 84.

4 Heather Pristash, Inez Schaechterle and Sue Carter Wood, 'Identity, Embroidery, and Sewing: The Needle as Pen: Intentionality, Needlework, and the Production of Alternate Discourses of Power', in *Women and the Material Culture of Needlework and Textiles, 1750–1950*, ed. Maureen Daly Goggin and Beth Fowkes Tobin (Farnham, 2009), p. 27.

5 For more discussion of decorative needlework and counter narratives in the past see Ann Rosalind Jones and Peter Stallybrass, *Renaissance Clothing and the Materials of Memory* (Cambridge, 2000), pp. 134–71.

6 Rozsika Parker, *The Subversive Stitch* (London, 1984), p. 215.
7 Susan Frye, *Pens and Needles: Women's Textualities in Early Modern England* (Philadelphia, PA, 2010).
8 Parker, *The Subversive Stitch*, p. 199.
9 Mary Lowndes, *On Banners and Banner-Making* [1909], reprinted as Appendix 5 in Lisa Tickner, *The Spectacle of Women: Imagery of the Suffrage Campaign, 1907–14* (London, 1987).
10 Museum of London, shield-shaped banner, *c.* 1908, 115 × 91 cm, museum no. 2016.22.
11 Jean-Jacques Rousseau, *Émile* [1762] (London, 1974), pp. 335 and 92.
12 D. C. Bloomer, *Life and Writings of Amelia Bloomer* (Boston, MA, 1895), pp. 65–81.
13 Annie Jenness Miller, *Physical Beauty and How to Obtain and How to Preserve It* (New York, 1892), pp. 171–7. See also *Mother and Babe* (New York, 1892).
14 William Morris, 'Beauty of Life' [19 February 1880], in *Hopes and Fears for Art: Five Lectures by William Morris* [1882] (London, 1919), pp. 71–113.
15 William Morris, 'The Lesser Arts of Life (A Lecture Delivered 21 January 1882)', in *Lectures on Art Delivered in Support for the Society for the Protection of Ancient Buildings* (London, 1882), pp. 225–6.
16 Charlotte Perkins Gilman, *The Dress of Women*, originally published in 1915 in instalments in Gilman's monthly journal *The Forerunner*, reprinted in book form as *The Dress of Women: A Critical Introduction to the Symbolism and Sociology of Clothing*, ed. Michael R. Hill and Mary Jo Deegan (Westport, CT, 2002), pp. 3 and 131–3.
17 For more on The Men's Dress Reform Party see Barbara Burman, 'Better and Brighter Clothes: The Men's Dress Reform Party 1929–1940', *Journal of Design History*, VIII/4 (1995), pp. 275–90.
18 Elizabeth Wilson, *Adorned in Dreams: Fashion and Modernity* (London, 1985), p. 14.
19 Otto von Busch, '"A suit, of his own earning": Fashion Supremacy and Sustainable Fashion Activism', in *Routledge Handbook of Sustainability and Fashion*, ed. Kate Fletcher and Mathilda Tham (Abingdon, 2015), pp. 275–82.
20 Georgia Murray and Poppy Thorpe, '3 Women on the Joy of Making Your Own Clothes', www.refinery29.com, 3 April 2020.

21 Seamwork, www.seamwork.com, accessed 11 January 2023.
22 Nasrin Himada, 'Things Needed Made', in *The New Politics of the Handmade: Craft, Art and Design*, ed. Anthea Black and Nicole Burisch (London, 2021), pp. 171–9.
23 Murray and Thorpe, '3 Women on the Joy of Making Your Own Clothes'.
24 Naomi Alice Clarke, 'Exploring the Role of Sewing as a Leisure Activity for Those Aged 40 Years and Under', *Textile: Cloth and Culture*, XVIII/2 (2020), pp. 118–44.
25 Mary Danielson Perry, 'How We Talk About Size', https://curvysewingcollective.com, 15 July 2014.
26 Katie Whittle, 'Androgynous Fashion', www.seamwork.com, July 2016. See also The Sewcialists, 'Who We Are: My Queer Making Story', www.thesewcialists.com, 21 March 2018. For more on sewing as politics and resilience, see Sew Queer, 'Our Mission', www.sewqueer.org, accessed 3 February 2023
27 See www.openstylelab.org, accessed 11 January 2023.
28 See www.theablelabel.com, www.lucyjonesdesign.com and 'The Family Caregivers' Guide to Adaptive Clothing', www.thecaregiverspace.org. Sweden's Independent Living Institute supported the Fashion Freaks advice site for wheelchair users, https://en.fashionfreaks.se, all accessed 11 January 2023.
29 Sarah Corbett, *How to Be a Craftivist: The Art of Gentle Protest* (London, 2017), pp. 248, 149–69.
30 Personal communication with the author. See also Sara Impey, *Text in Textile Art* (London, 2013).
31 See www.violetprotest.com, accessed 11 January 2023.
32 Lynn Setterington, 'Community Involvement', www.lynnsetterington.co.uk, accessed 11 January 2023.
33 Social Justice Sewing Academy, www.sjsacademy.org, accessed 11 January 2023.
34 Amy Twigger Holroyd and Emma Sherciff, *Stitching Together: Good Practice Guidelines* (Bournemouth, 2020), and www.stitchingtogether.net, accessed 11 January 2023.
35 Anthea Black and Nicole Burisch, 'From Craftivism to Craftwashing', in *The New Politics of the Handmade: Craft, Art and Design*, ed. Black and Burisch (London and New York, 2021), pp. 13–32.

8 Into the Fray

1 Anna König, 'A Stitch in Time', *Culture Unbound: Journal of Current Cultural Research*, V/4 (2013), pp. 569–85.

2 John Taylor, 'The Praise of the Needle', in *The Needles Excellency: A New Booke wherein are divers Admirable Workes wrought with the Needle, Newly invented and cut in Copper for the pleasure and profit of the industrious* (London, 1631).

3 See www.repaircafe.org, accessed 12 January 2023.

4 Glenn Adamson, *Fewer, Better Things: The Hidden Wisdom of Objects* (London, 2018), pp. 73–5.

5 Thérèse de Dillmont, *Encyclopedia of Needlework* (Dornach, 1886), p. 15.

6 To be seen in various museum collections. A number survive from the famous Quaker school at Ackworth, Yorkshire, England. See Carol Humphrey, *Sampled Lives: Samplers from the Fitzwilliam Museum* (Cambridge, 2017), pp. 190–92; Gillian Vogelsang-Eastwood, 'Darned! Darning Samplers, a Hidden History', *Selvedge*, 102 (2021), pp. 62–4.

7 Proceedings of the Old Bailey, 'January 1785, Trial of William Moore [t17850112-2]', www.oldbaileyonline.org, accessed 5 February 2023.

8 Proceedings of the Old Bailey, 'February 1795, Trial of Ann Gibbons [t17950218-29]', www.oldbaileyonline.org, accessed 5 February 2023.

9 Proceedings of the Old Bailey, 'April 1853, Trial of Edward Harding Berkley and others [t18530404-510]', www.oldbaileyonline.org, accessed 5 February 2023.

10 Linda Baumgarten, *What Clothes Reveal: The Language of Clothing in Colonial and Federal America* (Williamsburg, VA, 2002), p. 185. Jefferson's garments are in the collection at Monticello, Charlottesville, Virginia. Chapter 6, pp. 182–207, gives an overview of alterations in eighteenth-century clothing well illustrated from surviving examples in the Colonial Williamsburg Collection.

11 Proceedings of the Old Bailey, 'December 1792, Trial of John Hodgson [t17921215-98]', www.oldbaileyonline.org, accessed 5 February 2023.

12 Man's doublet of quilted satin, Victoria and Albert Museum, object number 347-1905, illustrated in Avril Hart and Susan

North, *Seventeenth and Eighteenth-Century Fashion in Detail* (London, 2009), pp. 26–7, 112, 138.

13 Kay Staniland, *In Royal Fashion: The Clothes of Princess Charlotte of Wales and Queen Victoria, 1796–1901* (London, 1997), p. 171.

14 Julie A. Campbell, 'Wearily Moving Her Needle: Army Officers' Wives and Sewing in the Nineteenth-Century American West', in *Culture of Sewing: Gender, Consumption and Home Dressmaking*, ed. Barbara Burman (Oxford, 1999), pp. 129–39.

15 Elizabeth Bishop, 'Efforts of Affection: A Memoir of Marianne Moore' [*c.* 1969], in Bishop, *Prose* (London, 2011), p. 124.

16 Jervoise of Herriard Family Papers, Hampshire Record Office, HRO 44M69/M2/1/16.

17 WRAP, 'Refashion and Upcycle', www.loveyourclothes.org.uk, accessed 28 October 2020. See also Ellie Violet Bramley, 'Forget Fast Fashion! Six Ways to Bring Clothes Back to Life – from Darning to Stain Removal', *The Guardian*, 29 April 2020, www.theguardian.com.

18 Joan Haslip, 'John Lewis Memory Store', www.johnlewismemorystore.org.uk, accessed 10 July 2020. By kind permission of the John Lewis Partnership Archives.

19 Eithne Farry, 'A Stitch in Time', *The Guardian*, 28 April 2008, www.theguardian.com.

20 Daniel Miller, *The Comfort of Things* (Cambridge, 2009), p. 61.

21 WRAP, 'Clothing Longevity and Circular Business Models Receptivity in the UK', www.wrap.org.uk, October 2022.

22 Flora Klickmann, ed., *The Cult of the Needle* (London, 1914), p. 90.

23 Maud Pember Reeves, *Round About a Pound a Week* [1913] (London 1994), p. 166.

24 Helen Reynolds, '"Your Clothes are Materials of War": The British Government Promotion of Home Sewing during the Second World War', in *Culture of Sewing*, ed. Burman, pp. 327–39. See also Julie Summers, *Fashion on the Ration: Style in the Second World War* (London, 2015); and Imperial War Museums, 'Make Do and Mend', www.iwm.org.uk, accessed 3 February 2023.

25 Amelia Womack, 'Fashion Brands Should Be Obliged to Help You Repair What You Wear – It Will Help Tackle the Climate Crisis', *The Independent*, 18 February 2020, www.independent.co.uk.

26 WRAP, 'Citizen Behaviour Change: Love Your Clothes', www.wrap.org.uk/taking-action, October 2022.

27 Katrina Rodabaugh, *Mending Matters* (New York, 2018), p. 43.

28 WRAP, 'Clothing Longevity and Circular Business Models Receptivity in the UK'.

29 See www.tomofholland.com, accessed January 2022.

30 Claire Wellesley-Smith, *Slow Stitch: Mindful and Contemplative Textile Art* (London, 2015) p. 63.

31 National Army Museum, London, NAM.2002–12–1–1. See www.collection.nam.ac.uk, accessed 18 April 2023.

32 Victoria Kelley, 'Time, Wear and Maintenance', in *Writing Material Culture History*, ed. Anne Gerritson and Giorgio Riello (London, 2015), pp. 191–7.

33 Carpenter's words quoted here come from 'Simplification of Life', a paper he gave in 1886 to the Fellowship of the New Life, a group of activists in London experimenting – not entirely successfully! – with a combination of high ideals, communal living and manual labour. The paper appeared in Edward Carpenter, *England's Ideal and Other Papers on Social Subjects* (London, 1887), pp. 86, 95–6.

34 Sheila Rowbotham, *Edward Carpenter: A Life of Liberty and Love* (London, 2008), p. 456.

35 Ibid., p. 254.

36 Kate Fletcher, 'Other Fashion Systems', in *Routledge Handbook of Sustainability and Fashion*, ed. Kate Fletcher and Mathilda Tham (Abingdon, 2015), p. 18.

37 WRAP, 'Citizen Behaviour Change, Love Your Clothes'.

38 Kate Fletcher and Lynda Grose, *Fashion and Sustainability: Design for Change* (London, 2012), pp. 101, 155–6.

39 Ibid., pp. 67–9.

40 Drapers, 'Sustainability and the Consumer 2021', www.drapersonline.com, accessed 3 February 2023.

41 Katrina Rodabaugh, *Mending Matters: Stitch, Patch, and Repair Your Favourite Denim and More* (New York, 2018), p. 80.

42 See www.collectivemendingsessions.com, accessed 12 January 2023.

43 Sara Impey, *Social Fabric*, studio quilt and cotton, 116 × 117 cm, International Quilt Museum, Lincoln, Nebraska, USA, object no. 2017.089. 0002. See www.internationalquiltmuseum.org, accessed 5 January 2023.

SELECT BIBLIOGRAPHY

Akselson, Caroline, and Alexandra Bruce, *The Great British Sewing Bee: Sustainable Style: 27 Garments to Sew for a More Considered Closet* (London, 2020)

Almond, Kevin, and Elaine Evans, 'A Regional Study of Women's Emotional Attachments to the Consumption and Making of Ordinary Clothing, Drawing on Archives in Leeds, West Yorkshire, 1939–1979', *Costume*, LVI/I (2022), pp. 74–100

Amos, Johanna, and Lisa Binkley, eds, *Stitching the Self: Identity and the Needle Arts* (London, 2021)

Atkins, Jacqueline Marx, *Shared Threads: Quilting Together Past and Present* (New York, 1994)

Balfour-Paul, Jenny, *Indigo* (London, 1998)

Baudry, Mary C., *Findings: The Material Culture of Needlework and Sewing* (New Haven, CT, 2006)

Baumgarten, Linda, *What Clothes Reveal: The Language of Clothing in Colonial and Federal America* (Williamsburg, VA, 2002)

Beckert, Sven, *Empire of Cotton: A New History of Global Capitalism* (London, 2015)

Bedat, Maxine, *Unraveled: The Life and Death of a Garment* (New York, 2021)

Black, Anthea, and Nicole Burisch, eds, *The New Politics of the Handmade: Craft, Art and Design* (London, 2021)

Brooks, Andrew, *Clothing Poverty: The Hidden World of Fast Fashion and Second-Hand Clothes* (London, 2015)

Burman, Barbara, ed., *The Culture of Sewing: Gender, Consumption and Home Dressmaking* (Oxford, 1999)

—, 'Home Sewing and Fashions for All, 1908–1937', *Costume*, XXVIII/I (1994), pp. 71–80

——, '"What a deal of work there is in a dress!": Englishness and Home Dressmaking in the Age of the Sewing Machine', in *The Englishness of English Dress*, ed. Christopher Breward et al. (Oxford, 2002), pp. 79–96

Byrde, Penelope, *Jane Austen Fashion: Fashion and Needlework in the Works of Jane Austen* (Ludlow, 2008)

Clarke, Naomi Alice, 'Exploring the Role of Sewing as a Leisure Activity for Those Aged 40 Years and Under', *Textile*, XVIII/2 (2020), pp. 118–44

Corbett, Sarah, *How to Be a Craftivist: The Art of Gentle Protest* (London, 2017)

Crawford, Matthew, *The Case for Working with Your Hands; or, Why Office Work Is Bad for Us and Fixing Things Feels Good* (London, 2009)

——, *The World Beyond Your Head: How to Flourish in an Age of Distraction* (London, 2015)

Csikszentmihalyi, Mihaly, *Flow: The Classic Work on How to Achieve Happiness* (London, 2002)

Cunningham, Patricia A., *Reforming Women's Fashion, 1850–1920: Politics, Health and Art* (Kent, OH, 2003)

Davidson, Hilary, *Dress in the Age of Jane Austen: Regency Fashion* (London, 2019), plain sewing pp. 91–7

Davidson, Rosemary, and Arzu Tahsin, *Craftfulness: Mend Yourself by Making Things* (London, 2018)

Dormer, Peter, *The Art of the Maker: Skill and Its Meaning in Art, Craft and Design* (London, 1994)

——, ed., *The Culture of Craft: Status and Future* (Manchester, 1997)

Edwards, Nina, *On the Button: The Significance of an Ordinary Item* (London, 2011)

Emery, Joy Spanabel, *A History of the Paper Pattern Industry: The Home Dressmaking Fashion Revolution* (London, 2014)

Finlay, Victoria, *Fabric: The Hidden History of the Material World* (London 2021)

Fletcher, Kate, *The Craft of Use: Post-Growth Fashion* (Abingdon, 2016)

——, *Sustainable Fashion and Textiles: Design Journeys* (Abingdon, 2014)

——, and Mathilda Tham, eds, *Routledge Handbook of Sustainability and Fashion* (Abingdon, 2015)

Flintoff, Jean-Paul, *Sew Your Own*, ebook (London, 2010)

Frye, Susan, *Pens and Needles: Women's Textualities in Early Modern England* (Philadelphia, PA, 2010)

Gale, Colin, and Jasbir Kaur, *Fashion and Textiles: An Overview* (Oxford, 2004)

—, and —, *The Textile Book* (Oxford, 2002)

Gamber, Wendy, *The Female Economy: The Millinery and Dressmaking Trades, 1860–1930* (Urbana, IL, 1997)

Garson, Barbara, *All the Livelong Day: The Meaning and Demeaning of Routine Work* (London, 1994)

Gauntlett, David, *Making Is Connecting: The Social Power of Creativity, from Craft and Knitting to Digital Everything* (Cambridge, 2020)

Goggin, Maureen Daly, and Beth Fowkes Tobin, eds, *Women and the Material Culture of Needlework and Textiles, 1750–1950* (Farnham, 2009)

Gordon, Beverly, *Textiles: The Whole Story, Uses, Meanings, Significance* (London, 2014)

Gordon, Sarah, *'Make It Yourself': Home Sewing, Gender, and Culture, 1890–1930* (New York, 2009)

Green, Nancy L., *Ready-to-Wear and Ready-to-Work: A Century of Industry and Immigrants in Paris and New York* (Durham, NC, 1997)

Guth, Christine M. E., *Craft Culture in Early Modern Japan: Materials, Makers, and Mastery* (Oakland, CA, 2021)

Gwilt, Alison, Alice Payne and Evelise Anicet Rüthschilling, eds, *Global Perspectives on Sustainable Fashion* (London, 2019)

Harris, Beth, ed., *Famine and Fashion: Needlewomen in the Nineteenth Century* (Aldershot, 2005)

Harris, Jennifer, ed., *5000 Years of Textiles* (London, 1993)

Holroyd, Amy Twigger, *Folk Fashion: Understanding Homemade Clothes* (London, 2017)

Howell, Geraldine, *Wartime Fashion: From Haute Couture to Homemade, 1939–1945* (London, 2013)

Hunter, Clare, *Threads of Life: A History of the World through the Eye of a Needle* (London, 2019)

Impey, Sara, *Text in Textile Art* (London, 2013)

Ingold, Tim, *Making: Anthropology, Archaeology, Art and Architecture* (Abingdon, 2013)

Klickmann, Flora, ed., *The Cult of the Needle* (London, 1914)

Kneebone, Roger, *Expert: Understanding the Path to Mastery* (London, 2020)

Knight, Lynn, *The Button Box: Lifting the Lid on Women's Lives*
    (London, 2016)
Korn, Peter, *Why We Make Things and Why It Matters: The*
    Education of a Craftsman (London,
Krause, Elizabeth L., *Tight Knit: Global Families and the Social Life*
    of Fast Fashion (Chicago, IL, 2018)
A Lady, *The Workwoman's Guide* (London, 1840)
Ling, Elenor, Suzanne Reynolds and Jane Munro, eds, *The Human*
    Touch: Making Art, Leaving Traces (Cambridge, 2020)
Long, Bridget, '"Regular Progressive Work Occupies My Mind Best":
    Needlework as a Source of Entertainment, Consolation and
    Reflection', *Textile*, XIV/2 (2016), pp. 176–87
McBrinn, Joseph, *Queering the Subversive Stitch: Men and the Culture*
    of Needlework (London, 2021)
McLean, Marcia, '"I dearly loved that machine": Women and the
    Objects of Home Sewing in the 1940s', in *Women and the*
    Material Culture of Needlework and Textiles, 1750–1950, ed.
    Maureen Daly Goggin and Beth Fowkes Tobin (Farnham, 2009),
    pp. 69–89
Martin, Jane, *Women and the Politics of Schooling in Victorian and*
    Edwardian England (London, 1999)
Martindale, Addie, and Ellen McKinney, 'Why Do They Sew?
    Women's Motivations to Sew Clothing for Themselves', *Clothing*
    and Textiles Research Journal, XXXVIII/1 (2020), pp. 32–48
Maynard, Margaret, *Dressed in Time: A World View* (London, 2022)
Miller, Lesley Ellis, Ana Cabrera Lafuente and Claire Allen-Johnstone,
    eds, *Silk: Fibre, Fabric and Fashion* (London, 2021)
Padovani, Clio, and Paul Whittaker, *Sustainability and the Social*
    Fabric: Europe's New Textile Industries (London, 2019)
Parker, Rozsika, *The Subversive Stitch: Embroidery and the Making*
    of the Feminine (London, 1986)
Pye, David, *The Nature and Art of Workmanship* (London, 1995)
Pym, Celia, *On Mending: Stories of Damage and Repair* (Stroud, 2022)
Richmond, Vivienne, *Clothing the Poor in Nineteenth-Century*
    England (Cambridge, 2013)
Riello, Giorgio, *Cotton: The Fabric that Made the Modern World*
    (Cambridge, 2013)
Robinson, Elizabeth Margaret, 'Women and Needlework in Britain,
    1920–1970', PhD thesis, Royal Holloway, University of London,
    2012

Robinson, Ken, and Lou Aronica, *Finding Your Element: How to Discover Your Talents and Passions and Transform your Life* (London, 2014)

Rodabaugh, Katrina, *Mending Matters: Stitch, Patch and Repair your Favorite Denim and More* (New York, 2018)

Rogers, Gay Ann, *An Illustrated History of Needlework Tools* (London, 1983)

Rose, Mike, *The Mind at Work: Valuing the Intelligence of the American Worker* (London, 2014)

St Clair, Kassia, *The Golden Thread: How Fabric Changed History* (London, 2019)

Schoeser, Mary, *Textiles: The Art of Mankind* (London, 2012)

Sekules, Kate, *Mend! A Refashioning Manual and Manifesto* (London, 2020)

Sennett, Richard, *The Craftsman* (London, 2008)

Singer, Ruth, *Sew Eco: Sewing Sustainable and Re-Used Materials* (London, 2010)

Smith, Joe, 'The World in a Wardrobe: Expressing Notions of Care in the Economy and Everyday Life', in *Routledge Handbook of Sustainability and Fashion*, ed. Kate Fletcher and Mathilda Tham (Abingdon, 2015), pp. 139–46.

Spyer, Patricia, 'The Body, Materiality and the Senses', in *Handbook of Material Culture*, ed. Christopher Tilley, Webb Keane, Susanne Küchler, Michael Rowlands and Patricia Spyer (London, 2006), pp. 125–9.

Stalp, Marybeth, *Quilting: The Fabric of Everyday Life* (Oxford, 2007)

Tallis, Raymond, *The Hand: A Philosophical Inquiry into Human Being* (Edinburgh, 2003)

Tarlo, Emma, *Clothing Matters: Dress and Identity in India* (London, 1996)

Thanhauser, Sofi, *Worn: A People's History of Clothing* (London, 2022)

Thomas, Dana, *Fashionopolis: The Price of Fashion and the Future of Clothes* (London, 2019)

Thomas, Sue, *Fashion Ethics* (Abingdon, 2017)

Thompson, Emma Katelin, 'Sew What: An Ethnographic Exploration of Contemporary Garment Sewing Practices in Kingston Ontario', PhD thesis, Queen's University, Kingston, Ontario, 2021

Tickner, Lisa, *The Spectacle of Women: Imagery of the Suffrage Campaign, 1907–1914* (London, 1987)

Turkle, Sherry, *Evocative Objects, Things We Think With* (Cambridge, MA, 2011)

Weiner, Annette B., and Jane Schneider, eds, *Cloth and Human Experience* (Washington, DC, 1989)

Wellesley-Smith, Claire, *Resilient Stitch: Wellbeing and Connection in Textile Art* (London, 2021)

—, *Slow Stitch: Mindful and Contemplative Textile Art* (London, 2015)

Wilson, Frank R., *The Hand: How Its Use Shapes the Brain, Language, and Human Culture* (New York, 1999)

Young, Esme, *Behind the Seams* (London, 2022)

ASSOCIATIONS AND WEBSITES

Changing Markets Foundation
Campaigns for sustainable global markets including fashion
and textiles
www.changingmarkets.org

The Craft of Use
Studies of real-life post-growth fashion
www.craftofuse.org

Crafts Council (UK)
Research on the social, economic and cultural value of craft
www.craftscouncil.org.uk/about/research-and-policy

Curvy Sewing Collective
https://curvysewingcollective.com

Ellen MacArthur Foundation
The circular economy including fashion and textiles
www.ellenmacarthurfoundation.org

Haptic and Hue
Website, podcast and online U.S. and UK bookshop on how cloth
'speaks to us and the impact it has on our lives'
www.hapticandhue.com

Helen Howes
Expert and mender of old sewing machines
www.helenhowes-sewingmachines.co.uk

International Sewing Machine Collectors' Society
www.ismacs.net

King's Fund on social prescribing
www.kingsfund.org.uk/publications/social-prescribing

Labour Behind the Label
Not-for-profit campaigning for workers' rights in the clothing industry,
UK home of Clean Clothes Campaign
https://labourbehindthelabel.net

Love Your Clothes
Working with consumers on how they buy, use and dispose
of their clothing
www.loveyourclothes.org.uk

Seamwork
U.S. motivational and practical site for sewing clothes
www.seamwork.com

Lynn Setterington
UK textile artist working with stitch on social and community issues
www.lynnsetterington.co.uk

SewQueer
U.S. project at intersection of sewing and queer identity
www.sewqueer.org

Ruth Singer
UK textile artist-maker and writer
https://ruthsinger.com

Claire Wellesley-Smith
UK textile artist, writer and researcher within arts, heritage
and community well-being
www.clairewellesleysmith.co.uk

WRAP
Climate action UK-based NGO working globally including
on fashion and textiles. Home to SCAP: Sustainable Clothing
Action Plan
https://wrap.org.uk

ACKNOWLEDGEMENTS

My late mother started it all. She sewed throughout my childhood and beyond, alongside all her other work, and by example showed just how many life lessons the practice of sewing can offer. I think she'd have enjoyed the idea that she's like a seam running through this book.

My first professional steps towards *The Point of the Needle* began with the remarkable women of Hampshire who gave their time in 1995 to be interviewed at length about their sewing. They were an inspiration, the founding godmothers of my work in this field. They welcomed me into their homes and shared so much, including much humour and untold quantities of tea and cake. That period of work, in association with the wonderful Wessex Film and Sound Archive, led in 1999 to the book *The Culture of Sewing: Gender, Consumption and Home Dressmaking*, a collaboration in which I was joined by eighteen other scholars who also recognized the need to excavate more of sewing's history and significance and to whom I remain indebted. It was a project that signposted more routes forward.

Approaching *The Point of the Needle*, it seemed obvious that another oral history project should be the next step, after all a lot has changed since 1995. COVID-19 lockdowns threw a big spanner into that plan. So, I started *Our Sewing Stories* as an alternative way to continue the journey. It was an invitation to contributors – all genders, young and old – to write their own sewing stories, in effect their stitching autobiographies. It gave me the chance to be in touch with many more people than live interviews would have allowed. I owe them all so much; my thanks go to everyone involved. Sewing and generosity seem to go hand in hand. It's a matter of regret not meeting them all in person but what a pleasure it has been to read all those stories. I would have cited everybody if there had been room to do so in the book, but the stories of those not quoted directly are valued just as much as those who are. All the accounts of their sewing lives – frank, positive, wise, funny, sad, surprising, perceptive – have shaped the book's themes and shown in so many ways why sewing really does matter. *Our Sewing Stories* gradually grew into an original archive in its own right, one I hope to preserve in the public domain. Thank you to Julia Burge for keeping it all in good shape.

The COVID-19 pandemic also closed archives and libraries, some of my favourite spaces, so I thank the staff of the London Library who valiantly kept postal loans of books flowing during the lockdowns. In rural exile, the sound of their parcels landing on my doormat was music to my ears.

Many other people kept me company on the journey to *The Point of the Needle*. For their support and contributions, I am hugely grateful. Will Brown, Claire Mackaness, Cathy Spencer and Marie Willey so generously shared their workspaces and time with me and let me see their skills in action close-up; they are stars. I really wish I could have stayed a lot longer in their creative company. Along the way, the photographs of Louise Jasper, Liz Rideal and Syd Shelton were inspirational.

For information, advice and their confidence in the book, I send a big thank you to Lesley Miller and Bridget Long and to Penny Ruddock, who also persuaded me to pick up my pen in the first place. And my thanks are due to Polly Leonard at Selvedge, the Southern Counties Costume Society, Carol Tulloch at the University of the Arts London for those opportunities to think out loud about stitching and stitchers past and present, and to Sara Impey, Etka Kaul, Vivienne Richmond and Claire-Wellesley Smith for sharing their invaluable insights.

Verity Wilson read the book at manuscript stage. Her wise counsel shored me up when I most needed it, her astute questions raised the game, and I am immensely thankful to her for that generous contribution. Of course, the book's shortcomings are all my own responsibility.

At Reaktion, to Phoebe Colley, Martha Jay, Helen McCusker and the team, thank you for all your expertise behind the scenes. Although she doesn't sew and once stapled a skirt together, my editor Vivian Constantinopoulos initiated this book. She 'got' the direction of travel from the word go and I am indebted to her for her vision and patience.

Last, never least, a huge thank you to my family and friends for their forbearance during the journey; to Alba and Stanley for play time; to Theo Baines and Charlie Gardner, fine writers both, for sharing their thoughts; and to dear Tom, my human sunshine, for being there, for everything.

Photo p. 6: Getty Images (H. Armstrong Roberts/ClassicStock).

INDEX